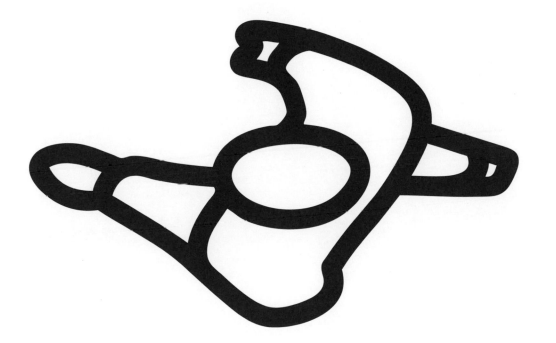

instant lettering

didot 36pt REPLICA STD
usa pica 42pt

320pp
Order no MUTEBOOK001

AAAAAAAAAABBBBBB
CCCCCDDDDDDDEE
EEEEEEEEEEEFFFFF
GGGGGHHHHHHIIIIIIIII
JJJJJJKKKLLLLLLL
MMMMMMNNNNNN
OOOOOOOPPPPPQQ
RRRRRRSSSSSSSSS
TTTTTTTUUUUUUUU
VVVVVWWWWXXXX
XXXYYYYYZZZ111222
333444555666777888
999000!!!!!&&&%£££
///@@@???€€€$$$
##©©℗

C595

instant lettering
SPACEMATIC
heat resistant

WITH OVER 2,000
ILLUSTRATIONS

MUTE

A VISUAL DOCUMENT

FROM 1978 →
TOMORROW

TERRY BURROWS
WITH DANIEL MILLER

 Thames & Hudson

MUTE548 → MUTE666

BONG1 → BONG43

DUNG7 → DUNG32

YAZ1 → YAZ8

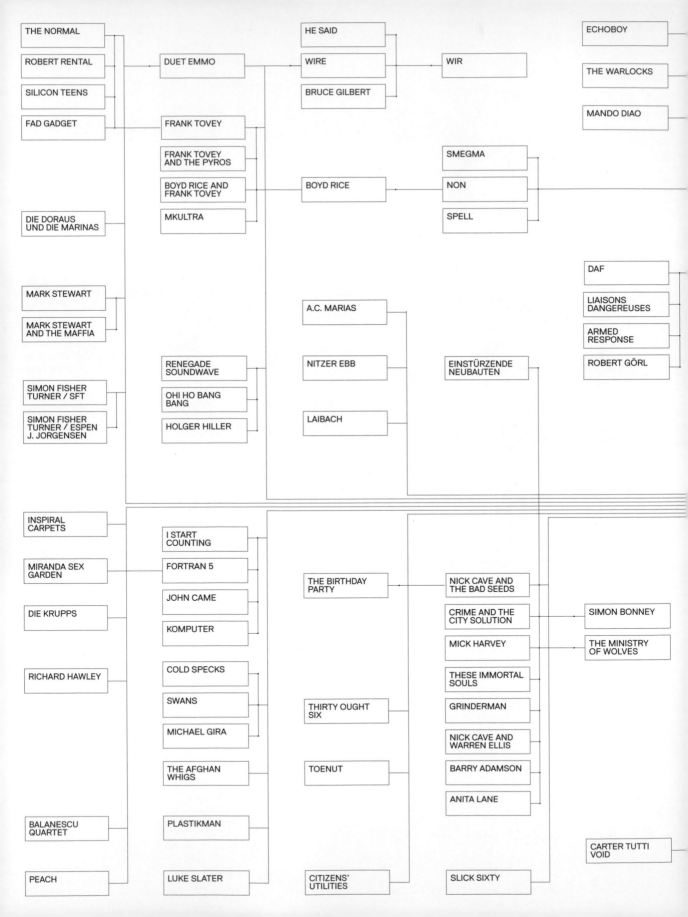

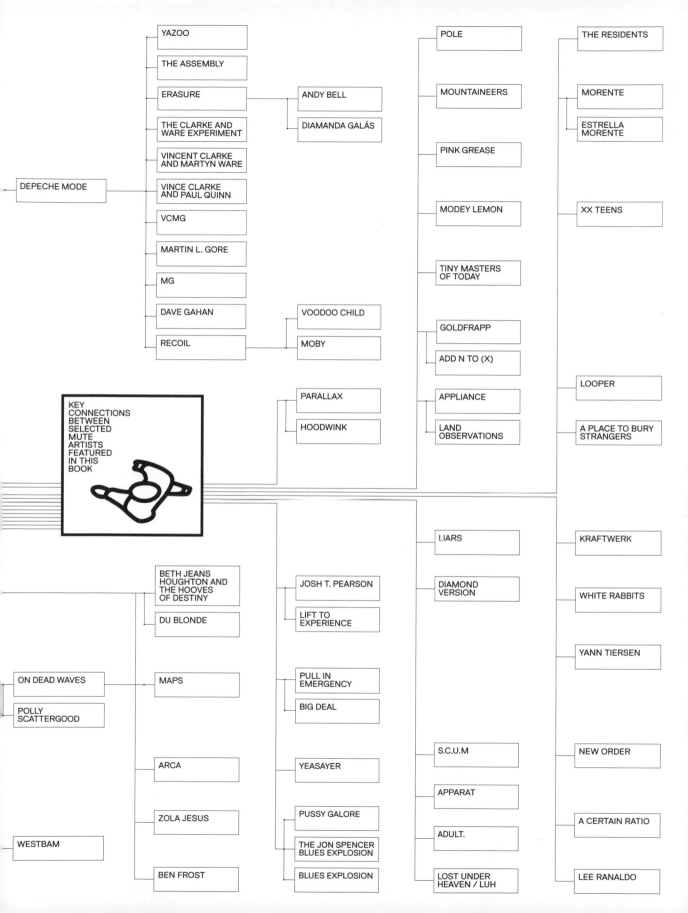

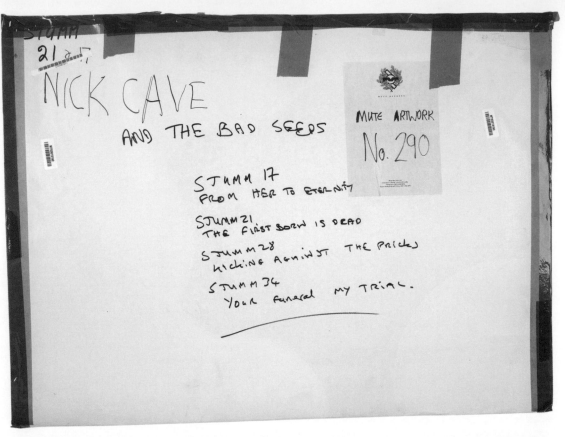

STUMM
21 & 7

NICK CAVE
AND THE BAD SEEDS

MUTE ARTWORK
No. 290

STUMM 17
FROM HER TO ETERNITY

STUMM 21
THE FIRST BORN IS DEAD

STUMM 28
KICKING AGAINST THE PRICKS

STUMM 34
YOUR FUNERAL MY TRIAL.

MUTE

38

Depeche

Black Celebration

MUTE
ARTWORK
NO. 38.

CONTENTS

008–009   BONG9 / Depeche Mode / 'It's Called A Heart' / 1985 /
           Photographic montage from the music video shoot by
           Peter Care, filmed on location in Berkshire.
010–011   MUTE185 / Nick Cave And The Bad Seeds + Kylie Minogue /
           'Where The Wild Roses Grow' / 1995 / Photograph by David
           Tonge, taken on the set of the video shoot in Surrey; this
           photo session was used to create the artwork and visual
           campaign for the single by Intro Design Studio.
012–013   STUMM188 / Goldfrapp / *Felt Mountain* / 2000 / Alison
           Goldfrapp art directed the creation of this mirror image at the
           Mute offices in Harrow Road using Joe Dilworth's split-tone
           photographic print. It was destined for Goldfrapp's debut album.

014–015   STUMM387 / Yeasayer / *Amen & Goodbye* / 2016 /
           Installation created by sculpture artist David Altmejd
           and used as the front cover. The band collaborated
           with Altmejd in creating a world that referenced previous
           Yeasayer artworks, controversial figures from history
           and popular culture, as well as the musicians themselves.
           They described it as '*Sgt Pepper* meets Hieronymous
           Bosch meets Dalí meets Pee-wee's Playhouse'.
←   Mute artwork folders / Folders containing artwork masters
           and photography for Depeche Mode's *Black Celebration*
           album and the first four albums by Nick Cave And The
           Bad Seeds.

           ' ' *All quotations featured throughout this book
           are by Daniel Miller, unless otherwise indicated.*

I saw electronic music as being more punk than punk: you didn't have to learn any chords, just press down on the keyboard and an interesting sound would come out.

→ DANIEL MILLER / 2013

IN

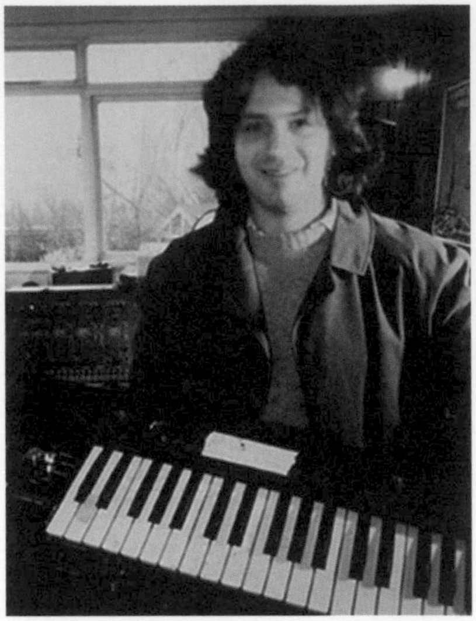

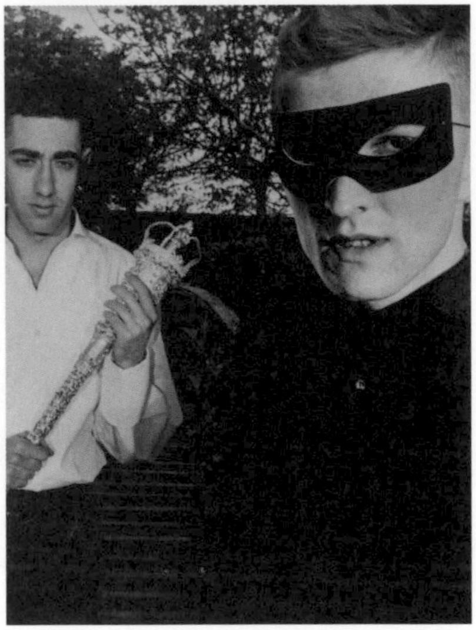

OD

TI

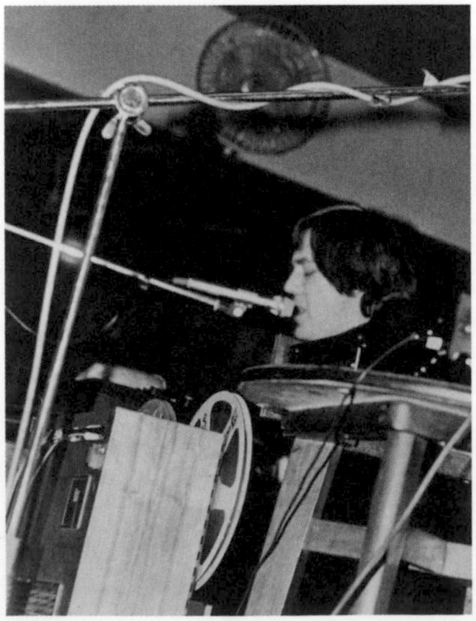

TR 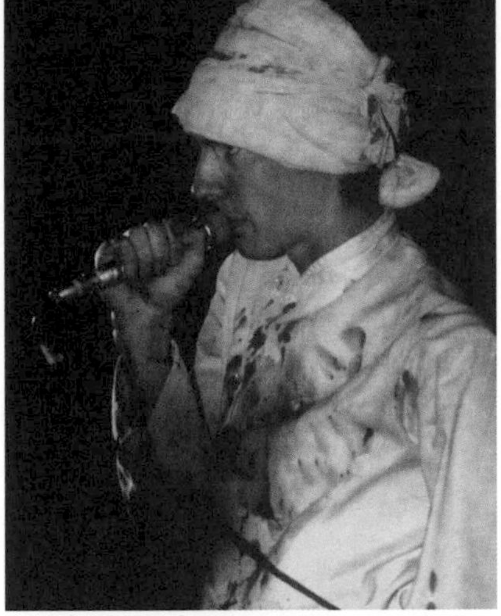

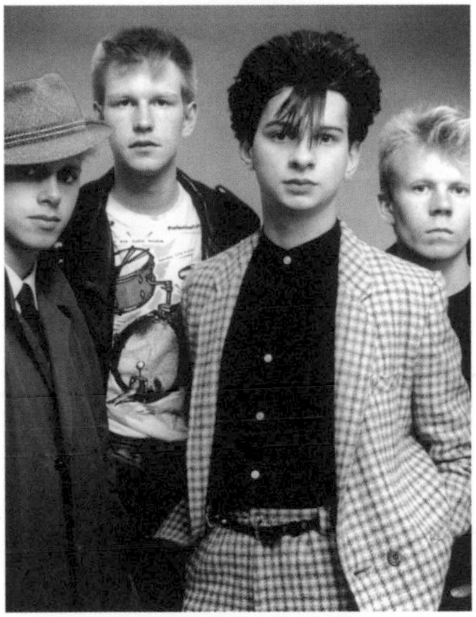 UC

ON 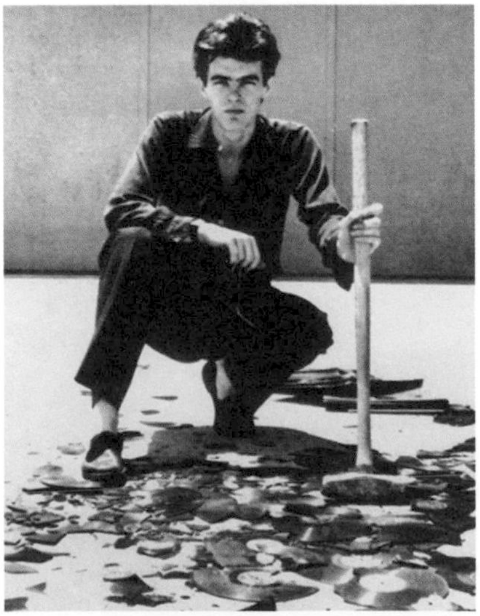

01

02

03

MUTE: THE ACCIDENTAL LABEL

The idea of putting out my own record came to me at the
end of the punk era. Like many of my generation, I was
inspired by the raw noise, the attitudes and the DIY ethos
of punk. The music itself didn't always interest me that
much – though I loved the energy, I found a lot of it quite
conservative. It did, however, reinforce the idea that it
was possible to make music without necessarily being
a virtuoso musician.

As a teenager I was completely obsessed with music.
Yet apart from playing guitar (badly) and saxophone (worse)
in a school blues band, growing up I had little in the way of
a musical background. It was during my time at art school
in the late 1960s that I became interested in the idea of
experimenting with electronic sound. There was also a lot
of very interesting music being produced at that time: I was
drawn in particular to artists from Germany like Can, Amon
Düül II, Neu! and Kraftwerk, who, in spite of their diverse
sounds, were lumped together by the music press under
the horrible term 'krautrock'.

The biggest problem for anyone who wanted to make
electronic music in those days was that the equipment
was inaccessible and so expensive. Or else you had to be
clever enough to build your own. It was only when Japanese
companies like Korg and Roland began to produce synthesisers
that people like me could start thinking about owning one.

I saw electronic music as being even more punk than
punk: you didn't have to learn any chords but could just
press down on the keyboard and an interesting sound would
come out. In early 1978, I recorded two tracks at home using
a cheap second-hand Korg 700S synth and a four-track tape
recorder – set up at my mother's house in Decoy Avenue,
north-west London, where I was living at the time – and
recorded my first single. Using the name The Normal, I'd
intended it really as a one-off experiment, and wondered
how I'd manage to shift the 500 copies I was planning to
press. As a name for the label, I went with Mute – a word
that had drifted into my consciousness from spending
my days working in film-editing suites. 'T.V.O.D.'/'Warm
Leatherette' was released in April 1978 and received a
surprising amount of night-time airplay and positive press
reviews. Within three months I'd sold around fifteen
thousand copies, distributed by Rough Trade.

I'd also begun to get demo tapes through the post, sent
to Mute Records at Decoy Avenue. (For years afterwards,
fans of Depeche Mode from all over the world would turn
up at my mum's doorstep. She loved it!) At that time, though,
I had no real interest in starting a label, and I didn't really
like anything that I heard. That was until I was introduced
to Frank Tovey – or Fad Gadget, as he called himself. I was
blown away by his home recordings and could really relate
to his music and lyrics. I suggested we go to into a studio
to record two of the songs. We released 'Back To Nature'
as a single, and that was effectively the beginning of Mute
Records as a *real* record label. For the first two years we
just released singles, until I received a visit from a German
group called Deutsch Amerikanische Freundschaft. In 1980,
I took them over to Cologne, where we recorded the first
Mute album with legendary producer Conny Plank.

04

05

06

I first saw Depeche Mode in late 1980. They were supporting Fad Gadget at the Bridge House pub in Canning Town. We shook hands and agreed to put out a single.

It was the release of the first two Depeche Mode singles in 1981 that carried Mute into the commercial world. They performed 'New Life' on *Top of the Pops* and their album *Speak & Spell* reached the UK Top 10. And even when Vince Clarke, who wrote most of the songs, moved on almost immediately, they continued to evolve, becoming one of the most important bands of their generation. Not long after that, Yazoo, the first of Vince's numerous other projects, gave us our first No.1 album.

The early releases on the label reflected my own personal interests in electronic and experimental music, and over time Mute became increasingly diverse. We also set up joint ventures with several specialist labels. There was Blast First, which licensed American bands like Sonic Youth and Dinosaur Jr. Around the same time, we also co-founded Rhythm King: inspired by the house music that had begun arriving in the UK from Chicago, Detroit and New York, we released chart hits by British artists like S-Express and Bomb The Bass. We ran our own Novamute label, specialising in techno and introducing producers like Plastikman (Richie Hawtin) and Speedy J. In addition to developing new artists, we also set up The Grey Area to keep in print influential experimental albums by important artists such as Can, Throbbing Gristle and Cabaret Voltaire, whose work either pre-dated the existence of Mute or had originally been released by other labels. More recently, we even ventured into the world of technology, producing

a pair of hand-held Mute Synths. This is an area I'd love to develop further.

When the idea for this book was first suggested, it was immediately clear to us that it shouldn't be a standard biography, but rather something that presented the story of the label visually – through design, artworks, photography and packaging. And this makes perfect sense. Although Mute is, above all, concerned with the music, the way our artists and releases are presented has always been such an important part of the label. Yet from the very beginning, I was clear that I wanted to avoid a consistent Mute 'look'. This is because most of our artists have very clear ideas of their own about the way they want to be presented, some of them even taking complete control of the design and photography. And that's an ethos we've always supported. Elsewhere, we've also worked with some outstanding and influential designers and photographers: names like Anton Corbijn, Brian Griffin, Peter Saville and Adrian Shaughnessy.

Mute Records has now been going for almost forty years. Which is not bad for a label that began more or less by accident. As for the future? Well, I really have no plans to retire....

Daniel Miller
London

01 Frank Tovey (Fad Gadget) / Promo Photo / 1981
02 David Gahan (Depeche Mode) / Pasadena / 1988
03 Nick Cave (The Birthday Party) / Sydney / 1984
04 Blixa Bargeld (Einstürzende Neubauten) / Utrecht / 1989
05 Will Gregory / Alison Goldfrapp (Goldfrapp) / Promo Photo / 2005
06 Milan Fras (Laibach) / Leipzig / 2003

TiPiE production
Mercredi 21
FAD GADGET
+ THE NON
From San Diego California
Auditorium
E.N.T.P.E.
VAULX-EN-VELIN
Imprimerie Lugdunum — Villeurbanne
30 F
Location :
Bruit Bleu
Music-Land
Le Progrès
rom London
nvier 1981 21 h.

nvier 1981 21 h.

rom London

Imprimerie Lugdunum — Villeurbanne

VAULX-EN-VELIN

E.N.T.P.E.

Auditorium

+ THE NON

From San Diego California

FAD GADGET

Mercredi 21

TiPiE production

1978

1979

01

02

'WARM LEATHERETTE' AND LETRASET

When punk rock reared its noisy head, a seismic cultural shift was felt in the UK. BBC legend John Peel first became aware of those tremors in the violent complaints that came his way after unveiling tracks from the Ramones' debut album on his late-night radio show in May 1976. The punk revolution may not have been entirely successful in sweeping aside music's old guard, but it would nevertheless create a lasting legacy in the establishment of a vibrant independent music scene, as well as impacting other creative fields – art, design and fashion. By 1978, you could be forgiven for thinking that one orthodoxy had simply been dislodged by another, with many of punk's royalty comfortably signed up to the same old major record labels. *Plus ça change*.

For some, though, the legacy of punk was as much about attitude as the music itself. In April 1978, Daniel Miller, a twenty-seven-year-old art school graduate, now plying his trade as a freelance film editor with television company ATV, unleashed a modest revolution of his own. Miller had been inspired by the energy of punk but was ambivalent toward much of the music: 'It cleared away a lot of shit, but musically I found it quite conservative.'

Indeed, the musical structures of much of the new wave may have come with added noise and have been thrashed out with an impressive lack of finesse, but they were still broadly part of the same tradition that drove, for example, the Rolling Stones – a band that as much as any other had represented an establishment ripe for dethroning.

Although Miller is mildly disparaging about his course at Guildford School of Art, his time as a student was not wasted. He immersed himself in the films of Luis Buñuel (along with the great man's noted recipe for the perfect Martini cocktail) and directors such as Werner Herzog and Wim Wenders, who formed part of the Neuer Deutscher Film (*New German Cinema*) movement. He also discovered

written works by the likes of Hubert Selby Jr and J. G. Ballard, citing *Last Exit to Brooklyn* and *Crash* as books that 'resonated and gave me a sense of darkness that I maybe hadn't understood that I had. All of these things, I suppose, later fed into my own creativity.'

Like many British youngsters during the 1960s, Daniel Miller became aware of electronic music while watching the TV series *Doctor Who*. Its famous theme tune, and much of the programme's incidental music and sound effects, were created by Delia Derbyshire for the BBC Radiophonic Workshop using an assortment of *musique concrète* techniques, such as manipulation of electronic oscillators, filters and magnetic tape. But Miller's first direct experience came at art school in 1970. 'As a part of my film and television course at Guildford, we also did "complementary studies". Ron Geesin, who had recorded the soundtrack album *Music from The Body* with Roger Waters of Pink Floyd, came to the college to give us a talk. He brought along an EMS Synthi A, which he didn't really know how to use, and he just let us muck about on it for an hour or so. That was a really important moment for me.'

During his time at art school, Miller began to feel that British and American rock music had lost the experimental edge that he'd once found inspiring. He began looking to Europe for an alternative. Germany offered an altogether more cerebral fare; often allied with left-wing politics and philosophies, many of its leading players came from academic backgrounds at universities, art academies or music conservatories. Irmin Schmidt and Holger Czukay of Can – still one of the bands Miller most reveres – had both studied under Karlheinz Stockhausen; Schmidt had even once been regarded as one of Germany's most promising young classical conductors. And then there were the related bands Neu! and Kraftwerk. The minimalistic soundscapes and insistent repetitive 'motorik' drum rhythms of Neu! were adopted spectacularly in 1974 by Kraftwerk on the

group's first electronic album, *Autobahn* – and Kraftwerk's global commercial success paved the way for much of the synthesiser music that followed.

The impetus for Miller to create his own music came with the arrival from the Far East of the first generation of affordable synthesisers: 'Up until the mid-1970s, synthesisers were really expensive, and way out of the reach of most musicians, but as cheaper Japanese versions came on the market, they became accessible to people like me. It was great, messing around on a synth until you created a sound you thought was really good.'

During the height of punk, the synthesiser had been viewed with suspicion. Yet the immediate aftermath saw the beginnings of an influential new generation of electronic music bands in the UK, based almost entirely around the use of budget-priced technology – the Japanese Korgs and Rolands, or the even cheaper British EDP Wasps. Seemingly out of nowhere, a new wave of experimental artists – such as Throbbing Gristle, Cabaret Voltaire and The Human League – suddenly began rising to the surface. 'I was very conscious of the fact that the possibilities of electronic music hadn't been realised – in fact, it had generally been derided. But punk wasn't *really* anti-synthesisers, just *anti* the way they'd been used by a lot of the prog rock people. I just thought the synthesiser was the ultimate punk instrument because you didn't even have to learn those horrible three chords they told you you needed to play the guitar. I thought it was the next logical step. I was a useless musician, and that's one of the things I liked about electronic music – I thought I could use it to better express the things that were going on in my head than by using conventional instruments. If you had good ideas, you could make music out of electronics.'

This revolution in affordable music technology was accompanied by another emerging development: the idea of recording music at home. The mid-1970s saw multitrack tape recorders designed for home or small studio use

appearing for the first time. Instead of paying an hourly rate for using a professional studio, it became possible for musicians to devote as much time as they wanted to their recordings, experimenting with new sounds and ideas without being 'on the clock'.

By the middle of 1977, once again living at his mother's house in Decoy Avenue in the north-west London suburb of Temple Fortune, Daniel Miller had been able to set up his own synthesiser and four-track studio. 'I was a freelance film editor at the time and was working every hour I could, so I could get hold of some of this stuff. I bought a second-hand MiniKorg-700S synth, and although there was no manual with it, it was pretty clear what the switches and buttons did. I also picked up a used Teac A-2340 tape recorder. I couldn't afford a mixing desk, but used the mix-down panel router that came with the Teac, so each of the four tracks could only be panned far left, far right or centre. I plugged it into the hi-fi and just started doing stuff. I was so excited the first time I did an overdub – a whole new world had opened up.'

Toying with the idea of releasing his own record, after several months of home experimentation Miller came up with a suitably matching pair of tracks. 'T.V.O.D.' and 'Warm Leatherette' were two sparse pieces of electronic minimalism constructed from short, simple repeating note sequences with a classic motorik rhythm – all generated using the monophonic Korg. Inspired by J. G. Ballard's *Crash*, the lyrics perfectly matched the stark sound, delivered as they were by Miller in a deliberate, clipped, emotionless monotone. The name he chose for his one-man band was The Normal.

Punk had seen the emergence of numerous bedroom record labels, most of whom produced no more than one or two records before calling it a day. One of Miller's inspirations for releasing his own music was a London punk band called The Desperate Bicycles. Formed with the sole aim of recording and releasing a single, the Bicycles were

05

06

DIY evangelists: on the sleeve, they listed all of the costs involved in making the record (£153), and it even provided them with a lyrical hook, their rallying cry: 'It was easy, it was cheap – go and do it!' Although no more than a musical footnote, the single was well known in its time, and influenced a surprising number of fledgling musicians and label owners.

Miller had few expectations of his own single leading anywhere: 'I just saw it as a one-off thing. I thought, why don't I make a record, put it out myself and then move on with my life?' He planned to press up 500 copies, although he freely admits to having expected 'most of them to end up under my bed'.

Before pressing the records, there was the small matter of coming up with a label identity: 'The idea of Mute came from film,' he recalls. 'Because I was working in a cutting room – an editing room – I saw this word "mute" everywhere.' And Mute was a certainly a suitably ironic name for a music label that didn't actually exist.

The sleeve design by Miller's close friend Simone Grant – who would work on many of Mute's early releases – made extensive use of Letraset, which would become a staple of the DIY music era. Not only was it used to provide the typography but also for the logo itself; the Mute 'walking man' – among the most iconic of music label identities – was simply selected from a Letraset sheet of architectural symbols. A stock industrial photograph of a pair of crash-test dummies completed the look. Mute001 was ready to roll.

Facing the daunting task of touting for business, Miller played 'Warm Leatherette' to Geoff Travis, owner of emerging independent music label and distributor Rough Trade. 'It was a big surprise and shock to me when he said they loved it and wanted to distribute it. I said, "Yeah, OK, whatever that means!"' Travis insisted that the initial pressing be upped to 2,000. 'It got some shockingly good reviews, and sold out immediately,' Miller recalls. Indeed, journalist Jane Suck of weekly music paper *Sounds* proclaimed it the 'Single of the

Century'. National airplay quickly followed when it was picked up by John Peel for his late-night show on BBC Radio 1.

Officially released in April 1978, within three months the single had sold thousands of copies. Arguably the first post-punk electronic single, it would be massively influential on the evolution of the UK electronic music scene. To Miller's amusement, two years later a very different version of 'Warm Leatherette' was recorded by singer Grace Jones.

It was at this time that Miller met Robert Rental at a Throbbing Gristle concert. Glaswegian Rental had also successfully released a DIY electronic single, 'Paralysis', on his own label. 'We were both invited separately by a concert promoter who wanted to put on a night of the new electronic bands. Neither of us thought we could do it on our own, so we decided we should to do it together. It was Throbbing Gristle, Cabaret Voltaire and us.' The concert received plenty of coverage in the music press: 'A lot of scene people were there,' he recalls, 'Siouxsie was there, John Lydon was there.'

Billed as Robert Rental And The Normal, the duo then took part in a Rough Trade tour, supporting Stiff Little Fingers. They quickly found their performances held limited appeal for fans of the Belfast punk band: 'They responded *very, very* badly! We had lots of stuff thrown at us. We never got a good reception anywhere...but after every gig there would always be one or two people come up to us and say it was the best thing they'd ever heard. And that made it worthwhile for us.'

The duo continued to perform live, with a residency in Paris and a UK tour: 'We played at Eric's in Liverpool, and in Manchester I met Tony Wilson when we played at the Factory Club, just as he was getting his label started.'

Apart from a one-sided album documenting the duo's performance at West Runton Pavilion, which was released by Rough Trade in 1980, that was as far as Daniel Miller decided to go with The Normal.

07

SILICON

08

Meanwhile, the cult success of Mute001 had yielded one rather unexpected result: Mute Records, the label that didn't actually exist, suddenly became a target for aspiring musicians in search of a record deal. Miller was perplexed: 'I don't really know why I put my address on the back of the cover – I thought it was something that you just *did*. But I was getting sent demo tapes, none of which I found very inspiring, and anyway at that point I really wasn't interested in starting a label.'

It was a chance meeting that changed his mind. Edwin Pouncey, better known as *Sounds*' resident punk cartoonist Savage Pencil, played Miller a tape recorded by his flat-mate Frank Tovey. Having recently returned to his native London from Leeds with a degree in visual arts and mime under his belt, Tovey – now calling himself Fad Gadget – had himself begun experimenting with tape recorders, cheap synthesisers and drum machines. It was the first demo tape Miller had heard that he'd liked. 'I met Frank, we got on really, really well, shared a lot of the same sensibilities, and a similar vision and I said, "Let's put a single out and see what happens." That really was the beginning of Mute Records as a label, as opposed to just being my own thing. When you start working with other people, it stops being a vanity project and you become responsible for someone else's career.'

Hiring out RMS, a budget eight-track studio in South Norwood, in a single day Miller produced Fad Gadget's doomy synthpop classic 'Back To Nature'. Released in October 1979, Mute002 – like Miller's debut – was another cult success, suddenly establishing Mute Records as a serious new name on the UK independent music scene.

A pioneering musician in his own right, Frank Tovey was one of the earliest electronic artists to make use of industrial effects in his sound. He was an engagingly eccentric and theatrical performer – a Fad Gadget show could make for an unnerving and unpredictable experience. 'He was probably the most extreme example of a person with a completely different on-stage persona,' Miller remembers. 'He was a very quiet, gentle, funny guy, but up on stage he could get pretty confrontational.'

Unsurprisingly, perhaps, Fad Gadget never achieved the same mainstream commercial success that came to some later Mute artists, but remained with the label, recording a dozen albums until he withdrew from the music world in 1993. Following his death in April 2002, Miller declared 'Frank was the first artist I ever worked with on Mute. He made some very special and influential records and played a big part in helping to lay the foundations of what the label was to become in the ensuing years.'

Although he had now put aside the notion of a musical career as The Normal, Miller nevertheless kicked off a second one-man project. Playing and singing snappy, electronic pop versions of classic rock 'n' roll hits, he presented himself as Silicon Teens. Billed as 'Probably the world's first teenage electronic pop group', the four fake band members were named as Darryl, Paul, Jacki and Diane. Released as Mute003 in August 1979, 'Memphis Tennessee'/ 'Let's Dance' received plenty of airplay; the following year, Miller would release two further singles and the album *Music for Parties* under the same secret identity.

With Mute Records now a bona fide label, Miller's own music would gradually move to the background as he focused on developing what was soon to become one of Britain's most influential independent music labels.

05 Daniel Miller / Promo Photo / 1978
06 Robert Rental / 1978
07 Frank Tovey (Fad Gadget) / Amsterdam / 1983
08 Silicon Teens (Darryl / Diane / Jacki / Paul) / Science Museum / London / 1980

„the normal"

MUTE001

«warm   leatherette»

«T.V.O.D.»

the normal

"....feel the steering wheel...."

THIS IS A

MUTE

RECORD

"....stick the aerial into...."

16 DECOY AVENUE LONDON N.W.11   ENGLAND

Photograph courtesey of Motor Industry Research Association   Sole distributors ROUGH TRADE RECORDS   MUTE 001

MUTE001 / 'T.V.O.D.'/ 'Warm Leatherette' / Cover / 1978 / Daniel Miller's friend Simone Grant designed the sleeve for Mute's first single release. 'Warm Leatherette' was inspired lyrically by the controversial J. G. Ballard novel *Crash*. 'The photograph we used on the front is a stock image of a crash test dummy. We wrote to the Motor Industry Research Association and they let us use it.' The reverse side of the sleeve features a pair of panels with cartoons depicting the two songs. Miller printed the address of his mother's house in Decoy Avenue, north-west London, on all of the early Mute releases. 'For years afterwards my mum had Depeche Mode fans turning up on her doorstep.'

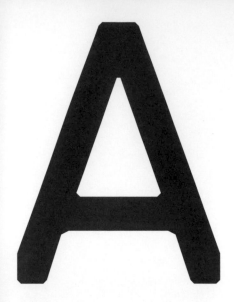

HOW TO MAKE A RECORD
BY DANIEL MILLER

I can actually remember a lot of the details about making 'T.V.O.D.' and 'Warm Leatherette' – I recorded, mixed and mastered the whole thing in twenty-four hours.

001	Buy a MiniKorg-700S synthesiser.
002	Buy a Teac A-2340 four-track tape recorder and a cheap microphone.
003	Buy a Teac AX-20 Mix-Down Panel – a four-channel router box – until you can afford to get hold of a mixer; buy an Allen & Heath Minimixer when you can.
004	Plug them into your hi-fi.
005	Play around with the Korg for a few months, get the hang of it – see what you like, see what you don't like.
006	Get hold of some free used quarter-inch tape.
007	Learn a bit about recording and how to overdub and bounce things down.
008	Record a couple of backing tracks.
009	Come up with some lyrics.
010	Mix the four tracks down to stereo.
011	Get your friend to design a sleeve.
012	Press up the record.

see opposite

'T.V.O.D.'
I didn't have a proper sequencer, but there's a repeating envelope on the Korg and that's what I used for the main 'T.V.O.D.' riff, so I got an arpeggiated bass sound that I liked. But what was really great about the 700S was that it had a second section with a ring modulator, and noise that could be switched in and out at the same time as the riff was playing; when it was switched out I'd adjust the ring modulator, so I got a different sound every time. So that went down on one track of the tape.

Next I did the 'drums', again using the Korg. One part, the snare sound, used just white noise, and I used a low sine wave with a short decay for the kick-drum sound. And I would just switch between white noise and sine wave to get the rhythm. I had to play along in real time like a real drummer, only by hitting the keys. So that went down on a second track.

Then I did the TV sounds. A friend lent me a TV set that had push-button channel changing, so I could switch between stations in time with the music. I had to do that quite a few times before I got something I liked. That went down on a third track.

Then I bounced down two of the tracks onto one, leaving two tracks free. On one of them I did the vocal and then I did a little synth melody line over the top on the other. And that was it.

'WARM LEATHERETTE'
There was a slightly different process used for 'Warm Leatherette', as it wasn't built around the same 'sequencery' effect. I started with the drums. The rhythm I basically stole from Jaki Liebezeit [of Can]. It was an approximation, obviously – I mean, it was nothing near what he did, but *inspired* by him. So I played that manually all the way through on one track.

The bass part uses the 700S filter. (It's such a great synth, you know, so underrated – there are so many things about it that are very unique.) The filter is a high-pass/low-pass that can be controlled together using a slider called the 'Traveler'. I got the effect on that synth sound by opening and closing the filter.

And then I did the vocal. And then there's the little high-pitched melody. So that was just four tracks – no bouncing down.

By this time, I'd got hold of a mixer – a used Allen & Heath six-channel Minimixer – and I also rented a Roland Space Echo for the day, which I hardly used in the end – I wanted a really dry sound and I only used it for the ADT on the synth on 'Warm Leatherette'.

I had to finish everything in one day, as I'd booked the mastering studio – Utopia in Primrose Hill – for the following day. So that gave me a deadline. I did the cut for the single having had no sleep. The engineer at Utopia listened to the two songs and told me not to give up my day job, so I thought I must be on to something.

The minimum number of records you could press was 500, and my expectation was that I'd give some to my close friends and family and that nobody else would be interested, and the rest would be sitting under my bed forever. But that didn't happen.

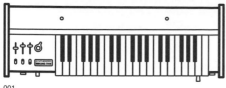

001

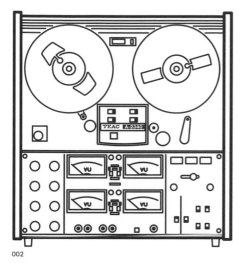

002

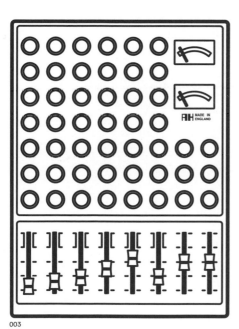

003

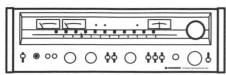

004

MUTE001

GIVING.

When you are in love giving is so important. Be sure. Give her T.V.O.D. the unique new single by The Normal on Mute Records.

A very special gift for a very special love.

MUTE001 / Audio Equipment 001 → 004 / 1970s / Minikorg-700S / Teac A-2340 / Allen & Heath Minimix / Generic 1970s Domestic Hi-Fi Amplifier.

MUTE001 / Record / Poster / 1978 / Simone Grant designed the labels and the inappropriately kitsch poster for 'T.V.O.D': *I don't need a TV screen / I just stick the aerial into my skin / Let the signal run through my veins / T.V.O.D.*

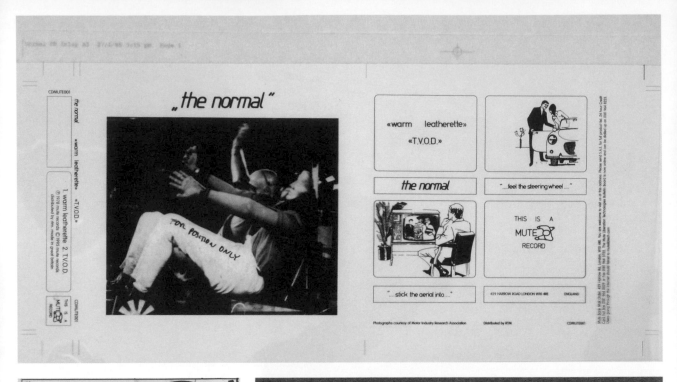

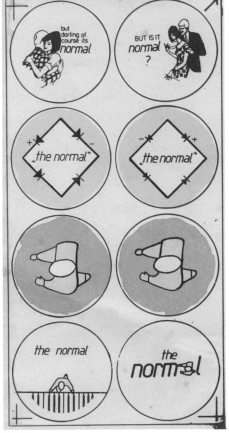

MUTE001

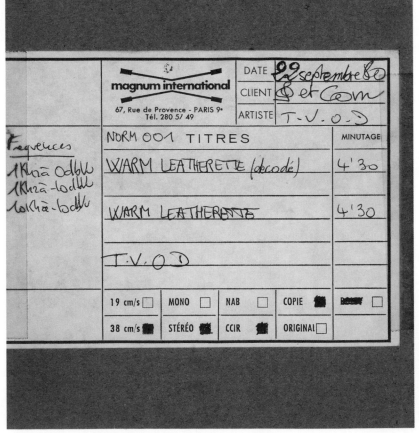

1978 – 1979

THE NORMAL

MUTE001 / 'T.V.O.D.'/'Warm Leatherette' / Artwork Proof / Master Tape Box / Promotional Badge Designs / 1978–80 / Proof sheet from the sleeve printer, Delga Press; master tape for the French release of the single on the Celluloid label (LTM202); set of four promotional badges designed by Simone Grant ('These were produced after the record came out').

Robert Rental And The Normal / Stills from *The South Bank Show* / 1979 / In 1979, Robert Rental and Daniel Miller toured the UK supporting Belfast punk band Stiff Little Fingers. ITV's *The South Bank Show* produced a 30-minute documentary about the tour. 'This music has no obvious audience,' the programme's narrator wryly observes of their performance.

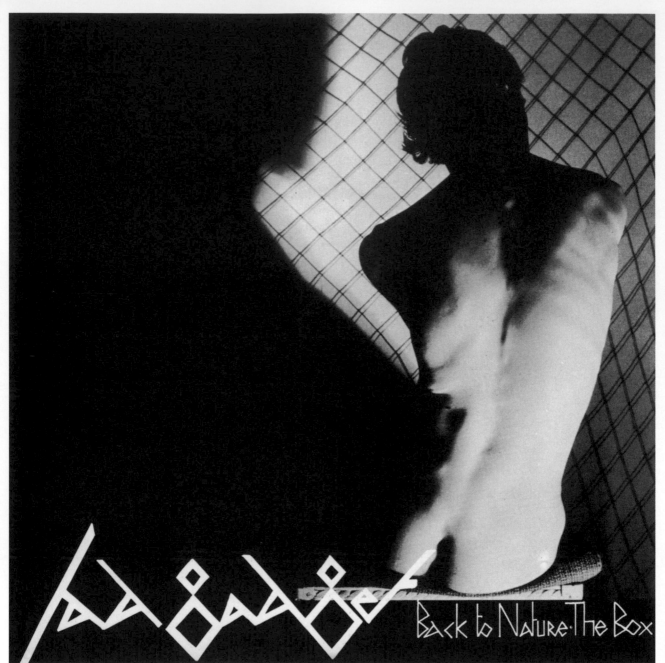

MUTE002

Photography B J Frost · design simone grant   16 Decoy Avenue London NW11   MUTE 002   distributed by ROUGH TRADE
Recorded at RMS Studios London

ꓥꓥ's ꓚꓷꓷꓚ꓾ꓼ·sꓠꓴꓚ꓾ꓼiʒ꓾ꓷ·vꓯic꓾·꓾ꓲꓮcꓵꓷꓯnicꓑiꓯnꓯ·ꓣꓠꓲꓬmnꓚ꓾n꓾ꓷꓯꓵꓷꓷ·

MUTE002 / 'Back To Nature' / Cover / 1978 / 'This record is the beginning of Mute Records as a label, for me,' says Daniel Miller. He produced Fad Gadget's debut single, 'Back To Nature', which featured striking cover images taken by Frank Tovey's girlfriend, Barbara Frost. Tovey had studied art at Leeds Polytechnic, alongside Soft Cell's Marc Almond. He called himself Fad Gadget because, in his own words, 'I didn't want people to think there was only one person in the group.' His compelling live shows often blurred the boundaries of music and performance art: he dived off the mixing desk during a concert in Amsterdam in the early 1980s, snapping both his ankles – the remainder of his tour had to be cancelled.

Although Silicon Teens didn't exist, our press release claimed they were the world's first teenage all-electronic pop band. That hadn't actually happened yet. But I knew it was going to happen some time soon.

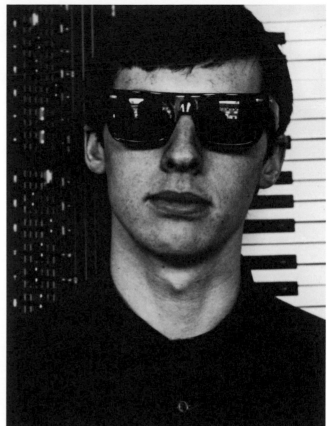

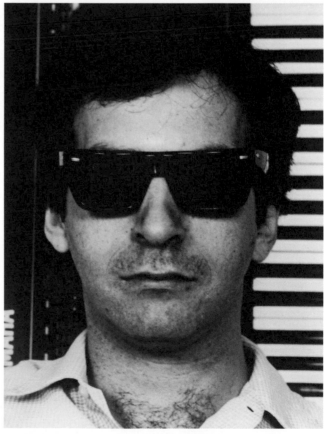

MUTE RECORDS Present

'JUDY IN DISGIUSE'

The second single from the world's first all electronic pop group

Silicon TEENS

DISTRIBUTED BY ROUGH TRADE
01·727 4312

AND

SPARTAN RECORDS
01·903 4753 / 4

JUDY IN DISGUISE C/W CHIP 'N ROLL

MUTE 004

MUTE004

MUTE003 / 'Memphis Tennessee' / Poster / 1979 / 'Simone [Grant] designed this for the first Silicon Teens single. The idea was that they were supposed to be a bunch of teenagers – rather than me on my own in the studio – and we wanted it to look as if the sleeve had been put together in one of their bedrooms. That's why the logo was hand-drawn on school book graph paper.'

MUTE004 / 'Judy In Disguise' / Poster / 1980 / Like its predecessor, the second Silicon Teens single was a cover version of a classic pop song – 'Judy In Disguise (With Glasses)', originally a hit in 1967. 'It was only while going through the layouts for this book that we spotted, nearly forty years too late, that we'd spelled "Disguise" as "Disgiuse"!' Was it deliberate?

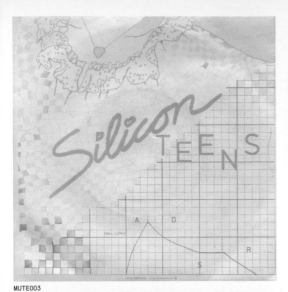

MUTE003

MUTE004

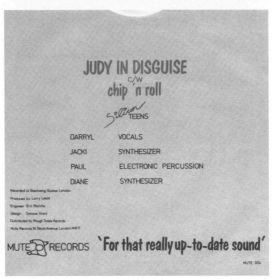

MUTE008

EARLY MUTE DESIGN

As a product of the British art school system, it's hardly surprising that Daniel Miller would place a certain emphasis on the way the Mute label output was presented. Yet although there is clear common musical ground among the first generation of Mute artists, from the beginning Miller took a very conscious decision that there shouldn't be a specific Mute look.

'Quite a lot of the labels of that time, especially Factory and 4AD, had their own look,' Miller says. 'With 4AD it was Vaughan Oliver, with Factory it was Peter Saville, and they basically designed everything. It was a good concept, creating a label aesthetic – and it's an idea you can relate back to Blue Note or Motown. I think because I was a recording artist, I couldn't conceive of putting out a record and being told who was going to do the artwork. I just didn't want the label to be predominant – I wanted that to be the musicians. I just felt that any design consistency we used should be specific to the artist rather than the label.'

Adrian Shaughnessy, founder of the design group Intro, who has worked extensively with Mute, offers his own thoughts: 'The Mute design approach is flexible, non-dogmatic and, usually, artist-led. By this I mean that although they take a keen interest in the visual presentation, it's the artists that ultimately decide. This explains the diversity of Mute cover art. As a designer, it can sometimes lead to frustration – especially if an artist has a view about visual matters that is too personal and subjective – but usually it results in good sleeve art – and covers that accurately reflect the music.'

Designer Simone Grant was a significant figure in the look of the early Mute sleeve designs. A close friend of Miller, Grant worked on most of the label's early releases, including singles and albums by The Normal, Silicon Teens, Fad Gadget and early Depeche Mode: 'I've known Daniel nearly fifty years. I was trained as a photographer and was just starting to do design work, and he asked me if I'd put the sleeve design for his first single.'

To keep the costs to a minimum, the sleeve had to be black and white, and also needed to reflect the stark musical content of the record. 'I did all of it using Letraset, even the tiny writing,' she explains. 'Daniel liked German typefaces, so I used a sheet of DIN. I also did the record labels and some posters...they were very silly posters, actually...all very kitsch!'

A dry-transfer system used by graphic designers, a Letraset sheet comprised multiple letters and numbers of a specific font that could be applied permanently to a surface by rubbing down on the sheet. In the days that predated computer desktop publishing, Letraset was the only alternative to expensive typesetting for creating professional-looking typography. It would some become a staple for every independent record label of the day. Letraset not only provided the typography but also the famed 'walking man' Mute logo that Miller had selected from a sheet of architectural symbols.

Reinforcing the aesthetic of the first single, Grant also produced promotional pictures: 'I photographed Daniel at Brent Cross, which had only just been built and was very stark and industrial-looking. He didn't want close-ups, just him in the distance, so they were very graphic.'

Like others involved with the Mute label, Grant fondly remembers working with Frank Tovey. 'He was such a creative and interesting man...Daniel asked me to do the first Fad Gadget single. The thing I'm most proud of is designing his logo, which was all handmade – there wasn't any lettering like that around at all back then. In the early days it was nearly all spot colour to keep the costs down. As Mute got more successful we started doing full-colour sleeves.'

The artwork for fake teenage band Silicon Teens – in reality, Miller on his own in the studio – was deliberately designed to reflect the DIY aesthetic of a tiny independent record label. 'It was meant to look as if it was them doing all their own artwork,' Grant reveals. 'A bit like The Desperate Bicycles, who lived around the corner and had just done their own DIY thing. We used graph paper and I made a handwritten font so that it looked like one of the members of the band had done it in their bedroom.'

Some artists had more specific ideas about what they wanted. 'A lot of the musicians we've worked with over the years have had art backgrounds or wanted to take control of their own visuals to some extent,' remarks Miller.

'DAF were a lot more definite about what they wanted,' Grant recalls. 'For one of their singles, the band sent in a drawing, and rolls of gift-wrap tape with hearts on, which I had to cut up.'

A wide variety of visual approaches have been used on subsequent Mute sleeve designs, yet they remain unified by a sense of playfulness. 'If there's one thing common to almost all of the Mute artists right since the beginning,' Miller concurs, 'it is that they seem to share a certain sense of humour.'

MUTE003 / 'Memphis Tennessee' / MUTE004 / 'Judy In Disguise' / MUTE008 / 'Sun Flight' / Covers / 1979–80 / 'All of the original artworks for Silicon Teens were created by Simone Grant. When I was a kid I had a book from Germany about space flight; it was very graphic and I loved the pictures. I gave it to Simone as a reference point for the kind of images I was looking for. It definitely influenced the Silicon Teens look.'

1980

1982

01

02

TAKING THE CHARTS

Having found cult success with The Normal, Fad Gadget and Silicon Teens, Daniel Miller kicked off the new decade, 'mucking about in the music business, helping out at Rough Trade and wondering what to do next'.

One immediate answer came in the form of a five-piece experimental electro-noise band based in Düsseldorf, Germany. Deutsch Amerikanische Freundschaft (DAF) were at the forefront of Die Neue Deutsche Welle ('New German Wave'), a loose movement of bands that roughly combined the energy and aggression of punk with harsh electronic soundscapes. Unusually for the time, these bands also took against the prevailing rock orthodoxy by singing in their native German tongue.

'As I'd been hugely influenced by krautrock, I was interested to know what was going in Germany at that time,' Miller reveals. 'DAF came to meet me at the Rough Trade shop. They'd had one experimental album out in Germany on the Ata Tak label but now they had a few songs. They played me "Kebabträume" and I thought that was great.'

It made perfect sense for the band to relocate to the UK. Vocalist 'Gabi' Delgado-López would later recall: 'At that time if you wanted to do new music you'd go to London because that was the centre, not Düsseldorf.'

'They were wild guys – and completely broke,' Miller remembers. 'I was living at my mother's house and they ended up sleeping on the floor, setting up all their gear. It was all crazy!'

DAF joined Mute Records, and the single 'Kebabträume' made for another critically acclaimed cult release.

In March 1980, Miller took the band to Cologne, where they recorded tracks with German studio legend Conny Plank for what would be Mute's first album release. 'I could afford three days at Conny's studio,' Miller remembers, 'and to work with Conny was like being in heaven. I think I must

have been really irritating because all the time I was going, "What are you doing? How are you getting that sound?" And he would say, "I don't know, I'm just plugging stuff in and seeing what it sounds like...."'

It was also a critical business decision that almost backfired: 'I put all of my money in those three days with Conny Plank,' Miller admits. 'And nothing happened for the first two days because everyone was just arguing about stuff. But Conny kept saying, "Don't worry it'll be fine...."'

In the end, they managed to record enough material for just over one side of an album; the second side was filled out with a powerful live recording made at the Electric Ballroom in Camden Town, London. The ensuing album, *Die Kleinen Und Die Bösen* ('The Small And The Evil'), may not have sold in huge quantities, but it helped further establish the label's emerging credentials in the experimental electronic field.

Soon after its release, DAF slimmed down to a duo of 'Gabi' Delgado-López and Robert Görl, losing Chrislo Haas, the synthesiser player who had been the main musical driving force in the band. Miller continues to hold Haas, who died in 2004, in the highest regard: 'He was one of the true electronic geniuses I've worked with.' Haas would re-emerge with Mute in 1982 as part of the short-lived but similarly influential trio Liaisons Dangereuses.

Leaving Mute in favour of a major-label deal with Virgin Records, DAF took on a heavier, more commercial electronic sound and within a year had become genuine pop stars in their native Germany. Even now, the band's 'defection' still seems to sting: 'I was really upset when DAF left,' Miller recalls.

Another early Mute curiosity to appear in 1980 was a shared seven-inch single by an unusual pair of American artists, Boyd Rice (using the name NON) and Smegma. Undoubtedly the label's most uncompromising and experimental release, one side comprised a set of three 'locked grooves' by Rice, creating the vinyl equivalent

03

04

of an ever-repeating tape loop. Furthermore, the single had a second hole that could be placed over the turntable's spindle, so the record could be played off-centre. 'The second hole had to be drilled one record at a time,' Miller says with a laugh. 'Anyone who happened to be around would take it in turns to have a go with the drill!' Boyd Rice has continued to record albums for Mute into the 21st century.

It was, of course, Depeche Mode whose success elevated Mute Records to the ranks of the UK's most commercially successful independent labels. Yet an accomplishment of this type would surely not have been too much of a surprise to the man who had conceived Silicon Teens. 'That was a made-up band [Miller alone in the studio], but the press releases claimed it was the world's first all-electronic teenage pop band – which hadn't happened yet, but I knew it was going to happen some time.'

And Depeche Mode *were* a bunch of teenagers armed with cheap synthesisers and an ear for a catchy melody. Born and bred in Basildon, Essex, they all still lived with their parents and famously practised together in near-silence under headphones, only their fingernails tapping away at the keyboards audible to the outside world.

Schoolmates Vince Martin and Andy Fletcher had teamed up with Martin Gore early in 1980 to form a doomy combo called Composition of Sound. Radio exposure to synthesiser bands like The Human League and Orchestral Manoeuvres in the Dark inspired them to pack away their guitars in favour of electronic instruments. When Martin heard Dave Gahan, then a student at Southend College of Technology, singing David Bowie's 'Heroes' during a jam in a neighbourhood scout hut, the singer was invited to complete the line-up.

It was Gahan who suggested a change of name, Depeche Mode deriving from a similarly titled French fashion magazine (its literal meaning is 'fashion news' or 'fashion update'). At the same time – fearing possible social security troubles

– Vince Martin, who was still signing on, adopted the new surname of Clarke.

With a growing live reputation on the local music scene, and in Vince Clarke a pop songwriter of rare talent, Depeche Mode soon became desperate to make a record. On 11 November 1980, they were booked to support Fad Gadget at the Bridge House in Canning Town, east London. Daniel Miller was also there that night: 'I saw them at the sound-check and I thought they were a right bunch of spotty, pseudo-New Romantics. But as soon as they started playing, I thought "What the fuck is this? It's incredible!" It was *exactly* the kind of thing I'd been hoping would happen. These were teenagers – seventeen or eighteen years of age – they'd chosen synthesisers as their instruments...and they were making great pop music.' But it was more than just the concept that appealed: 'The arrangements using three simple monophonic synths and a drum machine, the great songs – and Dave who was about seventeen but looked thirteen. Every song they played was better than the one before.'

At this time, Depeche Mode were also being wooed by Stevo Pearce, then in the throes of getting his fledgling Some Bizarre label off the ground. Miller, by contrast, offered them almost nothing tangible, just the same suggestion he'd made to Frank Tovey: 'Why don't we make a single?' In fact, there *were* no contracts at Mute Records at this time. The financial arrangements were a simple fifty fifty split of net profits between the label and the artist. 'They were all handshakes, no written contracts,' Miller says. 'I thought as long as you're fair with the artists, and you pay them, then why get lawyers involved?' Years later, Vince Clarke would remark: 'We all agreed that he [Miller] was the first one that we could trust; he said that if either party didn't like the other, we'd call it a day.' As it happened, it was a relationship that would continue for the next thirty years.

01 Deutsch Amerikanische Freundschaft (Wolfgang Spelmans / Gabriel Delgado-López / Michael Kemner) / Düsseldorf / 1979
02 Liaisons Dangereuses (Chrislo Haas / Krishna Goineau / Beate Bartel) / Promo Photo / 1981
03 NON (Boyd Rice) / Los Angeles / 1979
04 Depeche Mode (Vince Clarke / Martin Gore) / Essex / 1981

05

06

A session at Eric Radcliffe's Blackwing Studios, located in a deconsecrated church in Southwark, produced a debut single, 'Dreaming of Me'. It topped the UK independent charts, although in spite of daytime airplay on BBC Radio 1 throughout February 1981, it stalled outside the Top 50. But their appearance on the scene didn't go unnoticed. Suddenly, Miller muses, 'Every label in the country was after them...all the majors told them Mute could never have hits or international success, so I wanted to prove them wrong....They [the band] said, "No, we'll stay with you – see how it goes."'

Depeche Mode returned to Blackwing a month later to record another pair of Vince Clarke songs. The single 'New Life'/'Shout!' gave Depeche Mode – and Mute Records – their first genuine hit single. And a first television appearance on BBC's *Top of the Pops* chart show. In June 1981, the single peaked at No.11, selling around half a million copies.

'Two of them [Andy Fletcher and Martin Gore] still had day jobs when they first did *Top of the Pops*,' Miller remembers. 'But they left work soon afterwards and were making money straight away. Depeche didn't need big advances or anything like that, it was all pretty self-contained. Obviously, as they became bigger, they built up their own team around them – a tour manager, accountant, lawyer – but they didn't have a manager for a long time.'

The hits continued. September 1981 saw Depeche Mode in the Top 10 for the first time, when 'Just Can't Get Enough', with its catchy main synth riff, peaked at No.8 in the UK singles chart. One of Clarke's most commercial pop tunes, it also become a popular football terrace anthem. This was followed a month later by *Speak & Spell*, the band's debut album. Co-produced with Daniel Miller, and containing both Top 20 hits, in spite of very mixed reviews in the music press it reached No.10 in the UK album chart and was certified gold.

Shockingly, with the band's career taking off, Vince Clarke then announced his intention to leave Depeche Mode. 'Up to that point he was the main songwriter and driving force behind the band. But it wasn't a complete surprise to us,' Miller admits. 'They did a tour in Europe and I could see him disengaging from the others a bit – he hardly talked to them at all – I could see there was something going on in his head but I didn't know what it was. And then he broke the news.'

Clarke was not about to leave the band stranded, though. 'He was really good about it because he told us his plans in September '81, but said he'd see out all his commitments for the rest of the year. And then move on,' says Miller.

There was a strong defiance in the Depeche camp. 'They knew in Martin they had another good songwriter, and they were all pissed off with Vince and wanted to prove they could carry on without him.' In January 1982, Alan Wilder was recruited as a touring keyboard player, before joining as a permanent band member. Any doubts about the future of Depeche Mode were quickly dispelled when the single 'See You' reached the Top 5. The following September, *A Broken Frame*, the first Depeche Mode album without Vince Clarke, leapt straight into the Top 10.

'It was a very different way of making records,' Miller remarks. 'Vince had a very clear idea of the arrangements, whereas Martin would come in with a very basic song – we used to call it "Casio and foot-tap" – and everything became more collaborative. I had a bit more input into the arrangements and creating the sounds, and Eric Radcliffe, who was the engineer, also played a really important role.'

Although one of the reasons Clarke was said to have left Depeche Mode was a growing dislike of the public aspects of success, he later admitted that at the same time he was worried that leaving the band might have lost him his record deal. Looking for a new project to offer Miller, he quickly emerged with a new partner, Alison 'Alf' Moyet, a singer

07

08

he'd known from the music scene in Basildon. Clarke's appealing synthesised pop and Moyet's deep, bluesy voice made for an unusual combination. The duo called themselves Yazoo. (A legal issue would result in their being forced to shorten it to Yaz for the American market.)

'Vince played me "Only You",' Miller recalls. 'I wasn't sure whether it was the right thing to release at first, but I decided to go with it.' It proved to be an astute move, as the single reached No.2 in April 1982 (kept off the top only by Germany's Eurovision-winning song 'A Little Peace'). The follow-up single, 'Don't Go', hit No.3. These were also, notably, the first two Mute releases to make an impact on the US *Billboard* charts. The duo's debut album, *Upstairs at Eric's* (named after Eric Radcliffe of Blackwing Studios, where it was recorded) was no less popular, peaking at No.2 in September 1982, and achieving platinum status on both sides of the Atlantic.

'Vince and Alison became very successful very quickly all over the world – it's incredible when I think about it,' Miller admits now. But the relationship quickly began to sour. 'They only did one tour and by then they weren't getting on at all well. Somewhat reluctantly they agreed to make a second album.'

In fact, by the time they began recording *You and Me Both*, Clarke and Moyet were barely talking at all. Clarke would go into Blackwing in the mornings to record the backing tracks and then leave before Moyet arrived in the afternoon to do her vocal parts. It was left to Eric Radcliffe to bridge the two parties. Shortly before the album was released, Yazoo announced publicly that they had disbanded. Ironically, the album was a massive posthumous hit, giving Mute Records a first taste of life at the top of the album charts.

'In spite of their falling out, they still made a great record,' Miller reflects. 'But Alison told me it'd all been too much. She'd been playing in a pub rhythm-and-blues band and before she knew it she was on *Top of the Pops* and then

on TV all over the world. It was all too fast for her. In the end, she was overwhelmed. She told me, "I just want somebody to take over and tell me what to do," and I said, "Sorry, I'm just not that person." And with my blessing she went off and signed with CBS. We've stayed friends, though.'

As it happened, Alison Moyet's solo career would be immense, her debut album, *Alf*, one of the biggest sellers of 1984. Vince Clarke, meanwhile, kicked off a new project with Eric Radcliffe. The intention behind The Assembly was to produce a series of singles, each one with a different vocalist. Their first release, 'Never Never', was recorded with Feargal Sharkey, former singer with Irish punk band The Undertones. Although it was a Top 5 hit, the ever-restless Clarke quickly moved on.

05   Depeche Mode / 'New Life' / TV Performance / *Top of the Pops* / 1981
06   Depeche Mode (David Gahan / Martin Gore) With Engineer John Fryer / Blackwing Studios / London / 1982
07   Yazoo (Alison Moyet / Vince Clarke) / Promo Photo / 1982
08   The Assembly (Eric Radcliffe / Vince Clarke) / Splendid Studio / London / 1984

NON + SMEGMA

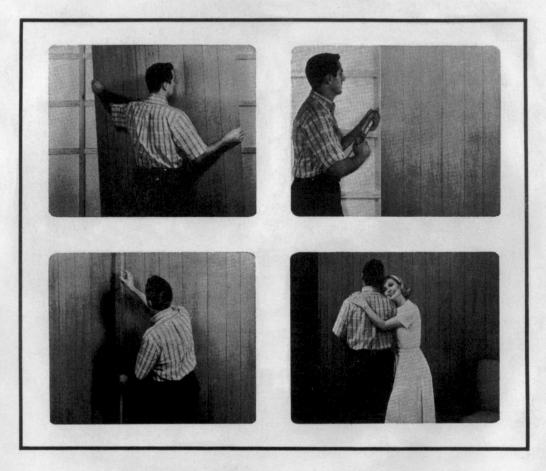

SMEGMA + NON

MUTE007

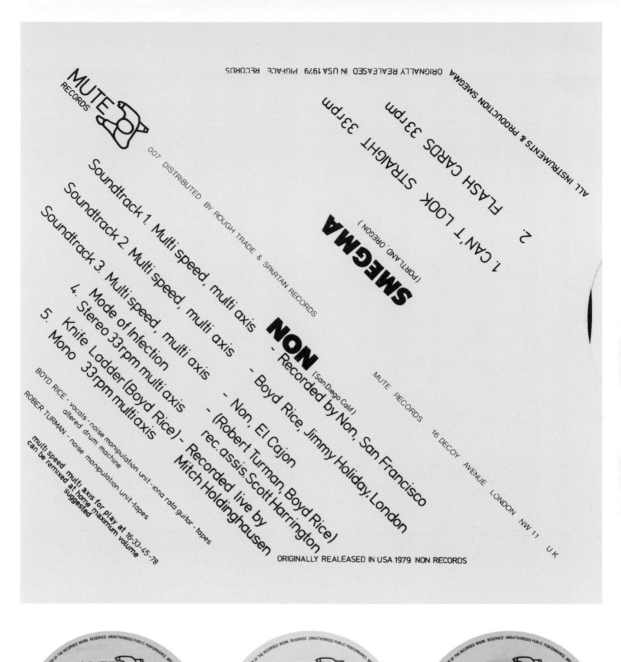

MUTE RECORDS

007 DISTRIBUTED BY ROUGH TRADE & SPARTAN RECORDS

ORIGINALLY REALEASED IN USA 1979 PIGFACE RECORDS

ALL INSTRUMENTS & PRODUCTION SMEGMA

SMEGMA
(PORTLAND OREGON)

2. FLASH CARDS 33rpm

1 CAN'T LOOK STRAIGHT 33rpm

Soundtrack 1. Multi speed, multi axis

Soundtrack 2. Multi speed, multi axis

Soundtrack 3. Multi speed, multi axis

4. Mode of Infection
Stereo 33rpm multi axis

5. Knife Ladder (Boyd Rice)
Mono 33rpm multi axis

NON
(San Diego Calif.)

- Recorded by Non, San Francisco

- Boyd Rice, Jimmy Holiday, London

- Non, El Cajon
(Robert Turman, Boyd Rice)

- Recorded live by
rec. ass is Scott Harrington
Mitch Holdinghausen

MUTE RECORDS 16 DECOY AVENUE LONDON NW 11 U.K.

BOYD RICE - vocals - noise manipulation unit - iona rola guitar - tapes

ROBER TURMAN - noise manipulation unit - tapes

multi speed multi axis for play at 16-33-45-78
can be remixed at home
maximum volume suggested

ORIGINALLY REALEASED IN USA 1979 NON RECORDS

MUTE007 / NON + Smegma / Cover / Record Labels / 1980 / A shared single with American experimental artists NON and Smegma taking a side each. 'This was a "concept single" with two holes; the NON side featured locked-groove loops that could be played at any speed using either hole. It was an early example of turntablism, where you are using the record as an instrument. The second hole had to be hand-drilled as the pressing plant couldn't do it – I did some of them...Frank Tovey did some...David Simmonds [Fad Gadget keyboard player]...Epic Soundtracks [Swell Maps] did some...each record is unique.'

MUTE010

ROBERT RENTAL
ON LOCATION

ROBERT RENTAL   ~   voice . bass guitar . synthesizer . studio .
ROBERT GÖRL   ~   drums . studio .
THOMAS LEER   ~   piano on Double Heart . studio .
Eric Radcliffe John Fryer Daniel Miller ~ studio .
Blackwing Studios London August 1980
Hilary Farrow Liz Farrow ~ cover
Mute Records 16 Decoy Avenue London NW11
Distributed by Rough Trade & Spartan Records

MUTE 010

MUTE010 / 'Double Heart' / Cover / 1980 / Although he was to establish himself as a significant figure during the early days of the British experimental electronic music scene, Robert Donnachie (Robert Rental) released only a pair of solo singles and a collaborative album each with Thomas Leer and Daniel Miller. 'I met Robert at a Throbbing Gristle gig. We'd both already released our own singles but didn't feel comfortable with the idea of playing live on our own. So we teamed up, calling ourselves Robert Rental And The Normal.'

He was probably the greatest example of someone having a completely different on-stage persona. He was a very quiet, gentle, funny guy but on stage he could become extremely confrontational.

MUTE006

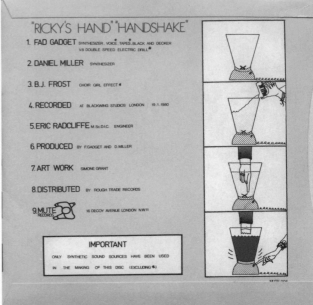

MUTE009

STUMM3

MUTE006 / 'Ricky's Hand' / Cover / MUTE009 / 'Fireside Favourite' / Cover / 1980 / 'Ricky's Hand' was Fad Gadget's second single. 'The drawings on the back of the sleeve were, for some reason, inspired by a joke: "What's green and turns red at the flick of a switch? A frog in a liquidiser!"' 'Fireside Favourite' was the lead single from Fad Gadget's debut album.

STUMM3 / *Fireside Favourites* / Record / 1980 / *Fireside Favourites* was the third album to be released on Mute. It was recorded at Eric Radcliffe's Blackwing Studios – soon to be second home to many Mute artists. The iconic 'Tumbling Man' logo was created by Rocking Russia's founder and creative director Alex McDowell.

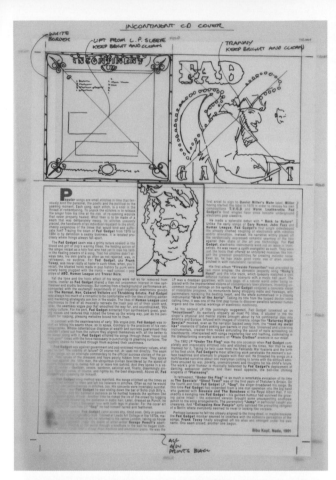

STUMM6

MUTE017

OUTER SLEEVE BACK

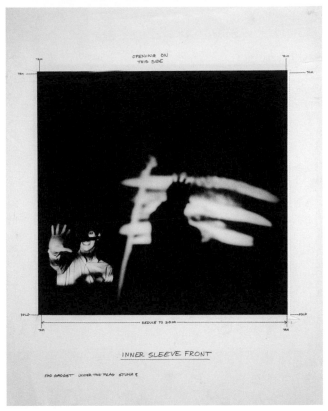

INNER SLEEVE FRONT

STUMM8

STUMM6 / *Incontinent* / Artwork Board / Front / MUTE017 /
'Saturday Night Special' / Poster / Cover / STUMM8 / *Under The Flag* /
Artwork Boards / 1981–82 / The second Fad Gadget album, *Incontinent*,
featured a striking portrait of Frank Tovey made up as Mr Punch and
photographed by Anton Corbijn.

'Frank was such an important figure in the evolution of Mute Records.
He was a really creative artist, very visually aware – he and Anton forged a
really strong collaborative relationship. This was our first project with Anton.'
Corbijn would also provide the design and photography for *Under The Flag*
a year later.

MUTE005

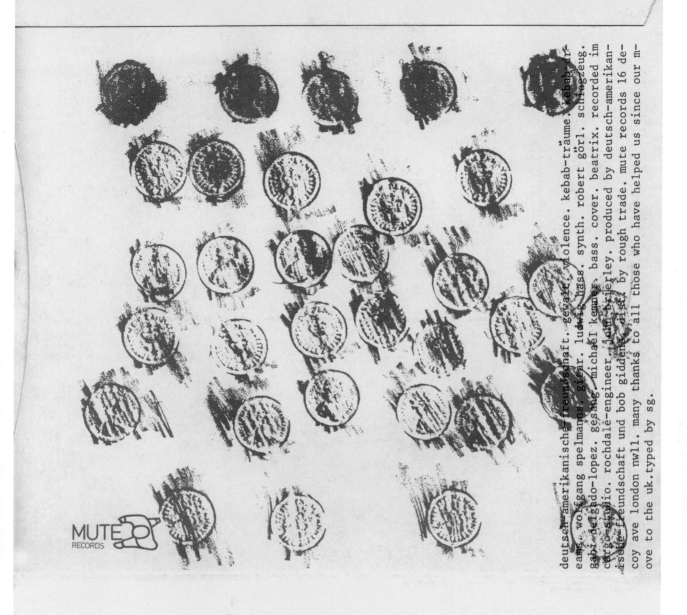

deutsch-amerikanische freundschaft. gewalt. violence. kebab-träume. kebab-dr-
eams. wolfgang spelmans. gitar. ludwig hass. synth. robert görl. schlegzeug.
gabi delgado-lopez. gesang. michael kemner. bass. cover. beatrix. recorded im
cargo-studio. rochdale-engineer. john brierley. produced by deutsch-amerikanische freundschaft und bob giddens. dist. by rough trade. mute records 16 decoy ave london nw11. many thanks to all those who have helped us since our m-
ove to the uk.typed by sg.

MUTE
RECORDS

MUTE005 / 'Kebabträume' / Cover / 1980 / 'DAF had released an improvised instrumental album on Ata Tak in Germany [*Produkt Der Deutsch-Amerikanischen Freundschaft*], but by the time I met them they'd started writing songs. "Kebabträume" was the first track they played me and I loved it. When they first moved to London they were living on the floor at my mum's house with all of their equipment.' The single was released in March 1980. The cover artwork was originated by the band themselves.

STUMM1

DEUTSCH AMERIKANISCHE FREUNDSCHAFT

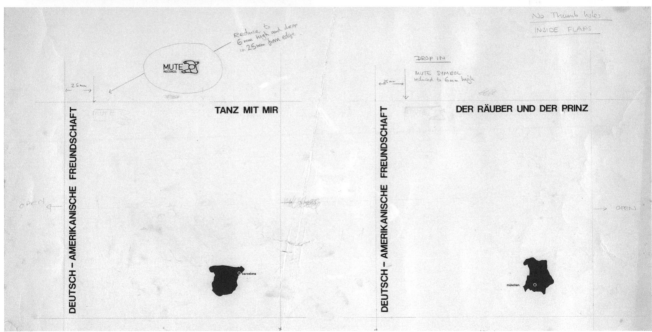

MUTE011

STUMM1 / *Die Kleinen Und Die Bösen* / Front / 1980 / '*Die Kleinen Und Die Bösen* was Mute's first album release, and was produced by the legendary Conny Plank at his studio in Cologne. Working with DAF inspired the "STUMM" prefix used at the start of the catalogue numbers for our albums – it's the German word for "mute".'

MUTE011 / 'Der Räuber Und Der Prinz'/'Tanz Mit Mir' / Cover / Artwork Board / 1981 / By the time of DAF's second and final single for Mute, 'Der Räuber Und Der Prinz'/'Tanz Mit Mir', the band had trimmed down to a duo of Gabi Delgado-López and Robert Görl. 'I was really upset when they decided to leave Mute and sign with Virgin.'

It's what I'd anticipated would happen. These were teenagers – seventeen and eighteen years old – and they'd chosen synthesisers over conventional instruments.

And they were making great pop music.

→ DEPECHE MODE / 1980
(DAVID GAHAN / ANDY FLETCHER / MARTIN GORE / VINCE CLARKE)

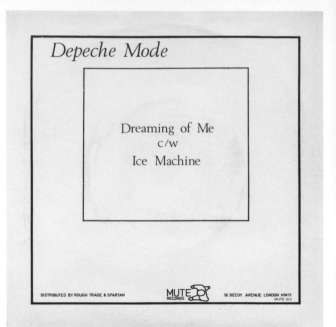

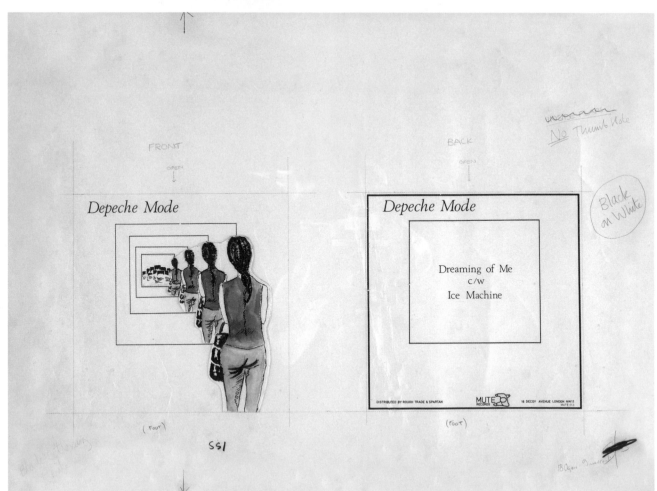

MUTE013

MUTE014   7"
12MUTE014   12"

MUTE016   7"
12MUTE016   12"

MUTE018   7"
12MUTE018   12"

MUTE022   7"
12MUTE022   12"

BONG1   7"
12BONG1   12"

BONG2   7"
12BONG2   12"

BONG3   7"
12BONG3   12"

BONG4   7"
12BONG4   12"

BONG5   7"
12BONG5   12"

BONG6   7"
12BONG6   12"

MUTE013 / 'Dreaming Of Me' / Cover / Artwork Board / 1981 / The artwork for the band's first single, 'Dreaming Of Me', was designed by Mark Crick, a Basildon school friend of theirs. Also a professional photographer, Crick would later write the well-known literary parodies *Kafka's Soup* and *Sartre's Sink*.

MUTE014 → BONG6 / Singles Discography / 1981–84 / 'New Life' (1981); 'Just Can't Get Enough' (1981); 'See You' (1982); 'The Meaning Of Love' (1982); 'Leave In Silence' (1982); 'Get The Balance Right!' (1983); 'Everything Counts' (1983); 'Love In Itself' (1983); 'People Are People' (1984); 'Master And Servant' (1984).

The 1980s saw a general vogue for longer or alternate takes of songs released as 12" 45 RPM singles. Unusually, the Depeche Mode singles offered completely different artworks between the 7" and 12" versions, making both types of release appealing to fans.

**DEPECHE MODE
SPEAK & SPELL**

Side 1

New Life

I Sometimes Wish I Was Dead

Puppets

Boys Say Go!

Nodisco

What's Your Name?

_____

Side 2

Photographic

Tora! Tora! Tora!

Big Muff

Any Second Now (Voices)

Just Can't Get Enough

_____

Synthetics, Voices Depeche Mode

Recorded at Blackwing Studios, London

Produced by Depeche Mode and Daniel Miller

Engineers Eric Radcliffe, John Fryer

Photography Brian Griffin

16 Decoy Avenue, London NW 11

Distribution by Rough Trade and Spartan Records

STUMM5

Depeche Mode

SPEAK & SPELL

STUMM5 / *Speak & Spell* / Cover Proof / 1981 / 'Brian Griffin did the photography for Depeche's first album *Speak & Spell*. Before we met, I'd been an admirer of his work with artists like Devo and Siouxsie. The photograph divided people – I've no idea what it means, and I'm not sure that Brian does either!' [Brian Griffin: 'Yes, Daniel is completely correct there!'] 'The graphic design was by legendary designer Barney Bubbles, who was well known for his work with Stiff Records, but earlier did the brilliant artwork for Hawkwind's *In Search Of Space* (1971). It was the beginning of a long creative relationship between Brian and Depeche Mode that lasted over five albums.'

ALL TYPE + KEYLINES MARKED ▬ PRINTS CREAM TO MATCH.
AREAS MARKED ▬ PRINTS WHITE OUT.
AREA MARKED ▬ PRINT 30% TINT BLACK.
ALL ON BLUE ▬ PANTONE 282 C

PANTONE
282C

BONG1

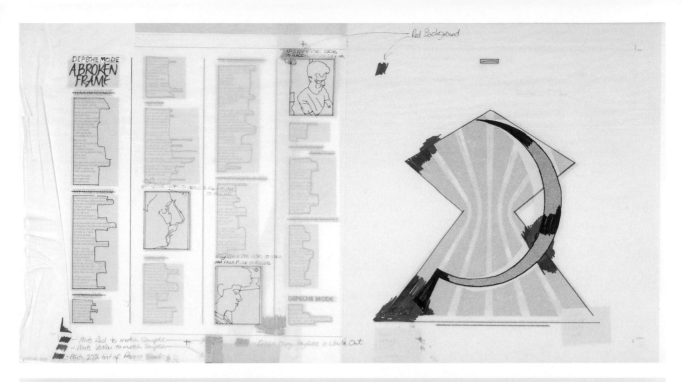

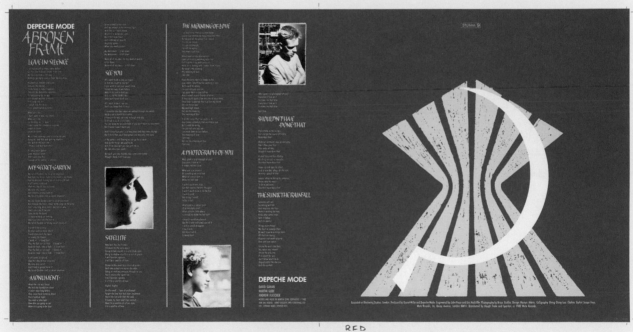

STUMM9

BONG1 / 'Leave In Silence' / Artwork Boards / Poster / 1982 / Depeche Mode's sixth single was the first to use the 'BONG' catalogue number, which lasted for the next 30 years. 'This was the first single from *A Broken Frame*. The artwork was created by Martyn Atkins, who did much of the graphic design on the Depeche Mode projects that Brian Griffin photographed.'

STUMM9 / *A Broken Frame* / Artwork Board / Inner Sleeve / 1982 / Martyn Atkins' inner sleeve for Depeche Mode's second album, *A Broken Frame*, took its visual cue – a scythe with a stylised wheatsheaf – from Brian Griffin's celebrated 'Russian peasant' photograph used as the cover image.

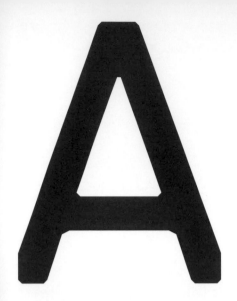

ICONIC PHOTOGRAPHY

Given the emphasis that Mute have always placed on the visual presentation of their artists and recordings, it's hardly surprising that over almost four decades they have engaged the services of some of the most important photographers of the period, among them celebrated figures such as Brian Griffin and Anton Corbijn.

Corbijn had a particularly strong early association with Fad Gadget, creating the striking artworks for his albums *Incontinent* (1981), *Under The Flag* (1982) and *Gag* (1984). Miller had met Corbijn as a photographer at the *New Musical Express*: 'He'd already photographed some of our artists, including an *NME* front cover for Depeche Mode. I'd always loved his work. Although he obviously worked with Depeche, he also had a great collaborative relationship with Frank Tovey. What I like about Anton's work is that somehow he seems to really understand exactly what the artist is all about – and that's been true of all the great photographers I've worked with. And he's got a sense of humour; that's important.'

Maintaining his flourishing career as a photographer, Corbijn would also quickly branch out into the newly emerging world of video production, memorably producing the accompanying film for Depeche Mode's 'Enjoy The Silence' single.

Brian Griffin has also enjoyed a long-standing and close relationship with Mute, and is particularly lauded for the iconic 'Russian peasant' photograph used on Depeche Mode's second album, *A Broken Frame* (1982). Griffin had, in fact, earlier supplied the contentious artwork to the band's 1981 debut, *Speak & Spell* – a sumptuous image of what the band's singer Dave Gahan described dismissively as 'a stuffed swan in a plastic bag'. Griffin had not been particularly fond of the band's music at that time and almost decided against taking the commission, but talking about it more than thirty years after the event,

he recalls: 'It was a crazy idea, but back then it was treated as almost abhorrent – someone said it was one of the worst album covers ever! It's only over recent years that people have warmed to it.'

Daniel Miller recalls how they met: 'The first real office we had was in Seymour Place, in London's West End. The building was owned by a photographer's agent who wanted me to meet one of his clients, Brian Griffin. He'd done some iconic photography in the early eighties and I thought he was an absolutely great photographer.'

Indeed, Griffin had taken images used on album sleeves by the likes of Devo, Elvis Costello, Ian Dury and the Blockheads, Siouxsie and the Banshees and many other innovative artists of the time, and often worked for Stiff Records with Barney Bubbles, one of the great masters of LP art design.

'On *Speak & Spell* I think I just told him to come up with something!' recalls Miller. 'But after that we built a more collaborative relationship. We would sit down, have a curry, get a pad out and some pencils and start mucking about over a few beers, and see if anything came out of it. And then he'd take it from there.'

Griffin's most noted work appeared on Depeche Mode's second album, *A Broken Frame*. Inspired by Soviet art – specifically, the Kazimir Malevich painting *Reaper* – the iconic image of a scythe-wielding Russian peasant woman was one of a large number of images he shot in September 1982 in a Cambridgeshire cornfield. As Griffin recalls: 'I was very lucky. It was a really blustery, torrential rainy day, but around midday the rain abated and the clouds opened...I balanced natural lighting with flash photography, which was something that wasn't being done very much back then – at least not outside of America. But it's an absolutely natural photograph – before the retouching and Photoshopping days.'

A widely acclaimed image, it appeared on the cover of the 1990 edition of *LIFE* magazine's *The World's Best Photographs 1980–1990*. In 1989, the *Guardian* newspaper described him as the 'photographer of the decade'. Griffin continued his association with Depeche Mode on *Construction Time Again* (1983), *Some Great Reward* (1984) and *Black Celebration* (1986). 'To me, it was also a political photograph. I come from a working-class background and I've always championed and promoted the worker if I had the chance,' Griffin concludes.

Another photographer to work with the label over a long period is Joe Dilworth. Combining a photographic career with drumming for Stereolab and Add N To (X), Dilworth has provided images for Goldfrapp, Nick Cave, The Jon Spencer Blues Explosion and many other Mute artists. 'His photographs just seem to get to the core of the artist's intention – which is really what's important,' Miller observes. 'With Mute, it's always more of a collaboration with the artist to make the images,' Dilworth remarks, 'and I got the feeling that once they had chosen the photographer to work with the artist, they just let them get on with it.'

Mute has always been prepared to let its artists lead the way if they have a particularly strong visual sense. Alison Goldfrapp provided all of the sleeve and promotional images for her 2017 album *Silver Eye*: 'She's an excellent photographer,' enthuses Miller.

STUMM9 / *A Broken Frame* / Photography / 1982 / STUMM13 /
Construction Time Again / Photography / 1983 / Brian Griffin images
from the photoshoot for the Depeche Mode albums *A Broken Frame*
(1982) and *Construction Time Again* (1983).

YAZOO
Only you
c/w
Situation
New single
7 MUTE020

MUTE020

7MUTE020

7YAZ001

7YAZ002

MUTE020 / 'Only You' / Poster / 1982 / Vince Clarke's first project
after leaving Depeche Mode was Yazoo, a duo that he formed with fellow
Basildon singer Alison Moyet. The poster for their debut single featured
the silhouetted images from the record's sleeve.

MUTE020 / 'Only You' / YAZ001 / 'Don't Go' / YAZ002 / 'The Other Side Of
Love' / Covers / 1982 / Yazoo enjoyed immediate success, their first two singles
becoming Top 3 UK hits. 'Some of Yazoo's photography was by Joe Lyons, who
also did a lot of work with Siouxsie and the Banshees around the same time.'

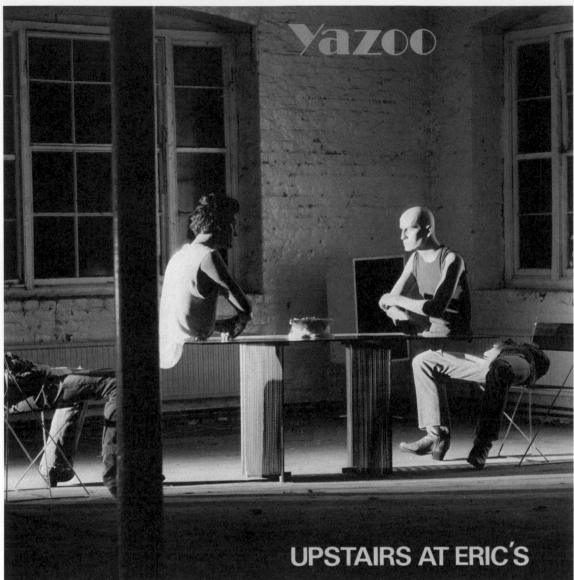

STUMM7

STUMM7 / *Upstairs At Eric's* / Front / Master Tapes / Test Polaroids / 1982 / Yazoo named their debut album after producer Eric Radcliffe's Blackwing Studios, which was directly above Vince Clarke's personal studio space. The cover portrait was by Joe Lyons. 'The polaroids were taken by Joe at the photoshoot for the album, but were never used; the image used on the cover of *Upstairs...*came about by accident, apparently.'

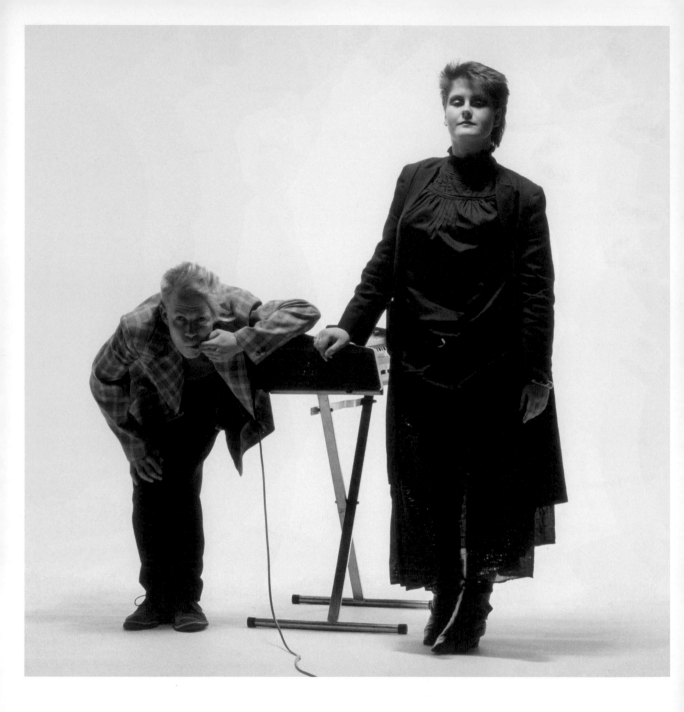

STUMM12

Yazoo / Promo Photo / 1983 / Photograph of Vince Clarke (left) and Alison Moyet (right) taken for their second album, *You And Me Both*. By the time Yazoo had finished recording the album they were barely speaking, and announced their break-up before it was even released. It nonetheless topped the album charts.

STUMM12 / *You And Me Both* / Front / 1983 / The artwork for *You And Me Both* was conceived by 23 Envelope (graphic designer Vaughan Oliver and photographer Nigel Grierson). 'Vaughan is well known for creating the visual identity for the 4AD label, but this was the only project he did for us. The image of two dogs fighting was unintentionally appropriate for the situation.'

1980 – 1982

MUTE023

MUTE019 / 'Fred Vom Jupiter' / Front / 1981 / 'This wasn't an original Mute release but one we licensed from our friends at Ata Tak in Düsseldorf, West Germany. We used to send each other all of our releases, and I just loved this, so we put it out in the UK. Andreas Dorau was a bit of a prodigy – he was only about fifteen or sixteen when he did this.'

MUTE023 / 'Los Niños Del Parque' / Front / 1981 / 'I already knew Chrislo Haas as he'd been one of the original members of Deutsch Amerikanische Freundschaft. Liaisons Dangereuses was Chrislo and Beate Bartel. We licensed it from the band as a one-off single. I think it's a classic.'

ANTON CORBIJN + DEPECHE MODE

Anton Corbijn is the name most closely associated with Depeche Mode's visual presentation. Since 1986, when he shot 'A Question Of Time', his first promotional film for the band, Corbijn has made more than twenty Depeche Mode videos and designed or photographed nearly all of their sleeves. Curiously, according to Dutchman Corbijn, his native country was one of the few areas of Europe not fully in thrall to the Depeche Mode sound.

With no formal training, Corbijn began his career as a music photographer in the Netherlands in the early 1970s. Late in 1979 he came to London to work for *New Musical Express*, and quickly made a name for himself with his stark black-and-white images – most memorably his session at a London underground station with Joy Division in 1979. It was during this time that he first came into contact with Daniel Miller via Fad Gadget.

'I took photographs of [Depeche Mode] in 1981,' Corbijn told Dutch TV in 2009. 'After that I was asked to work with them a couple of times, but I postponed it for five years because I didn't really like what they were doing that much.'

Corbijn began making videos in 1983, when he directed a promotional film for the single 'Hockey' by Palais Schaumberg, a Neue Deutsche Welle (New German Wave) band from Hamburg. He was no great fan of Depeche Mode when he was approached three years later to shoot a video for 'A Question of Time': 'The only reason I did that video was because it had to be made in the US – and I'd never worked in America at that time, so I put aside my artistic taste.'

Martin Gore, Depeche Mode's principal songwriter, was well aware of the way his band had been regarded before they worked with Corbijn: 'We struggled early on with an image problem and were seen really as just a pop band. We felt that Anton had a certain seriousness, a certain gravity to his work that would help us get away from that.'

Corbijn's videos for Depeche Mode truly hit their stride during the *Violator* period. 'I started to like their music more as it became more epic,' he says. One of his most remarkable videos was for the band's global hit 'Enjoy The Silence'. Depeche Mode were initially hostile to Corbijn's idea – based on Antoine de Saint-Exupéry's multi-layered children's book *The Little Prince* – of singer Dave Gahan dressed as a king, wandering around holding a deck chair. They were only persuaded after Corbijn explained that the king symbolised 'a man with everything in the world, just looking for a quiet place to sit'. The striking film was shot on location in the Scottish Highlands, the Swiss Alps and the Portuguese coast, and is widely regarded as a benchmark in the art of the music video. It certainly made an impact on a teenage Chris Martin. In 2008, his group Coldplay – by that time one of the most popular bands in the world – hired Corbijn to make a tribute video for their single 'Viva La Vida'. Indeed, the original video for 'Enjoy The Silence' was, according to Corbijn, 'the inspiration [for Chris Martin] to write the song – footage of the video became the content of his song – and he wanted his video to be a homage to the original'.

The importance Depeche Mode place on Corbijn's visual work is clear: 'I think he helped us to create a kind of cult status,' admits Martin Gore. 'But even though his work is very serious...he's actually a very funny person. He's constantly telling jokes and constantly making us laugh.'

Corbijn would continue to apply clever symbolism to other Depeche Mode videos, 'Barrel Of A Gun' referencing singer Dave Gahan's well-documented personal problems; featuring some striking images, Gahan sings, eyes closed, eyeballs crudely drawn on his eyelids. Corbijn admits that 'This was my commentary of their situation.'

By this time, Corbijn had been given almost complete control over Depeche Mode's visuals, including photography, videos, sleeve design and even the stage design for their world tours.

Unsurprisingly, with such a reputation, Depeche Mode were not alone in pursuing Corbijn's services. He has also maintained a long-standing relationship with U2, having created the iconic *Joshua Tree* sleeve image in 1987.

Corbijn's career evolved one stage further in 2007 when he directed his first feature film, *Control* – the biography of Joy Division singer Ian Curtis, whom Corbijn had photographed shortly before Curtis' death in 1979. Three years later, Corbijn had his first Hollywood experience when he directed George Clooney in the thriller *The American*. In spite of shifting seamlessly into this new world, he still maintains his key role as Depeche Mode's art director, having photographed and designed the band's fourteenth studio album, *Spirit*, in 2017.

BONG12 / 'A Question Of Time' / Video Stills / 1986 / Anton Corbijn's black-and-white video – his first for the band – helped transform the way Depeche Mode were perceived, adding gravitas as their sound evolved away from its synthpop roots.

I met Boyd in early
1978 and was intrigued
by his noise-generated,
multispeed locked grooves.
He's now been recording
for Mute for 35 years.

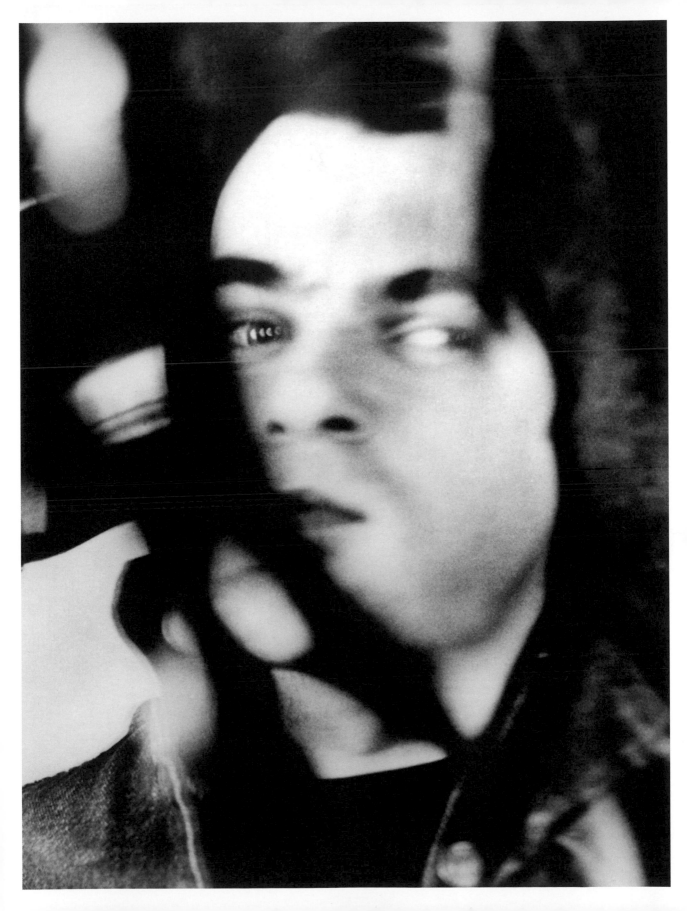

MUTE015

1980 – 1982   NON

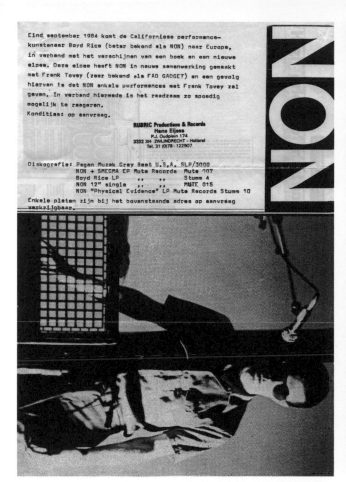

MUTE015 / 'Rise' / Front / Press Materials / 1982 / 'Boyd Rice – who is
NON – has been around since the early days of Mute. Although his music
has always been abstract and challenging, he's actually a big pop music fan.
He was there with me the first night I saw Depeche Mode playing live in 1980.
And he loved them. It's important to me that Mute continues to release music
by artists like Boyd.'

STUMM20

Boyd Rice
Frank Tovey

Easy Listening for the Hard of Hearing

STUMM4

STUMM10

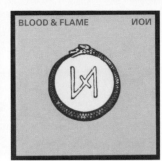

STUMM32

STUMM69

STUMM113

STUMM139

STUMM158

STUMM128

STUMM213

STUMM219

STUMM338

STUMM20 / *Easy Listening For The Hard of Hearing* / Front / 1984 /
Rice and Tovey's album of 12 'extractions' (producing sound from everyday objects) was made at Blackwing Studios. 'Boyd supported Frank on a tour of Europe in 1980. They found a creative connection and decided to do some recording together.'

STUMM4 → STUMM338 / Albums Discography / 1981–2017 / *Boyd Rice* (1981); *Physical Evidence* (1982); *Blood & Flame* (1987); *Easy Listening For*

Iron Youth: The Best Of NON (1989); *In The Shadow Of The Sword* (1992); *Might!* (1995); *God & Beast* (1997); *Receive The Flame* (1999); *Children Of The Black Sun* (2002); *Terra Incognita: Ambient Works 1975–Present* (2004); *Back To Mono* (2012).

'Although Boyd's records have never sold in large quantities, he's unquestionably an influential figure in the history of experimental electronic music.'

1983

1989

01

02

THE OTHER SIDE OF MUTE

Although Mute found itself diversifying into other less familiar musical areas as the 1980s progressed, an evolving electronic pop sound still proved to be the label's commercial driving force.

The first signs that Depeche Mode were shifting into new territory came with the 1983 singles 'Get The Balance Right!' and 'Everything Counts'. Both exhibited a darker, edgier sound, and lyrics that bordered on the cynical and world-weary. Daniel Miller remembers: 'It was very important for us to make big steps between each record at that time, both in terms of songwriting and the way they sounded.'

Construction Time Again, the parent album of 'Everything Counts', heralded the arrival of new technology in the form of digital drum machines and, most dramatically, the E-mu Emulator and Synclavier digital samplers. 'We were very excited about sampling at that time, Miller recalls. 'Every day, Martin [Gore] would come into the studio with a new exotic instrument or a children's toy piano, saying "Let's try this...."'

In spite of a gradual shift away from their synthpop beginnings, Depeche Mode's popularity had now spread across most of Europe. 'You could feel the support when they went out to play,' Miller remarks. 'Their fans were so committed to the band. Depeche had made three very different albums and the fans wanted to follow their path – and were excited by where it was going.'

The year 1984 saw Depeche Mode cement their reputation as one of the most significant British bands of the decade with the critically acclaimed *Some Great Reward*. This was followed by a world tour, including fifteen dates in the United States. The band had first played in America in early 1982. 'We started off getting played on alternative music stations, like KROQ in LA and WLIR in New York,' Miller recalls, 'but at that time people in the American music business told us Depeche would never break out of the club scene because they weren't a conventional "rock" band with drums and guitars.'

Depeche Mode's popularity in America was built up slowly and methodically until 1987's *Music For The Masses* broke into the *Billboard* Top 40, providing a glimpse of the adulation soon heading in their direction. The excitement was well captured in *101*, D. A. Pennebaker's concert film shot at the Pasadena Rose Bowl in 1988.

Meanwhile, Depeche Mode's former colleague Vince Clarke was staging his own return. A naturally reclusive figure, Clarke was always happier away from the limelight, engaged in his own projects, operating at his own pace. 'There was a period where he locked himself away in the studio and just spent his time experimenting. I don't think he really knew what he wanted to do at that point. Success with Depeche and Yazoo had come so quickly and I think he just wanted to slow things down. And then after being in hibernation for a bit, one day he told me, "I think I'll start looking for a singer."'

Enlisting the help of Flood – Mark Ellis, one of Mute's regular producers – they found Andy Bell at the beginning of 1985 after advertising in the back pages of the weekly music paper *Melody Maker*. 'That was the way you did things in those days, you know,' Miller remarks: '"Singer needed for electronic band, no time wasters!" That was also how Alan [Wilder] was brought into Depeche.'

Having already tried out a number of new singers, Miller recalls, 'I think Andy was the last one they auditioned. He and Vince just hit if off and gelled straight away.' The flamboyant Bell – who was then working by day in a women's shoe shop – admitted that Vince Clarke was one of his heroes. Erasure was born. 'Like a lot of Mute performers,' Miller says, 'Andy Bell has an operatic quality about him – and I don't mean just for his voice – I think the same can be said about Dave Gahan. And Nick Cave, too.'

03

04

Evolving his signature synth-and-singer formula, the music Clarke made for Erasure may have been more oriented toward the dance floor but was no less lacking the catchy hooks of his earlier work. Yet to everyone's surprise, Erasure made a slow start. 'The first album [*Wonderland*] was a flop, really,' Miller admits. 'And the first three singles didn't get any airplay. It was a frustrating time for all of us. I told Vince at the time, maybe if we couldn't break the next single he should try another label.'

The duo's fortunes were dramatically reversed with the release of that fourth single. 'Vince told me, "I think we might have a song, come and have a listen." I went to the studio, they pressed the "play" button, ran out off to the pub and left me to it. And that was "Sometimes" – it was clearly a hit, and that was what started the Erasure cycle of success.'

Co-written by Clarke and Bell – like nearly all of Erasure's output – 'Sometimes' reached No.2 in the UK charts; the album on which it appeared, *The Circus*, also generated three further Top 20 hits during 1987. And a year later, *The Innocents* gave Erasure the first of a string of UK No.1 albums through to the middle of the nineties. The duo have now sold over 25 million albums worldwide.

The perseverance shown towards Erasure during their early releases illustrates, perhaps, one way in which Mute stands apart from other record labels. Daniel Miller does genuinely seem to place commercial interests behind the promotion of the music that enthuses him. 'We're a business,' he declares, 'but we release records because we like the music – even if nobody else does! But if people *do* want it, then we're prepared to go all the way with it. We're certainly not shutting ourselves off from commercial possibilities. It's just that we're not driven by them.'

The middle of the 1980s also saw Mute Records taking a few steps away from the world of synthesised pop toward the *relative* conventionality of the electric guitar, as Miller signed Australian post-punks The Birthday Party – then

in the last throes of their time together. Moving from Melbourne to London in 1980, The Birthday Party had swiftly made their mark with a fearsome live sound; a cacophony of pounding drums, driving bass and clashing twin guitars fronted by the charismatic Nick Cave. By 1983, the band was on the verge of imploding, and disillusioned with life in London, were briefly rejuvenated by a move to Berlin – and another from 4AD to Mute.

Miller could hardly have been aware at the time that although The Birthday Party would only record one EP for Mute as a band (*Mutiny!*), it would ensure a seemingly never-ending supply of bands and collaborations over the next three decades.

'I met them in the very early days of Mute when they arrived from Australia,' Miller recalls. 'I went to see one of their first gigs over here at the Moonlight Club in West Hampstead, and thought they were not so much a band as an incendiary device! I'd have loved to have done something with them, but at that point I had DAF sleeping on my floor, I was completely broke and I realised they needed to be recorded in a good studio to capture their live sound. I just didn't think I could manage it, so I phoned Ivo [Watts-Russell] at 4AD and recommended them to him.'

Nick Cave himself recognised the four songs on *Mutiny!* as 'a documentary of the group in utter collapse'. And, sure enough, by the time it was released at the end of 1983, The Birthday Party had gone.

Unsurprisingly, the first, and most enduringly successful of The Birthday Party's offspring was based around front man Nick Cave. The Bad Seeds' ever-evolving line-up initially featured Cave's former band mate Mick Harvey along with Blixa Bargeld from Einstürzende Neubauten and ex-Magazine bassist Barry Adamson. The sparse, primal sound of The Bad Seeds couldn't have contrasted more with the anarchic clatter of The Birthday Party; above all it gave breathing space to Cave's increasingly epic lyrics.

01 Depeche Mode / 'Everything Counts' / Video Still / 1983
02 Erasure (Andy Bell) / 'Who Needs Love Like That' / Video Still / 1985
03 Erasure / *Wonderland* / Back Cover Photo / 1986
04 The Birthday Party (Nick Cave) / Hamburg / 1982

05

06

After their 1984 debut, *From Her To Eternity*, Nick Cave And The Bad Seeds recorded a succession of critically lauded albums, among them *The Firstborn Is Dead* (1985), *Kicking Against The Pricks* (1986), *Your Funeral...My Trial* (1986) and *Tender Prey* (1988). And Cave upped his credentials as a purveyor of Southern Gothic with a novel, *And The Ass Saw The Angel* (1989).

Miller recognises a significant influence on Nick Cave. 'It's important to say that Mick Harvey, who'd been Nick's musical partner since they were together in The Boys Next Door – their band before The Birthday Party – has been massively important. It was Mick who kept the ship afloat. He left at various times and whenever he was out of the picture things always became chaotic.'

For all of Cave's well-documented issues with heroin at this time, Miller was always impressed with his focus in the studio: 'Watching the way he worked was incredible. He was constantly writing – there were notes everywhere – and he got into the role really easily, He knew exactly what he wanted to do. And he got it down.' But, he concedes, 'Although musically it was all great, it might have been a difficult time for him personally.'

The second band to arrive at Mute via The Birthday Party was Crime And The City Solution. Revolving around singer Simon Bonney, several versions of the band existed in Sydney, Australia, during the late 1970s. Relocating to Berlin in 1985, Bonney formed a new version with Mick Harvey and his former band mate Rowland S. Howard, as well as Howard's brother Harry. Through cross-pollination with other members of the Mute family – still a frequent occurrence – Chrislo Haas (ex-DAF) was also recruited. With a fluid line-up, this version of the band recorded four albums for Mute before disbanding in the 1990s when Bonney moved to Los Angeles. Bonney re-formed Crime in 2013 with a new line-up and released the album *American Twilight* on Mute.

Rowland S. Howard would also front his own band, These Immortal Souls, alongside his brother Harry. Their own brand of gothic post-punk appeared on a pair of Mute albums.

Wire were already art-punk legends by the time they joined the Mute label, having recorded three seminal albums for the Harvest label: *Pink Flag* (1977), *Chairs Missing* (1978) and *154* (1979). Miller had first met the four members of Wire while performing with Robert Rental, both parties admiring each other's work. ('*Chairs Missing* is one of my favourite albums ever,' Miller reveals.)

'When Wire went on hiatus in 1980, Graham Lewis and Bruce Gilbert began working together as Dome,' explains Miller. 'We all happened to be working at Blackwing Studios at the same time and one of us suggested we did something together, and that became Duet Emmo – an anagram of Mute and Dome.'

Although Wire had made occasional use of electronic instrumentation on their early albums, by the time they reformed in 1986 they were actively embracing the use of synthesisers, sequencers and drum machines on new albums – such as *The Ideal Copy* (1987), *A Bell Is A Cup... Until It Is Struck* (1988) and *IBTABA* (1989).

One of the most controversial bands to find a home at Mute Records is Slovenian industrial avant-garde art troupe Laibach. Indeed, the first thing you see when you walk into Mute HQ in Albion Place, Hammersmith, is a press photograph of the band dressed in what – at first glance, at least – appears suspiciously like SS uniforms.

Formed in 1980 in the mining town of Trbovlje, in what was then Yugoslavia, Laibach were the musical wing of the provocative Neue Slowenische Kunst ('New Slovenian Art') movement. Their sound and presentation – variously described in the press as 'martial' or 'totalitarian' – not to mention a willingness to integrate futurist imagery into their work, would lead some observers to question their

07

08

politics, motives and meanings. The band have fed on this ambiguity, deflecting accusations with neatly oblique soundbites such as 'We are fascists as much as Hitler was a painter.' Over the years, they've been denounced not only as Nazis but also as extreme communists. Although, in truth, either argument misunderstands the band and their satirical deconstructions.

Miller remembers their first meeting: 'They were all living in London, washing dishes, and they popped in off the street into the office. I knew nothing about them but I liked the noise they made. They showed me their artwork, which really resonated with me.'

Laibach's sound quickly evolved from experimental industrial collages to the kind of slow, heavy sampled marching beats that would later all but provide a template for the Neue Deutsche Härte ('New German Hardness') bands such as Rammstein – who have acknowledged their seminal influence.

'I love their aesthetic. Their confrontational-ism! Their contrary-ism! The satire...and, of course, the music. I just totally got it. They were definitely trying to provoke a reaction – and they did it for a reason. The only way they could function under a totalitarian regime was by being provocative – or become part of the system. And then you realise that it's not just about totalitarianism, but liberal Western democracy as well.'

Since 1985, Laibach have recorded more than a dozen albums for Mute. In addition to their own compositions, they have also provided a fascinating selection of covers of the Beatles, the Rolling Stones, Queen, J. S. Bach, and, spectacularly, 1980s rock anthem 'The Final Countdown'. In 2015, they would find themselves at the heart of mainstream American culture when comedian John Oliver delivered a skit on HBO's *Last Week Tonight* about the (genuine) announcement that Laibach had been invited to perform in North Korea. The offer had come from the

Committee for Cultural Relations with Foreign Countries – itself a curious organisation, a private company based in Spain that officially represents the North Korean government. The first Western 'rock' band to receive such an honour, not only – Oliver added with growing incredulity – had Laibach agreed to the proposal, but they were planning to cover songs from *The Sound Of Music,* purportedly one of the few Hollywood movies North Koreans were allowed to see. Reporting on the event, American news network CNN noted that the politely reserved audience – predominantly middle-aged party officials – seemed 'puzzled' by the performance!

05   The Bad Seeds (Barry Adamson / Mick Harvey / Blixa Bargeld) /
      The Firstborn Is Dead / Outtake / 1985
06   Crime And The City Solution (Mick Harvey / Simon Bonney / Rowland S. Howard /
      Harry Howard / Epic Soundtracks) / *Room Of Lights* / Label Photo / 1986
07   Duet Emmo (Daniel Miller / Graham Lewis / Bruce Gilbert) / Promo Photo / 1983
08   Laibach (Dejan Knez) / Ljubljana / 1989

Robert Görl

MIT DIR.

7MUTE027

Robert Görl

BERÜHRT VERFÜHRT.

7 MUTE 027
DISTRIBUTED BY CARTEL & SPARTAN

ROBERT

Görl

DARLING DON'T LEAVE ME

7MUTE031

ROBERT

Görl

NIGHT FULL OF TENSION

STUMM16

STUMM11 / *Or So It Seems* / Poster / 1983 / 'With Wire on hiatus, Graham Lewis and Bruce Gilbert started their own project, Dome, and Duet Emmo was my collaboration with them. The inspired artwork was by The Brothers Quay [influential stop-motion animators] who were friends of Graham and Bruce.'

MUTE027 / 'Mit Dir' / Cover / MUTE031 / 'Darling Don't Leave Me' / Front / STUMM16 *Night Full Of Tension* / Front / 1983–84 / When DAF broke up (temporarily) in 1983, Robert Görl made a pair of singles and an album for Mute. 'He was friends with Annie Lennox; she sang on "Darling Don't Leave Me"; he'd played drums on the first Eurythmics album.'

DEPECHE MODE

Get The Balance Right!

DEPECHE MODE

The Great Outdoors!

7BONG2

DEPECHE MODE
EVERYTHING COUNTS

NEW SINGLE AVAILABLE ON BOTH 7 & 12" (EXTENDED MIXES)

BONG3 MUTE

BONG3

BONG2 / 'Get The Balance Right!' / Artwork / Cover / 1983 / When Martin Gore assumed songwriting duties after Vince Clarke's departure, Depeche Mode began to take on a darker tone. 'Martyn Atkins did the graphic design for "Get The Balance Right!" and "Everything Counts". Both of these sleeves give an early pointer that the band were beginning to move in a different direction musically.'

BONG3 / 'Everything Counts' / Poster / 1983 / 'This was the first single from *Construction Time Again*. However, it came out before we'd finalised the look of the project, which is why it seems different from the rest of the imagery.' The song gave Depeche Mode their joint-highest UK chart hit up to that point, eventually reaching No.6 ('See You', released in 1982, had achieved the same position).

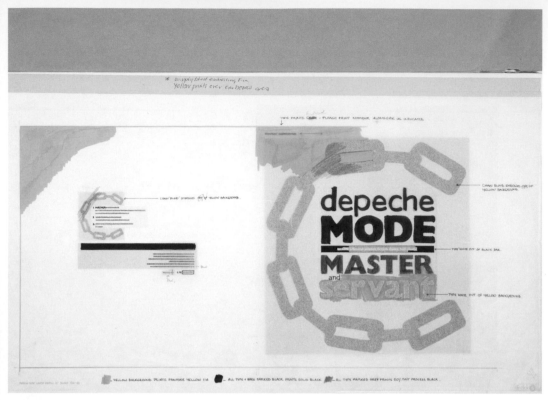

BONG6

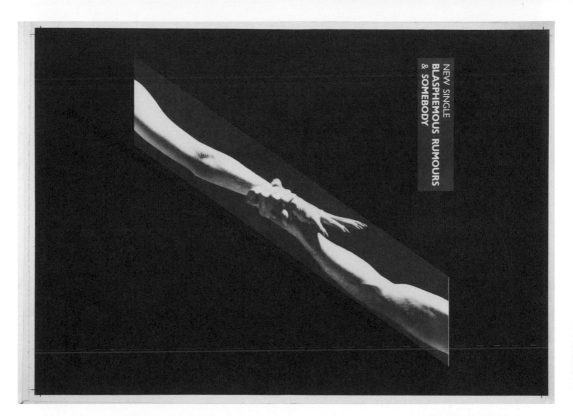

BONG6 / *Master And Servant* / Art Boards / Cover Proof / Poster / 1984 /
The first single from Depeche Mode's 1984 album *Some Great Reward* saw
the band moving rapidly away from their electronic pop roots. 'At this time

Martyn Atkins was creating a strong, consistent graphic look for Depeche's
developing sound. There's the new logo...the blocks of colour...it still looks
very powerful now.'

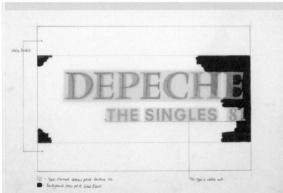

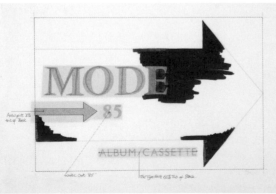

MUTEL1

THE SINGLES

PEOPLE ARE PEOPLE
MASTER AND SERVANT
IT'S CALLED A HEART
JUST CAN'T GET ENOUGH
SEE YOU
SHAKE THE DISEASE
EVERYTHING COUNTS
NEW LIFE
BLASPHEMOUS RUMOURS
LEAVE IN SILENCE
GET THE BALANCE RIGHT
LOVE IN ITSELF
DREAMING OF ME

DEPECHE MODE THE SINGLES 81 ——— 85 MUTEL1

DEPECHE MODE
THE SINGLES 81 ——→ 85

Mute Records Limited, 33 Kensington Gardens Square, London W2

MUTEL1 / *The Singles 81–85* / Artwork Boards / Posters / Proofs / 1985 / 'In the short space of four years – between 1981 and 1985 – Depeche Mode made four albums and were also touring heavily as well; nowadays it takes four years to make one album. This was the first Mute compilation, and is also the only time that Depeche Mode have ever posed specifically for an album cover shot. On the inner sleeve we printed press quotes, including some of the most hostile reviews they'd received. That was fun.' The catalogue number was MUTEL1 – a tongue-in-cheek nod to the KTEL compilations of the time.

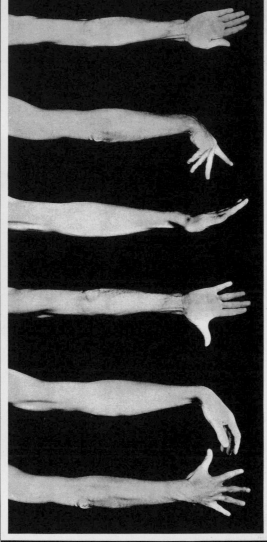

BRUCE GILBERT

THIS WAY

 L.P. BY BRUCE GILBERT
WITH MUSIC COMMISSIONED
BY MICHAEL CLARK
FOR DANCE-WORK »DO YOU ME? I DID«
MUTE RECORDS 1984 STUMM 18
DISTRIBUTED BY THE CARTEL AND SPARTAN

STUMM18

BRUCE GILBERT

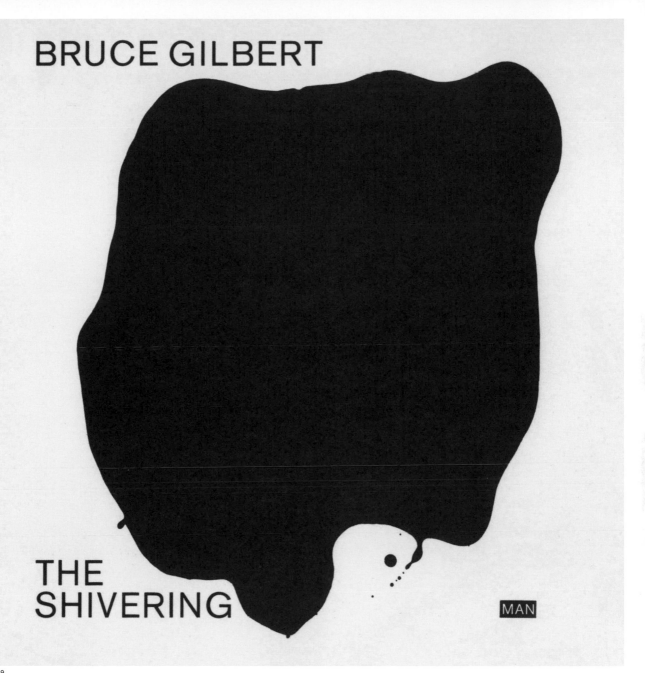

THE
SHIVERING

MAN

STUMM39

STUMM18 / *This Way* / Poster / 1984 / Bruce Gilbert's first solo album featured a commission from British ballet dancer and choreographer Michael Clark. A radical departure from the music that Gilbert played as guitarist with Wire, much of the album comprises rich electronic drones.

STUMM39 / *The Shivering Man* / Front / 1987 / 'After *154* [Wire album released in 1979], all the members of the band recorded their own experimental solo projects. We were lucky enough that Bruce wanted to record his albums for Mute and they still look and sound great.'

I went to see one of
their first gigs after
they arrived in the UK,
and thought they were
not so much a band as
an incendiary device.

→ THE BIRTHDAY PARTY / 1983 /
(NICK CAVE / MICK HARVEY / TRACY PEW / ROWLAND S. HOWARD)

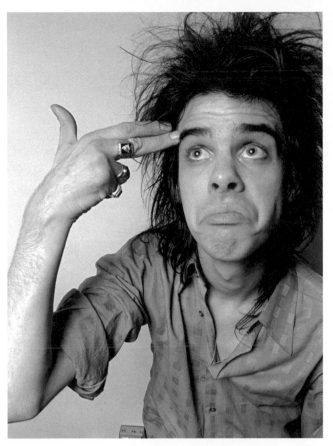

The Birthday Party (Nick Cave) and fans / Sydney / 1982 / 'They were an extraordinary band to see live. I'd have loved to have worked with them when I first met them in London, but I had no money and DAF had just come over from Germany and were sleeping on my floor. At that particular time I really wouldn't have been able to do them justice.' Photographs taken by Tasso Taraboulsi over two shows, three days apart.

12MUTE029

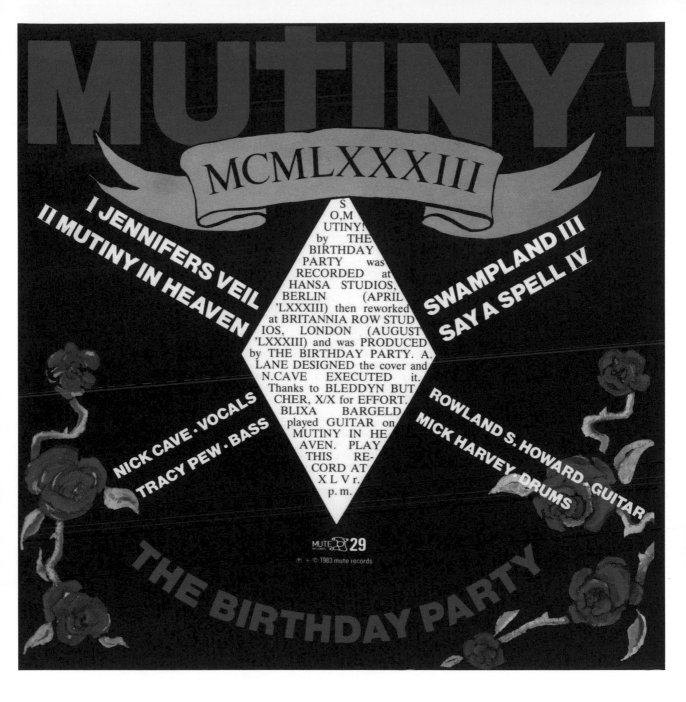

MUTINY!

MCMLXXXIII

I JENNIFERS VEIL
II MUTINY IN HEAVEN

SWAMPLAND III
SAY A SPELL IV

SOMUTINY! by THE BIRTHDAY PARTY was RECORDED at HANSA STUDIOS, BERLIN (APRIL 'LXXXIII) then reworked at BRITANNIA ROW STUDIOS, LONDON (AUGUST 'LXXXIII) and was PRODUCED by THE BIRTHDAY PARTY. A. LANE DESIGNED the cover and N.CAVE EXECUTED it. Thanks to BLEDDYN BUTCHER, X/X for EFFORT. BLIXA BARGELD played GUITAR on MUTINY IN HEAVEN. PLAY THIS RECORD AT XLV r. p.m.

NICK CAVE · VOCALS
TRACY PEW · BASS

ROWLAND S. HOWARD · GUITAR
MICK HARVEY · DRUMS

MUTE 29
℗ + © 1983 mute records

THE BIRTHDAY PARTY

MUTE029 / *Mutiny!* / Cover / 1983 / 'This was the first and only Birthday Party release on Mute. There was a swastika among the images on the back of the cover, and this created a problem when copies of the record were sent over to Germany – where displaying the symbol was against the law. So each copy we sent over first had to have the swastika blacked out by Mute staff using a felt pen!'

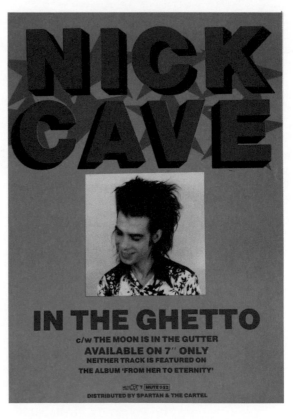

MUTE032

NICK CAVE

FEATURING

THE BAD SEEDS

FROM HER
TO ETERNITY

MUTE RECORDS STUMM 17

STUMM17

MUTE032 / 'In The Ghetto' / Artwork Boards / Poster / 1984 / The three layers of the original board artwork and the final printed poster for Nick Cave's first single. The track is a surprising cover of 'In The Ghetto', a ballad made famous in the 1960s by Elvis Presley. The band briefly performed as Nick Cave And The Cavemen before switching to The Bad Seeds – a name taken from the final Birthday Party release. Although issued on the same day as Cave's debut, *From Her To Eternity*, the single did not appear on the original album.

STUMM17 / *From Her To Eternity* / Colour Separation Sheet / 1984 / Many fans of The Birthday Party were surprised by Nick Cave's new sound. Gone was the high-speed aggression, in its place was a more focused sound that enabled Cave's lyrics to breathe. 'The Birthday Party was very much a group...and there was quite a specific sonic intention with that group and it was something, I think, that Nick had had enough of.' Mick Harvey, The Bad Seeds.

Neg 29
Neg 12

please crop so
the tattoo *illegible* is like this

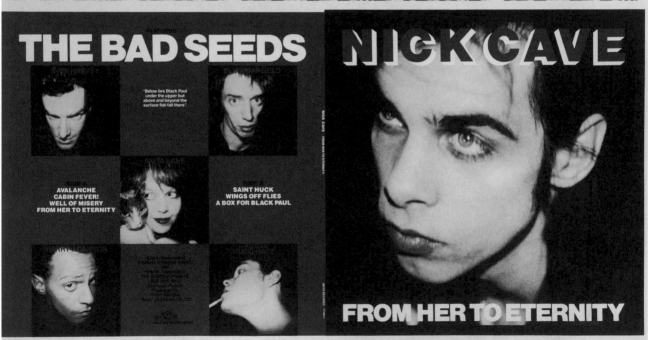

STUMM17

Cave's debut album saw a marked shift in sound from his days fronting
The Birthday Party. He later recalled, 'I wanted it to be more lyrically
orientated, and getting Blixa Bargeld from Einstürzende Neubauten in the
group made an incredible difference. He's a completely kind of atmospheric
guitarist and incredibly economical and it gave me room to breathe.'

STUMM21

STUMM28

STUMM21 / *The Firstborn Is Dead* / Poster Proof / 1985 / 'The whole idea of *The Firstborn Is Dead* was ostensibly to make a blues album [in inverted commas]; this was done in the full knowledge that we weren't capable of making a traditional blues album.' Mick Harvey, The Bad Seeds.

STUMM28 / *Kicking Against The Pricks* / Inner Sleeve Artwork Mock-Up / 1986 / A collection of cover versions, the title of the third Bad Seeds album derives from a biblical phrase that appears in Acts of the Apostles (in the King James Version of the Bible).

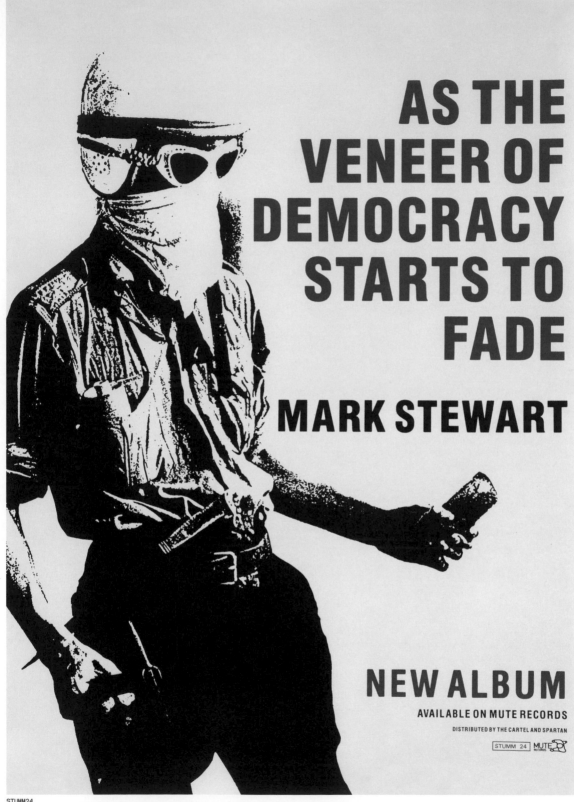

AS THE VENEER OF DEMOCRACY STARTS TO FADE

MARK STEWART

NEW ALBUM
AVAILABLE ON MUTE RECORDS
DISTRIBUTED BY THE CARTEL AND SPARTAN
STUMM 24 MUTE RECORDS

STUMM24

STUMM24

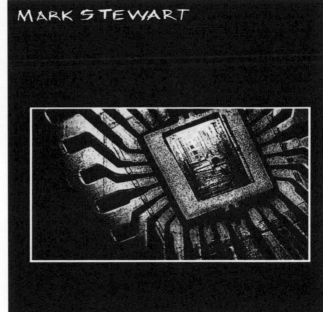

STUMM43

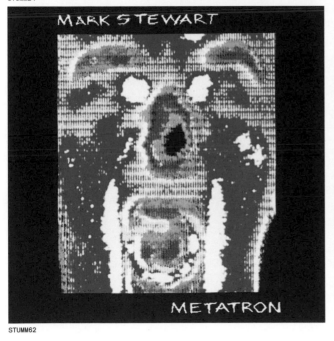

STUMM62

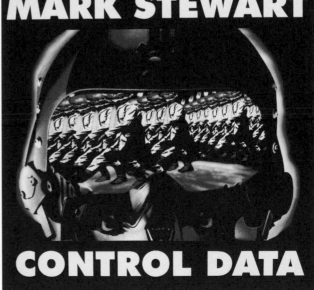

STUMM93

STUMM24 / *As The Veneer Of Democracy Starts To Fade* / Poster / 1985 / Mark Stewart established himself in the late 1970s singing with teenage Bristol agitprop band The Pop Group. 'Mark came up with the artwork – it's one of my favourite Mute posters'.

STUMM24 → STUMM93 / Albums Discography / 1985–96 / *As The Veneer*

Of Democracy Starts To Fade (1985); *Mark Stewart* (1987); *Metatron* (1990); *Control Data* (1995).

Recording four albums for Mute, Stewart worked regularly with On U Sound dub producer Adrian Sherwood, as well as musicians Doug Wimbish (bass), Keith LeBlanc (drums) and Skip McDonald (guitar) from the Sugarhill Gang band.

MUTE037

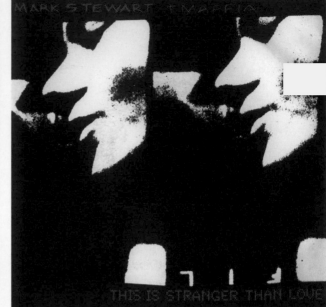

MUTE059

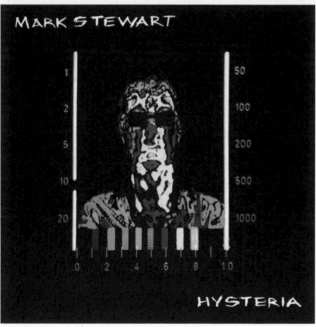

MUTE092

MUTE130

MARK STEWART

CONSUMED – THE REMIX WARS

MUTE213

MUTE037 → MUTE213 / Singles Discography / 1985–98 /
'Hypnotized' (1985); 'This Is Stranger Than Love' (1987); 'Hysteria'
(1990); 'Dream Kitchen' (1996); 'Consumed – The Remix Wars' (1998).

From his early days as a Bristol teenager in The Pop Group,
Stewart's work has always taken an avowedly political line,

encompassing radical philosophies, attacks on consumerism and
government behaviour. His music's pioneering mix of punk, funk
and dub was a massive influence on the industrial bands of the
1980s and the later Bristol trip-hop scene, including artists
such as Massive Attack, Portishead and Tricky. 'Another great
confrontational Mute artist.'

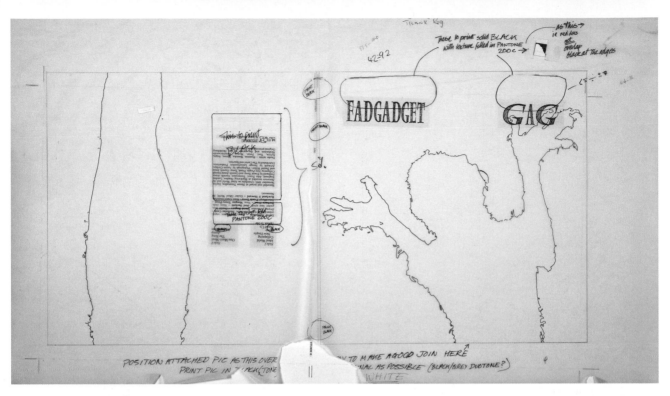

STUMM15

STUMM15 / *Gag* / Cover Photography / Artwork Board / Proof / 1984 / Less immediate than his earlier releases, the fourth album from Fad Gadget saw Frank Tovey effectively combining electronic and industrial sounds. It also featured 'Collapsing New People' (1984), a single recorded in Berlin with German band Einstürzende Neubauten – whose name translates as 'collapsing new buildings'. The artwork and design were once again created by Anton Corbijn.

MUTE039

frank tovey

LUDDITE JOE

SEVEN AND TWELVE INCH SINGLE

MUTE044

MUTE039 / 'Luxury' / Front / Poster / MUTE044 / 'Luddite Joe' / Poster / 1985–86 / In 1985, Frank Tovey decided to give himself a relaunch: 'Because of my reputation, Fad Gadget songs were hardly ever played on the radio, so I started using my own name.' His first single, 'Luxury', was as close as this uncompromising artist would ever come to having a mainstream hit record. 'Luxury' was designed by Paul White, who later founded Me Company.

STUMM3

STUMM6

STUMM8

STUMM15

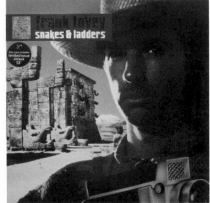

STUMM23

STUMM37

STUMM56

STUMM73

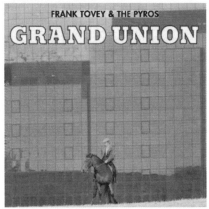

STUMM84

STUMM107

MUTEL7

MUTEL13

MUTE002

MUTE006

MUTE009

MUTE012

MUTE017

MUTE021

MUTE024

MUTE026

MUTE028

MUTE030

MUTE033

MUTE039

MUTE044

MUTE079

MUTE100

MUTE121

STUMM3 → MUTEL13 / Albums Discography / 1980–2006 / *Fireside Favourites* (1980); *Incontinent* (1981); *Under The Flag* (1983); *Gag* (1984); *Snakes & Ladders* (1985); *The Fad Gadget Singles* (1986); *Civilian* (1988); *Tyranny And The Hired Hand* (1989); *Grand Union* (1991); *Worried Men In Second-Hand Suits* (1992); *The Best Of Fad Gadget* (2001); *Fad Gadget By Frank Tovey* (2006).

MUTE002 → MUTE121 / Singles Discography / 1979–91 / 'Back To Nature' (1979); 'Ricky's Hand' (1980); 'Fireside Favourite'/'Insecticide' (1980); 'Make Room' (1981); 'Saturday Night Special' (1982); 'King Of The Flies' (1982); 'Life On The Line' (1982); 'For Whom The Bells Toll' (1982); 'I Discover Love' (1983); 'Collapsing New People' (1984); 'One Man's Meat' (1984); 'Luxury' (1985); 'Luddite Joe' (1986); 'Bridge St Shuffle' (1988); 'Sam Hall' (1989); 'The Liberty Tree' (1991).

CRIME AND THE CITY THE SOLUTION

THE KENTUCKY CLICK / ADVENTURE.

3 TRACK 12"

mute
12MUTE46

MUTE046

CRIME + THE CITY SOLUTION · POLICE

The Dangling Man E.P.

MUTE036

MUTE046 / 'The Kentucky Click' / 'Adventure' / Poster / MUTE036 / 'The Dangling Man' / Front / 1985–86 / Simon Bonney formed Crime And The City Solution in Sydney, Australia, in 1977. He moved to London in 1983 to work with fellow countrymen Mick Harvey and Rowland S. Howard of The Birthday Party, relocating to Berlin in 1986 for what he later described as 'the definitive years of the band'. A debut EP, 'The Dangling Man', was released in 1985. The cover images were by *New Musical Express* photographer Bleddyn Butcher, noted in particular for his work with Nick Cave.

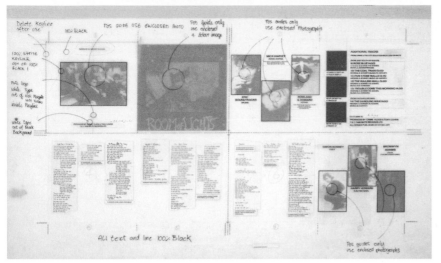
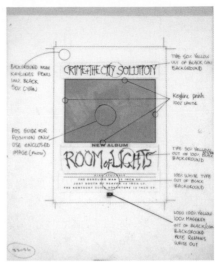
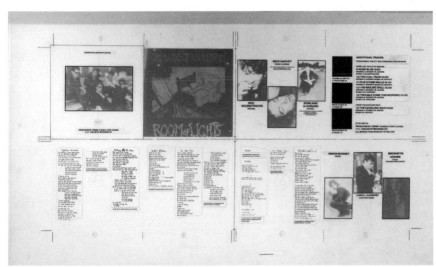
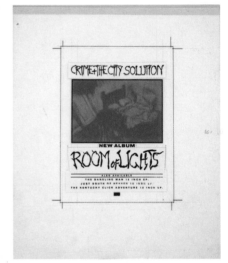

22STUMM36 / *Just South Of Heaven* / *Room Of Lights* / Cover Proof / Artwork Boards / Originally Released 1985–86 / Reissue Compilation 1988 / *Just South Of Heaven* was released as a mini-LP in 1985, followed a year later by a full debut, *Room Of Lights*. Paintings and illustrations for both releases came from Bronwyn Adams, who joined the band shortly afterwards;

she and Bonney would later marry, the couple moving Crime And The City Solution to Detroit in the early 1990s. In spite of the varied personnel across the decades, Bonney maintains that 'All bands with the name Crime have roughly the same ethos – a sense of adventure and a healthy disregard for rules.'

new *Album*

WONDERLAND.
by
erasure

STUMM25 / *Wonderland* / Poster / Proof / Colour Separation / 1986 / After two unsuccessful single releases, Erasure's 1986 debut album, *Wonderland*, stalled at No.71 in the UK album charts. 'This was a difficult period for all of us, because it was the first time Vince had done something that wasn't immediately successful. Maybe we were too complacent, and thought "Well he's done it three times before, he'll do it a fourth." But Vince and Andy worked really hard – going back to touring the clubs and universities in the back of a van.'

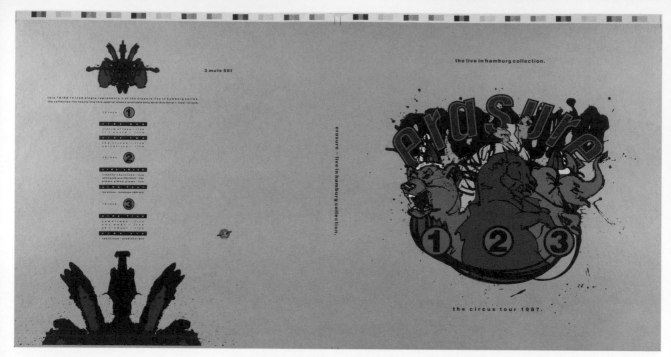

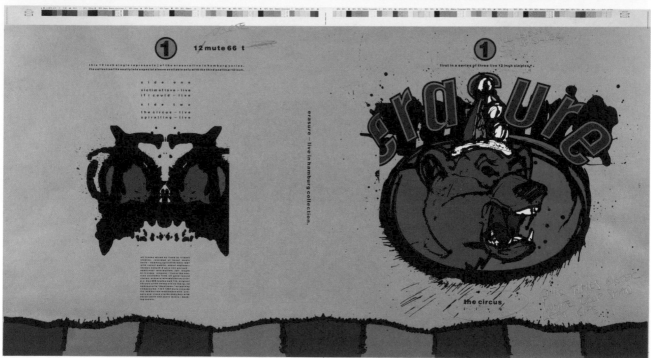

1MUTE66T

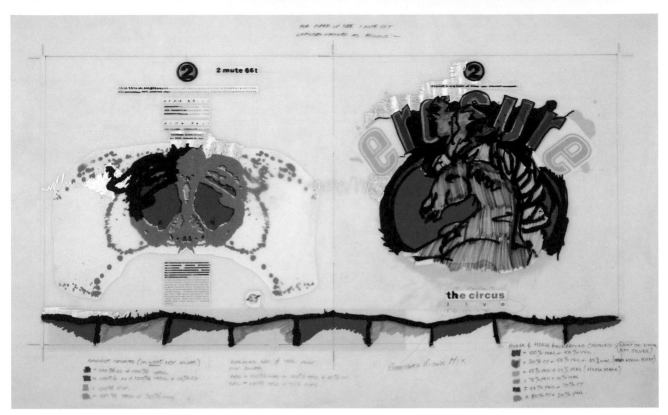

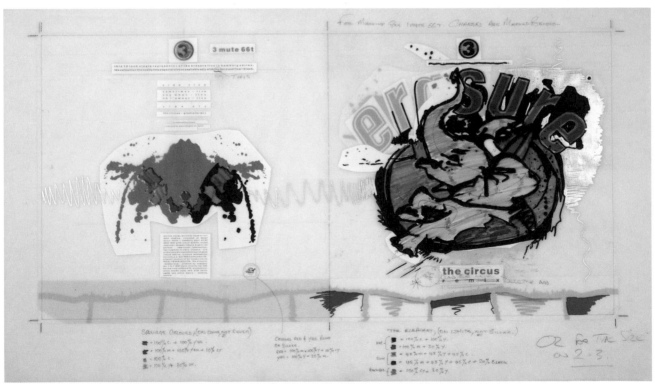

MUTE66T / *The Circus (Live)* / Proofs / Artwork Boards / 1987 /
'I remember when *Wonderland* hadn't worked my parents saying to me
"Are you going to get a proper job now?"' singer Andy Bell recalled. This
turned out to be unnecessary after the success of the duo's fourth single,
'Sometimes'. The ensuing breakthrough album, *The Circus*, peaked at No.6

in the UK charts and generated three further hit singles. Later in 1987,
Mute released a companion album, *The Two Ring Circus*, featuring remixes
by Flood, Pascal Gabriel, Little Louis Vega, Eric Radcliffe and Daniel Miller.
The artwork for both projects came from Me Company, founded by
graphic designer Paul White.

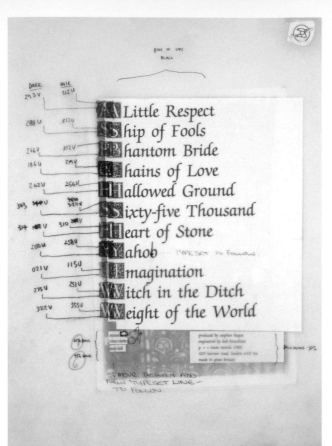

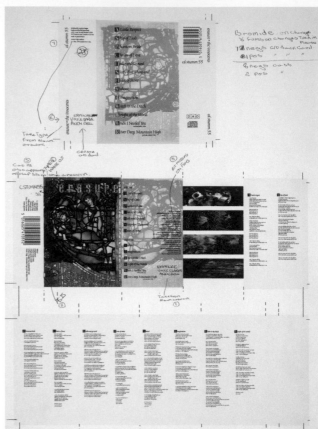

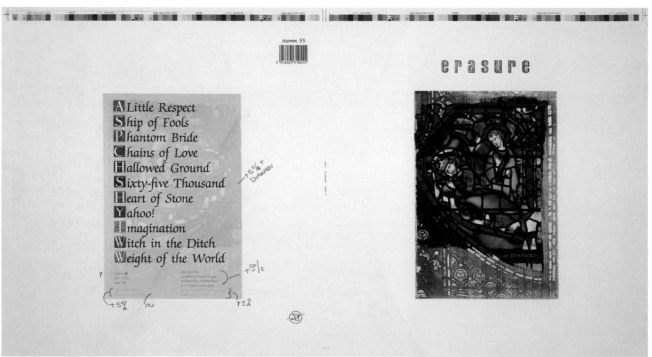

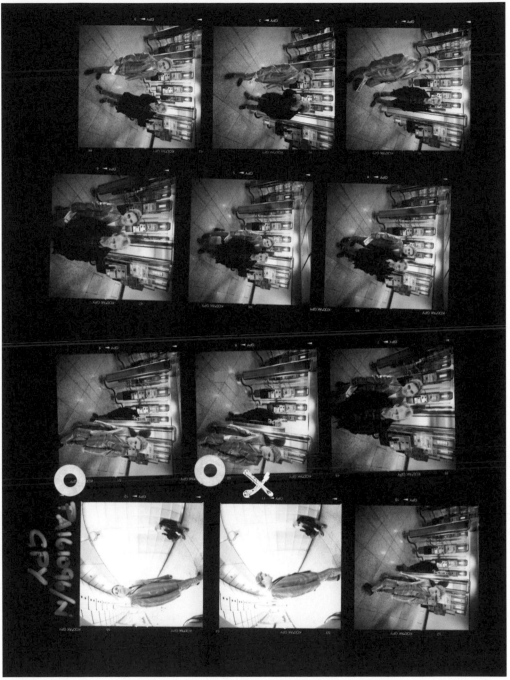

MUTE190

STUMM55 / *The Innocents* / Proofs / 1988 / Erasure's third album, *The Innocents*, topped the UK charts and took the duo into the US *Billboard* Top 50 for the first time. The album artwork was by Paul Khera and Slim Smith, the cover image featuring a panel from a stained-glass window in Chartres Cathedral in France; the image depicts the Emperor Charlemagne being visited in a dream by St James, who instructs him to wage a holy war against the Saracens.

MUTE190 / 'In My Arms' / contact sheet / 1996 / Erasure unexpectedly turned down the tempo for their 1997 synth ballad 'In My Arms'. Shown here is a contact sheet by music and fashion photographer Peter Ashworth containing images from which the sleeve artwork was selected. 'I think that everyone who's on Mute recognises that it's a very broad church, that's what makes it interesting for all the artists. If we weren't on Mute we'd probably have been dropped years ago!' Vince Clarke, Erasure.

STUMM25

STUMM35

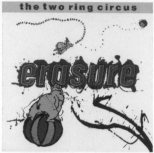

LSTUMM35

STUMM55

STUMM75

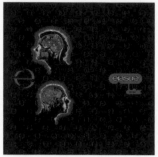

STUMM95

STUMM115

STUMM145

STUMM155

STUMM175

STUMM215

STUMM245

STUMM235

STUMM285

STUMM335

STUMM365

STUMM375

STUMM405

MUTEL2

XCDMUTEL16

MUTEL16

EDX5

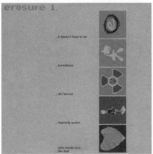

EBX1

EBX2

EBX3

EBX4

STUMM25 → STUMM405 / Studio Albums Discography / 1986–2017 / *Wonderland* (1986); *The Circus* (1987); *The Two Ring Circus* (1987); *The Innocents* (1988); *Wild!* (1989); *Chorus* (1991); *I Say I Say I Say* (1994); *Erasure* (1995); *Cowboy* (1997); *Loveboat* (2000); *Other People's Songs* (2003); *Nightbird* (2005); *Union Street* (2006); *Light At The End Of The World* (2007); *Tomorrow's World* (2011); *Snow Globe* (2013); *The Violet Flame* (2014); *World Be Gone* (2017).

MUTEL2 → EBX5 / Compilation Albums Discography / 1992–2016 / *Pop! The First 20 Hits* (1992); *Pop 2! The Second 20 Hits* (2009); *Total Pop! The First 40 Hits* (2009); *From Moscow To Mars* (2016); *1. Singles* (1999); *2. Singles* (1999); *3. Singles* (2001); *4. Singles* (2001).

Curated by Vince Clarke and Andy Bell, this is a sumptuous twelve-CD, thirtieth-anniversary anthology box-set package, also featuring a DVD, a hardback book, art prints, postcards, 'space passport' and a set of Erasure stamps.

'Erasure and I have worked with a wonderful array of talents for the album campaigns, many times with Paul White and Me Company, Intro Design (*Cowboy* and *Loveboat*), Assorted Images (*I Say I Say I Say*), Tom Hingston Studio (*Tomorrow's World*), Slim Smith (*The Innocents*), Blue Ink Creative (*Snow Globe* and *The Violet Flame*), sculptor Kate MacDowell (*Tomorrow's World*), artist Lucy McKenzie (*Union Street*), visual artist Rob Ryan (*Nightbird*), painter Louise Hendy (*World Be Gone*), illustrator Ashley Potter (*Erasure*) and of course Pierre et Gilles (*Wild!*).' Paul A. Taylor, art director, Mute.

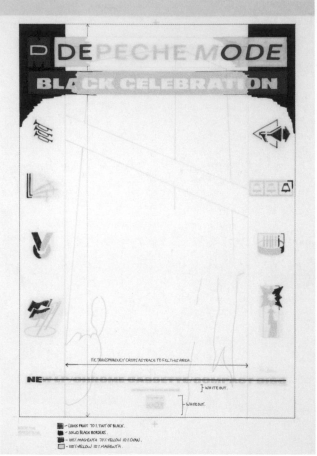

STUMM26

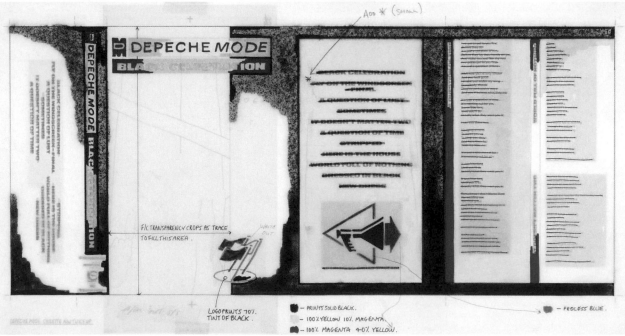

CSTUMM26

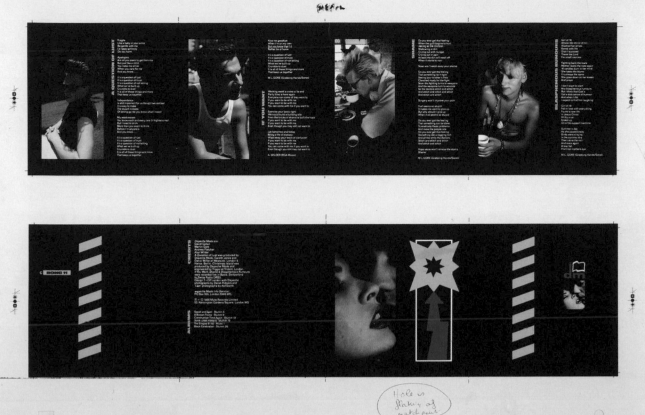

CBONG11

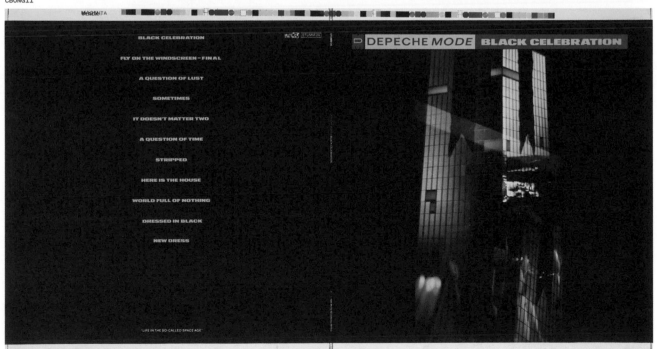

STUMM26

STUMM26 / *Black Celebration* / Artwork Boards / Poster / Proof / 1986 / BONG11 / 'A Question Of Lust' / Proofs / 1986 / 'This was the last album I did for Depeche Mode. The photograph is of a model I shot in my studio in Rotherhithe. I hold Mute as a label in the highest esteem, and thoroughly enjoyed the time I spent working with Daniel and Depeche Mode.' Brian Griffin, photographer.

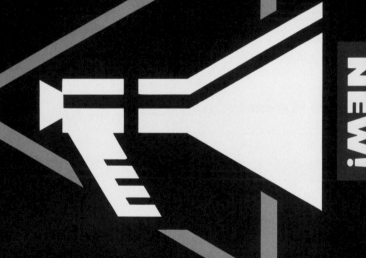

DEPECHE *MODE*

STRIPPED

NEW!

SINGLE

BONG10

BONG 13

STRANGELOVE · DEPECHE MODE ·

NEW SINGLE
DIE NEUE SINGLE
NYA SINGELN
LE NOUVEAU SINGLE

mute

BONG13

BONG10 / 'Stripped' / Poster / 1986 / 'Martyn Atkins and T&CP had been pushing iconography within their designs for Depeche Mode since they'd started working together. For *Black Celebration* and its singles, this was the first time we had used such a singular graphic design style throughout one campaign.' Paul A. Taylor, art director, Mute.

BONG13 / 'Strangelove' / Poster / 1987 / Depeche Mode embraced their growing global fan base with the poster for the 'Strangelove' single, using four different languages – English, German, Swedish and French – regardless of where it appeared. Daniel Miller created a slower version of the track for its appearance on the *Music For The Masses* album.

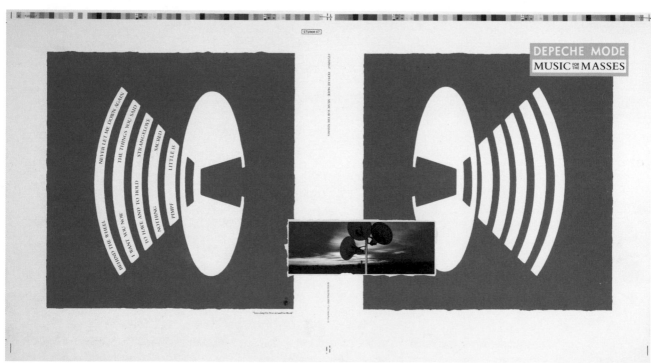

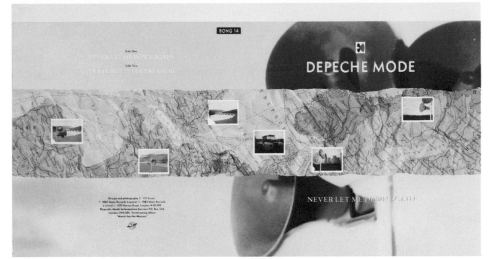

BONG14

L.12BONG14

12BONG14

STUMM47 / *Music For The Masses* / Test Shots / Proof / BONG14 / 'Never Let Me Down Again' / Proofs / 1987 / Depeche Mode's seventh studio album and its associated singles, featured a megaphone motif suggested by designer Martyn Atkins.

'He came up with this idea of a speaker, but to give the kind of ironic element….So you end up with this kind of eerie thing where you get these speakers or megaphones in the middle of a setting that doesn't suit it at all.' Alan Wilder, Depeche Mode.

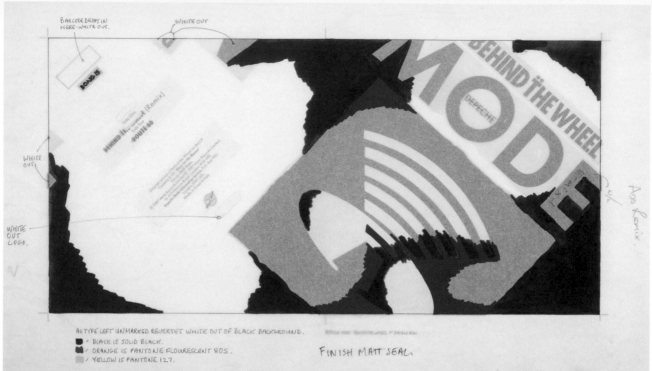

BARCODE DROPS IN
HERE·WHITE OUT.

WHITE OUT

WHITE
OUT.

WHITE
OUT
LOGO.

All TYPE LEFT UNMARKED REVERSES WHITE OUT OF BLACK BACKGROUND.

■ ✓ BLACK IS SOLID BLACK.
■ ✓ ORANGE IS PANTONE FLOURESCENT 805.
▨ ✓ YELLOW IS PANTONE 127.

FINISH MATT SEAL.

BONG15

L12BONG15

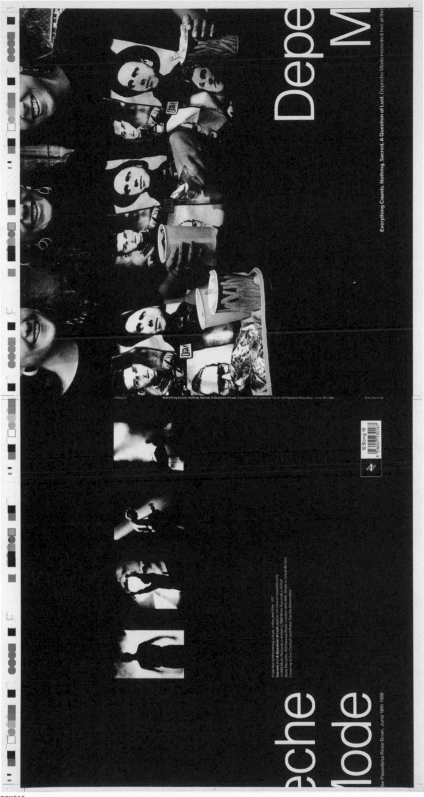

BONG16

BONG15 / 'Behind The Wheel' / Artwork Board / Proof / 1987 /
The overlay board artwork for the 'Behind The Wheel' single features
reprographic instructions from Martyn Atkins. Beneath it is shown the
printer's proof that was used for colour approval on the limited-edition
12" version of the single.

BONG16 / 'Everything Counts' / 'Nothing' / Proof / 1988 / 'The first Depeche
sleeve to feature Anton Corbijn's imagery, the design for "Everything Counts"
came from Paul West, then working for Peter Saville Associates; Paul later
worked with Anton on the design for the *Exciter* campaign.' Paul A. Taylor,
art director, Mute.

BONG7 7"   12BONG7 12"

BONG8 7"   12BONG8 12"

BONG9 7"   12BONG9 12"

BONG10 7"   12BONG10 12"

BONG11 7"   CBONG11 CASSETTE

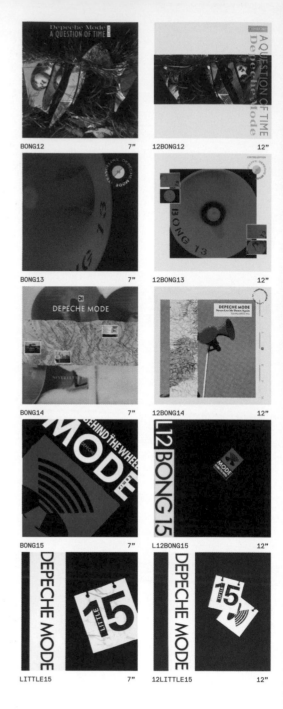

BONG12 7"   12BONG12 12"

BONG13 7"   12BONG13 12"

BONG14 7"   12BONG14 12"

BONG15 7"   L12BONG15 12"

LITTLE15 7"   12LITTLE15 12"

BONG16   7"

L12BONG16   12"

GBONG17   7"

12BONG17   12"

BONG18   7"

XL12BONG18   12"

BONG19   7"

L12BONG19   12"

BONG20   7"

L12BONG20   12"

BONG21   7"

L12BONG21   12"

12BONG22   12"

L12BONG22   12"

12BONG23   12"

L12BONG23   CD

12BONG24   12"

L12BONG24   12"

CDBONG25   CD

LCDBONG25   CD

BONG7 → BONG25 / Singles Discography / 1984–97 / [Page 152, left block] 'Blasphemous Rumours' (1984); 'Shake The Disease' (1985); 'It's Called A Heart' (1985); 'Stripped' (1986); 'A Question Of Lust' (1986). [Page 152, right block] 'A Question Of Time' (1986) 'Strangelove' (1987); 'Never Let Me Down' (1987); 'Behind The Wheel' (1987); 'Little 15' (1988). [Page 153, left block] 'Everything Counts' (1988); 'Personal Jesus' (1988) 'Enjoy The Silence' (1989); 'Policy Of Truth' (1990); 'World In My Eyes' (1990). [Page 153, right block] 'I Feel You' (1993); 'Walking In My Shoes' (1993); 'Condemnation' (1993). 'In Your Room' (1994); 'Barrel Of A Gun' (1996).

From the live version of 'Everything Counts' (BONG16) onwards, Anton Corbijn took over the sleeve visuals from T&CP and maintained the idea of different imagery for each format that the band had maintained since 'Dreaming Of Me'. The second 12" format for 'World In My Eyes' was packaged in a sealed blue PVC sleeve. The vinyl inside could not be accessed without cutting it open along the 'Violate here' instructional dotted line. (The track was the lead single from the *Violator* album.) The sleeve design for 'Walking In My Shoes' references the striking video for the song. When he heard the track, Corbijn remarked 'I see nuns, with beaks, skating.'

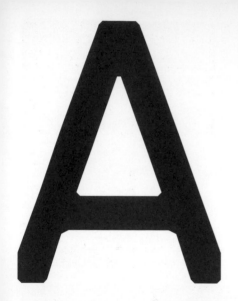

THE GREY AREA + THE TRIUMPHANT LEGACIES

The Mute label has always maintained an open catalogue – once issued, a release is generally never formally deleted; if the rights remain with the label, then at least one format of the recording will still be available. Mute also took an interest in keeping classic albums from other labels in print. 'There's music out there that isn't Mute in the sense that we didn't create the master recordings, but it is Mute in spirit,' explains Daniel Miller. 'And there's other material that is influential either to myself or the label.'

It all began when Throbbing Gristle approached Miller to look after their catalogue. 'When Throbbing Gristle terminated their mission, they closed down their label and asked us if we'd take over.' The first releases included *The Second Annual Report*, *D.o.A.* and perhaps their most significant album, *20 Jazz Funk Greats*. All are hugely influential in Britain's experimental and electronic underground scene.

In the late 1980s, Miller was approached by Spoon Records, the label owned and run by Can – one of the most important bands of the 1970s, and one of Miller's personal favourites – to represent their full catalogue outside Germany. 'They owned the rights to all of their original albums, and then later put them out on their own Spoon label,' Miller remarks, 'and then asked us if we'd take over.' Mute went much further; in close collaboration with Can's manager Hildegard Schmidt (wife of keyboard player Irmin) who ran Spoon, they made available a continuous stream of unreleased recordings and new collaborations, with the intention of keeping the Can legacy alive and allowing it to be revitalised and revisited every few years. By the time Can originally disbanded in 1979, they had released fewer than a dozen albums; there are now more than fifty in print, including solo works. Mute also gained access to the back catalogue of influential Sheffield industrial band Cabaret Voltaire, making available works such as *The Voice of America*, *Red Mecca*, *Three Mantras*, and later the band's Virgin and Parlophone releases.

Miller remarks that following the collaborations with Can and Cabaret Voltaire, 'We just decided to group them all together. The Grey Area Of Mute is simply a label of artists we love, who we think are important, and whose work should always be available.' John McRobbie, a former Mute general manager, coined the name in 1989 and ran the label, also instigating Mute's first steps into direct mail order to fans.

Since then, The Grey Area has reissued important works by pioneering giants such as Laibach and Einstürzende Neubauten, and also less well known yet nonetheless influential names such as SPK (standing for Sozialistisches Patienten Kollektiv, Surgical Penis Klinik and other variations), Monte Cazazza, Graeme Revell, Chris Carter, Thomas Leer And Robert Rental, Swell Maps, Buzzcocks and Virgin Prunes. Deutsch Amerikanische Freundschaft also returned to the label with the re-release of the three albums they made for Virgin Records after leaving Mute in 1981. The Grey Area was also responsible for a series of albums covering the pioneering electronic music of Delia Derbyshire and the BBC Radiophonic Workshop, widely known for the theme tune and incidental music to the TV science-fiction show *Doctor Who*. The five albums also include BBC station idents from the 1970s recorded by Derbyshire, John Baker and David Cain.

Miller has also tried unsuccessfully to create partnerships with some of his other 1970s Krautrock favourites. Frustratingly, attempts to license the Neu! catalogue were prevented by personal issues between the two members of the band. Although not strictly a part of The Grey Area, from 2004 to 2008 Mute also made available some of the early works and new recordings of seminal American avant-garde collective The Residents. A band that has never officially revealed the personal identities of its members (on stage they mask their faces with props such as giant eyeballs and prosthetics), they were a key influence on the early 1980s experimental music scene, releasing controversial works that included *The Third Reich 'n Roll*, a bizarre collage of twisted covers of 1970s American Top 40 hits, on their own Ralph Records.

The year 2014 saw the return to Mute of Swans, who had releases previously on the imprint Product, Inc. This included two new albums and an extensive reissue campaign in conjunction with Michael Gira's Young God label, through which he owns all of his catalogue.

A Certain Ratio also signed with Mute to look after their extensive catalogue after fellow former Factory Records label mates New Order recommended Mute as a good home for their work. Looper connected their sole Mute album *The Snare* with their other releases, offering Mute the rest of their early catalogue for the 2015 box-set release *These Things*. In 2017, Mute issued an under-appreciated master-piece from 2001 by Josh T. Pearson's original band Lift To Experience; the album was finally mixed as God intended.

One set of reissues of which Miller is particularly proud came about in 2009 when (still at that time part of EMI) Mute was able to reissue remastered versions of Kraftwerk's back catalogue dating back to 1974's *Autobahn*, arguably the album that created what would later become electropop. Miller admits to having been massively influenced by the Düsseldorf group, and many years later would even buy one of their bespoke vocoders. In their praise he simply remarks that, 'Everything Kraftwerk do just works!' Even though they haven't recorded a new album since 2003's *Tour de France Soundtracks*, Kraftwerk continue to be a highly successful touring entity.

Daniel Miller views The Grey Area and the label's other reissues as an ongoing programme.

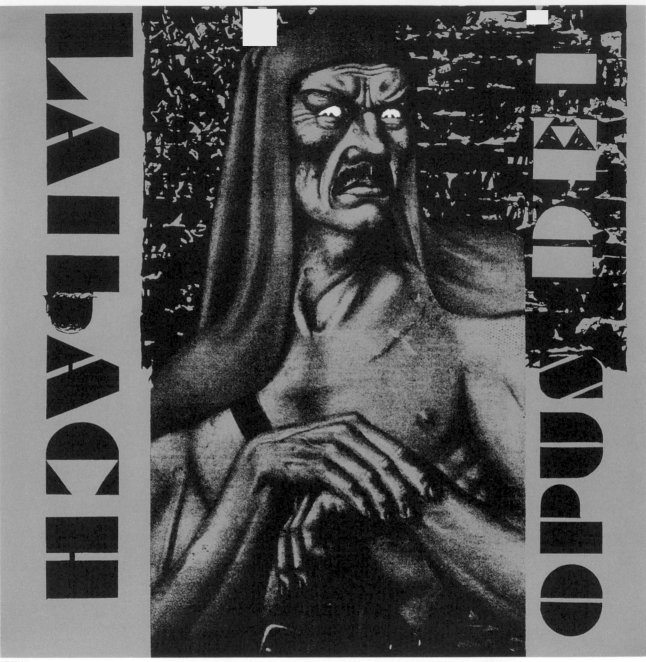

STUMM44

STUMM44 / *Opus Dei* / Front / 1987 / 'Like everything else in the group we also normally create visuals collectively, with collected ideas and debates and through Hegelian discourse of thesis, antithesis and synthesis, so to say. The execution of the final result is in the designer's hand. The *Opus Dei* album was at the time formally heavily inspired by Queen and Motörhead, so we were looking for an image for the front cover that would resemble Freddie Mercury and Lemmy Kilmister and also Laibach's front man [Milan Fras]. We found an image of a teutonic god of war, added the moustache and that was it.' Ivan Novak, Laibach.

Laibach / *Chess Für Vier* / 2003 / 'This photo was taken by Igor Škafar during the promotional activities for the *WAT* album [2003]. We play Laibach's diplomatic cross-chess for four up in the high mountains in Slovenia, where the famous First World War battle of the Isonzo (known to historians as the Isonzo Front) took place between June 1915 and November 1917. (Also partly described by Hemingway in *A Farewell To Arms*.) In the photo we are dressed in American military uniforms – the Americans were the only real winners of the First World War.' Ivan Novak, Laibach.

STUMM44

STUMM58

STUMM70

STUMM82

STUMM121

STUMM136

STUMM223

STUMM276

STUMM297

STUMM358

STUMM401

LPMUTE80

NSK1

NSK3

MUTEL12

LHN

LHN99

STUMM344

MUTEL23

STUMM44 → STUMM401 / Studio Album Discography / 1987–2017 / *Opus Dei* (1987); *Let It Be* (1988); *Macbeth* (1990); *Kapital* (1992); *Nato* (1994); *Jesus Christ Superstars* (1996); *WAT* (2003); *Volk* (2006); *Laibachkunstderfuge* (2008); *Spectre* (2014); *Also Sprach Zarathustra* (2017).

LPMUTE80 → MUTEL23 / Other Albums / 1990–2012 / *Sympathy For The Devil* (1988); *Ljubljana - Zagreb - Beograd* (1993); *M.B. December 21, 1984* (1997); *Anthems* (2004); *Volk Tour, London CC Club 16.04.2007* (2007);

Monumental Retro-Avant-Garde (2012); *Iron Sky* (2012); *An Introduction To ... Laibach* (2012).

Laibach / *We Are Millions Millions Are One* / Poster / 2014 / Laibach's 2014 tour supporting the *Spectre* album (which included the song 'We Are Millions, Millions Are One') saw the band visiting China for the first time. A year later Laibach became the first Western a rock band to play in North Korea. 'Not being allowed to enjoy – even if they maybe did – North Koreans were the perfect Laibach audience.' Ivan Novak, Laibach.

I love everything
about Laibach.
I love their aesthetic.

Their confrontational-ism!
Their contrary-ism!
The satire...

Everything.

LAIBACH THE SOUND PYONGYANG
OF MUSIC D.P.R.KOREA
AUGUST 19TH & 20TH 2015

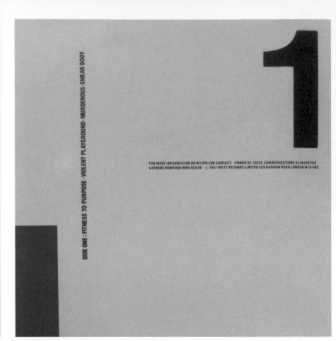

NITZEREBBPRODUKT1987

SIDE ONE : FITNESS TO PURPOSE : VIOLENT PLAYGROUND : MURDEROUS : SMEAR BODY

1

FOR MORE INFORMATION ON NITZER EBB CONTACT: POWER OF VOICE COMMUNICATIONS 35 MANSTED GARDENS ROMFORD RM6 4EO UK · © 1987 MUTE RECORDS LIMITED 429 HARROW ROAD LONDON W10 4RE

NITZER EBB : THAT TOTAL AGE

SIDE TWO : JOIN IN THE CHANT : ALARM : LET YOUR BODY LEARN : LET BEAUTY LOOSE : INTO THE LARGE AIR

NITZER EBB · NITZEREBBPRODUKT WOULD LIKE TO THANK: JOHN McDONALD · PHIL HARDING · MARTIN JEFFERYS · STAN MILLER · PAUL KENDALL · MIKE · RICHARD 23 · FRONT 242 · JO-ANNE · KATHY · TAMMY · CLARE · & ALL IN BELGIUM · CANADA · GERMANY · SPAIN · PRODUCED AND MIXED BY PHIL HARDING FOR BLUE AUGUST PRODUCTIONS · EXCEPT VIOLENT PLAYGROUND AND SMEAR BODY MIXED BY DUFFY · LET YOUR BODY LEARN RE-MIXED BY DANIEL MILLER & GARETH JONES. RECORDED AT THE GREENHOUSE LONDON N1 AND MIXED AT PWL LONDON SE1 ON AN SSL 4000E & AT HANSA STUDIOS BERLIN

2

STUMM45

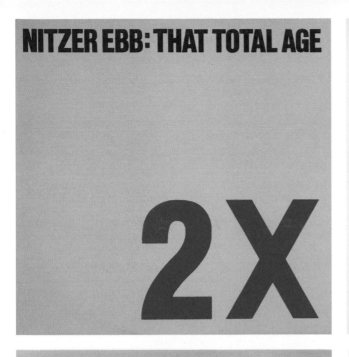

NITZER EBB: THAT TOTAL AGE

2X

RECORD ONE: SIDE TWO · MURDEROUS · SMEAR BODY

NITZEREBBPRODUKT 1987   LSTUMM45

12

RECORD ONE: SIDE ONE · FITNESS TO PURPOSE · VIOLENT PLAYGROUND

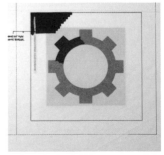

LSTUMM45

STUMM45 / *That Total Age* / Cover / Inner Sleeves / Remixes / Artwork Boards / 1987 / 'The idea of representing the sparse, hard sound through using black, red and grey was done to invoke totalitarian regimes and also to provoke the sensibility of the easily offended. The constructivist angle was intentional, and subconsciously perfect.' Simon Granger, designer.

NEB004

MUTE058

MUTE064

MUTE071

MUTE078

MUTE096

MUTE106

L12MUTE115

MUTE122

MUTE133

MUTE135

2/10MUTE145

MUTE155

MUTE164

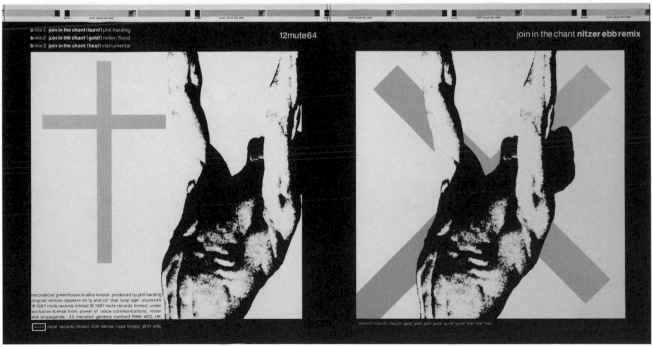

12MUTE064

NEB004 → MUTE164 / Singles Discography / 1986–95 / 'Murderous' (1986); 'Let Your Body Learn' (1987); 'Join In The Chant' (1987); 'Control I'm Here' (1988); 'Hearts & Minds' (1989); 'Shame' (1989); 'Lightning Man' (1990); 'Fun To Be Had' (1990); 'As Is' (1991); 'I Give To You' (1991); 'Godhead' (1991); 'Ascend' (1992); 'Kick It' (1995); 'I Thought' (1995).

MUTE064 / 'Join In The Chant' / Artwork Board / Proof / 1987 / 'The idea of the reduced aesthetic was a natural parallel with the music, it went from the militaristic to the minimalistic quite seamlessly. The later flouresecent orange and black was a deliberate move to subvert traditional industrial tags. As the music became more complex, so the artwork evolved.' Simon Granger, designer.

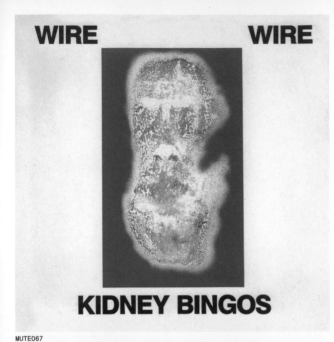

WIRE WIRE

KIDNEY BINGOS

MUTE067

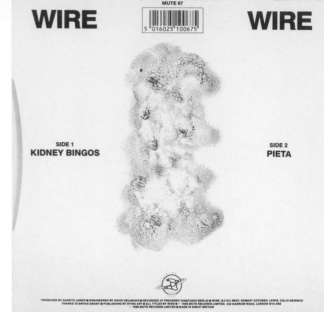

WIRE WIRE

MUTE 67

SIDE 1
KIDNEY BINGOS

SIDE 2
PIETA

PRODUCED BY GARETH JONES ■ ENGINEERED BY DAVID HEILMANN ■ RECORDED AT PREUSSEN TONSTUDIO BERLIN ■ WIRE: B.C.GILBERT, ROBERT GOTOBED, LEWIS, COLIN NEWMAN
THANKS TO BRYAN GRANT ■ PUBLISHING BY DYING ART ■ ALL TITLES BY WIRE ■ ℗ 1988 MUTE RECORDS LIMITED, 429 HARROW ROAD, LONDON W10 4RE
© 1988 MUTE RECORDS LIMITED ■ MADE IN GREAT BRITAIN

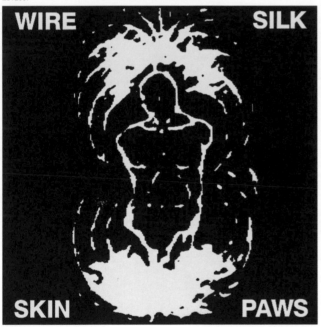

WIRE SILK

SKIN PAWS

MUTE084

MUTE 84

SILK SKIN PAWS
REMIXED BY DAVE ALLEN
GERMAN SHEPHERDS

SILK SKIN PAWS RECORDED AT PREUSSEN TONSTUDIO ■ PRODUCED BY GARETH JONES ■ ENGINEERED BY
DAVID HEILMANN ■ GERMAN SHEPHERDS RECORDED AT WORLDWIDE INTERNATIONAL ■ PRODUCED BY WIRE
ENGINEERED BY PAUL KENDALL ■ MIXED AT PREUSSEN TON STUDIO BY GARETH JONES ■ ENGINEERED BY
UWE HOFFMAN ■ WIRE: B. C. GILBERT, ROBERT GOTOBED, LEWIS, COLIN NEWMAN ■ SLEEVE: MAGNET MAN
BY RICHARD MACKNESS, LAYOUT BY SLIM SMITH ■ ℗ 1988 MUTE RECORDS LIMITED ■ © 1988 MUTE
RECORDS LIMITED ■ 429 HARROW ROAD, LONDON W10 4RE ■ MADE IN GREAT BRITAIN ■ ORIGINAL VERSION
OF "SILK SKIN PAWS" ON LP, CASSETTE, CD "A BELL IS A CUP UNTIL IT IS STRUCK".

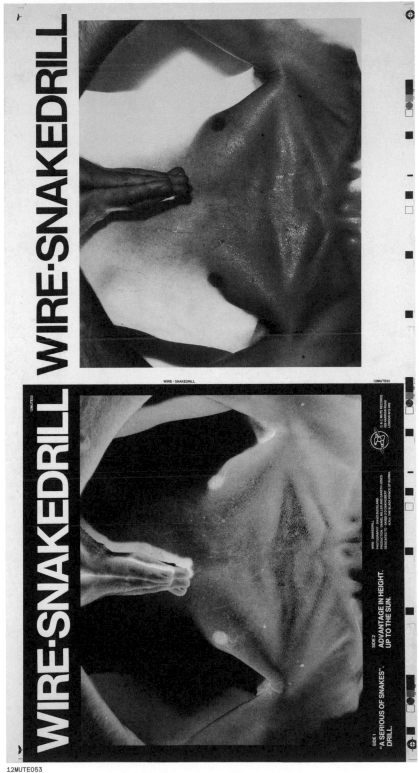

MUTE067 / *Kidney Bingos* / MUTE084 / *Silk Skin Paws* / Covers / 1988 /
When Wire regrouped in 1985, they refused to perform their earlier material,
instead hiring a Wire tribute band – Ex-Lion Tamers – as their opening act.
The EPs *Silk Skin Paws* and *Kidney Bingos* were released by Mute in 1988.

MUTE053 / *Snakedrill* / Proof / 1986 / Wire's first new recordings since
1980 appeared in the form of four tracks on this EP, which was co-produced
by Daniel Miller and Gareth Jones. The sleeve photograph was taken by
David Buckland.

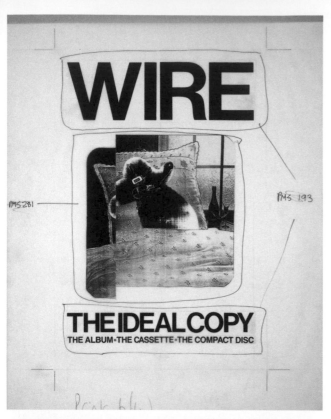

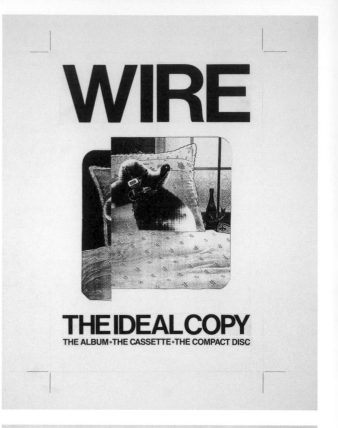

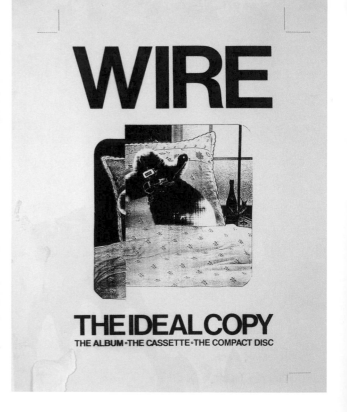

STUMM42

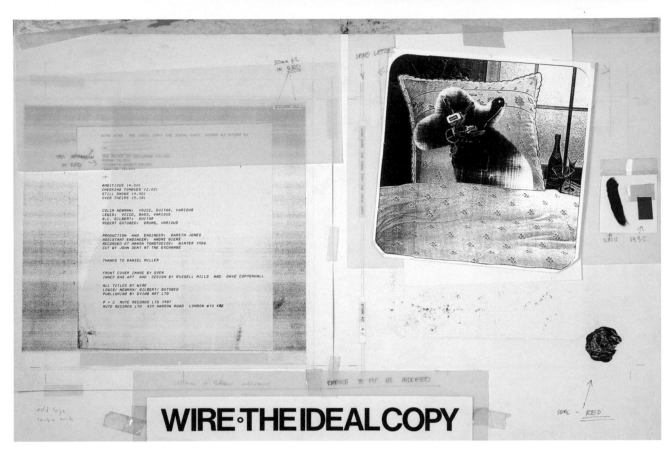

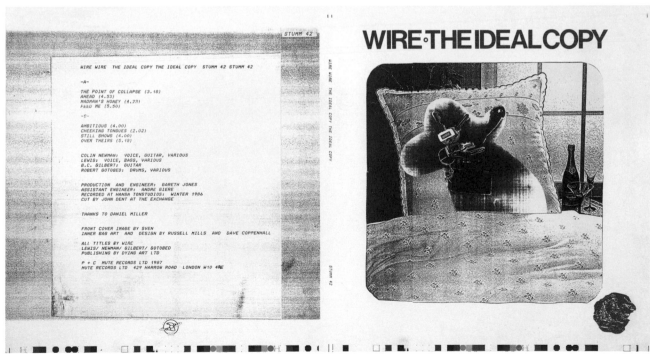

STUMM42 / *The Ideal Copy* / Artwork Boards / Proof / 1987 / Wire's first studio album since *154* in 1979 was hailed by critics as a masterful return. 'Wire are still one of my favourite bands of all time, and are still making great music now. I'm extremely proud to have worked with them.'

The cover image was credited to 'Sven' – actually Graham Lewis from the band – and the sleeve was available in four different colours. *The Ideal Copy* was also one of a small number of albums given a release in the pre-recorded Digital Audio Tape (DAT) format.

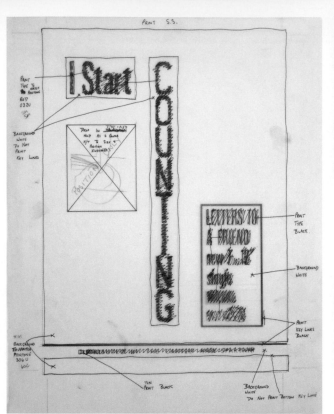

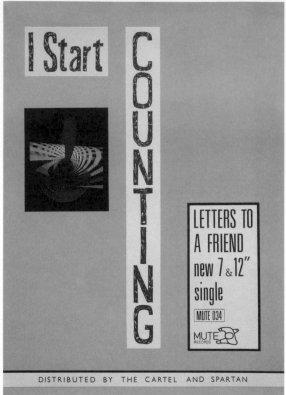

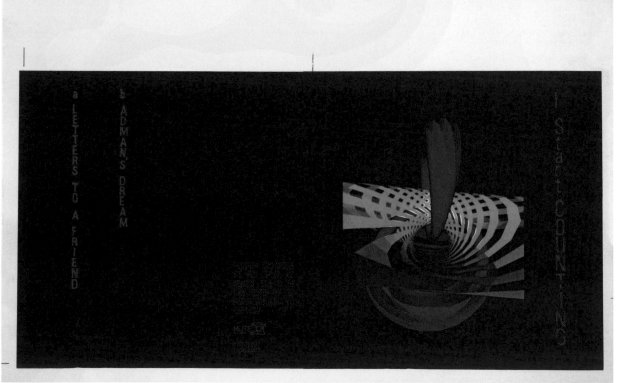

MUTE034

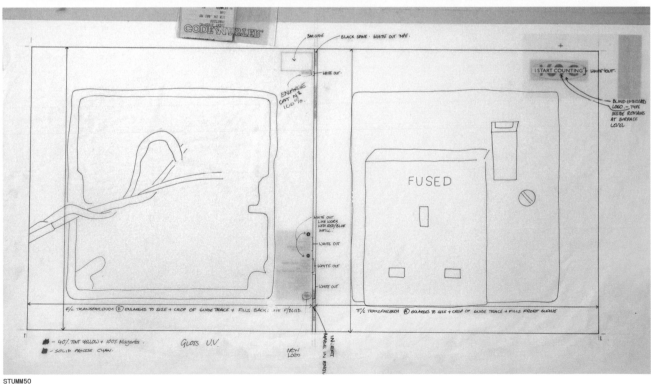

STUMM50

MUTE034 / 'Letters To A Friend' / Artwork Board / Poster / Proof / 1984 / Simon Leonard and David Baker met as students at Middlesex University, UK. The artwork for their debut single came from an academic paper called *Topology And Mechanics: Flows On The Torus*, written at Brown University in the USA.

STUMM50 / *Fused* / Proof / Artwork Board / 1988 / The second album by I Start Counting featured a strikingly simple sleeve design by T&CP Associates, who were working extensively for Mute Records during this period. The design studio's original name was Town & Country Planning Design.

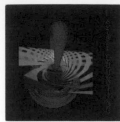

MUTE034

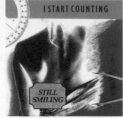

MUTE035

MUTE049

MUTE054

MUTE069

MUTE081

MUTE095

MUTE113

MUTE120

MUTE126

MUTE129

MUTE136

MUTE143

MUTE157

MUTE175

MUTE203

MUTE212

MUTE220

MUTE374

MUTE394

KONNECT-ING... I START COUNTING FORTRAN 5 KOMPUTER

CDMUTEL20

MUTE034 → MUTE394 / Singles Discography / 1984–2007 / Leonard and Baker have recorded for Mute as I Start Counting (1984–89), Fortran 5 (1990–95) and Komputer (since 1996). Much of their artwork was produced by Slim Smith, whose company Designland worked extensively for Mute from the late 1980s, including the Komputer album *The World Of Tomorrow* – the duo's nod to Kraftwerk as a response to Britpop's 1960s homages of the period.

MUTEL20 / *Konnecting* / Front / 2011 / 'While always being proud of our heritage and artists, Mute is continually looking at ways to reintroduce unappreciated classics. We were keen to join the dots for people with Simon and David's work and released the compilation *Konnecting... I Start Counting, Fortran 5, Komputer*, using the "K" as a nod to the Kraftwerk homage and a clean graphical typography from Louise Hendy at Blue Ink Creative.' Paul A. Taylor, art director, Mute.

THE SUBSIDIARIES

Over the course of almost forty years, Mute Records has either launched, partnered or financed a number of additional sub-labels, each with an identity and agenda of its own. Most have been curated by one or two individuals with specialist knowledge or interests, and administered by their parent company.

Blast First (1985–2004) Taking its name from a 1914 art magazine edited by Wyndham Lewis, the label was set up by Paul Smith and brought American recording artists Sonic Youth, Big Black, Butthole Surfers, The Afghan Whigs and Dinosaur Jr to prominence in Europe, while also providing an outlet for influential and experimental artists such as Pan Sonic, UT, Glenn Branca and Caspar Brotzmann. Blast First also released recordings from the influential Disobey series of live events that it founded. In 2004, Paul Smith left the Mute partnership and created the independent label Blast First Petite.

Mute America (1985→) Set up to provide North American releases for artists signed to Mute in the UK. In addition, the label has worked with artists outside the Mute roster that don't have an American label deal – in the past, this has included bands such as The Prodigy, M83, Jose Gonzales, The Knife, Fever Ray and The Acid.

Rhythm King (1986–1996) Originating in the mid-1980s, the dance label was set up by Martin Heath and James Horrocks and formed a successful partnership with Mute. Focusing on house music, hip hop/rap and the emerging sampling culture, the label enjoyed huge chart success with Bomb The Bass, S-Express, The Beatmasters and Betty Boo. Became independent from Mute in 1991, after which it entered into an agreement with Sony.

Mute Sonet France (1986–1990) A joint venture with the Sonet label in Paris to provide marketing support in France for Mute artists. The arrangement ended in 1990.

The Fine Line (1987→) Set up solely to release soundtrack albums, including music from the films of Derek Jarman, Todd Haynes, John Woo, John Hillcoat, Wim Wenders, Stephen Poliakoff and Clive Barker as well as compilations of music from TV and film by Mick Harvey, Barry Adamson, Irmin Schmidt and Simon Fisher Turner.

Product Inc. (1987–1990) Set up by Rob Collins, this label gave Mute its first association with Swans and also Jon Spencer (via the band Pussy Galore). Other releases included World Domination Enterprises, Young Gods, Acid Angels and The Bambi Slam.

The Grey Area (1990→) Set up by John McRobbie to give an outlet for previously released but unavailable music by influential and important artists such as Throbbing Gristle, Cabaret Voltaire, Can, A Certain Ratio, Einstürzende Neubauten, DAF, Buzzcocks, Swell Maps and SPK. The label's focus is on raising the profile of the artists and keeping their catalogues available.

Mute Czechoslovakia (1990–2002) Run from Prague in what is now the Czech Republic as a means of distributing the Mute catalogue to Eastern Europe. One of the only record labels in the country, Mute Czechoslovakia was the first international label to be based there after the Velvet Revolution.

Novamute (1991–2008 / 2017→) Set up as a specialist techno label by three members of the Mute staff: Pepe Jansz, Seth Hodder and Mick Paterson. Primarily released one-off 12-inch singles, but later branched out to occasional albums by the more successful artists. An influential label, it was responsible for the success of Richie Hawtin's Plastikman as well as releasing music by Speedy J, Luke Slater, Motor, Juno Reactor, Cristian Vogel, Miss Kitten, Moby's Voodoo Child, Mark Moor's Needledust, Cian Ciaran's Acid Casuals, and new remix releases by Nitzer Ebb and Throbbing Gristle. Novamute was deactivated in 2008 and reactivated in 2017.

13th Hour Recordings (1994–2000) Set up within Mute by staff members Shaun Connon, Nick Coquet and Paul A. Taylor to release music by British artists as an antidote to the Britpop scene. Deactivated in 2000.

Interpop (1995→) Set up to release Mute's interpretation of mainstream pop music; releases included DJ Quicksilver and The Brain.

Trophy Records (1995–1997) Moby's own label, on which he released electronic music he liked or had recorded under a different guise.

Parallel Series (1996–1997) Set up by staff members Roland Brown and PK to bring out new experimental music. Releases included works by Andrei Samsonov, Bruce Gilbert, Paul Kendall and Robert Hampson.

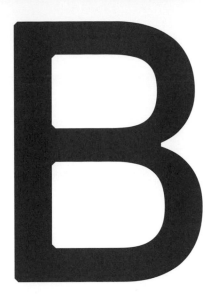

Future Groove (1999–2003) Trance and house label set up by Mute staff member Howard Corner; strongly involved in establishing the progressive house sound in the early 2000s.

Toast Hawaii (2003–2005) Set up by Andrew Fletcher from Depeche Mode. Released two albums by Client.

Live Here Now (2004→) Set up by Noggin, MJ and Iain Forsyth to record and produce CD releases of live performances available to buy at the end of the evening, and exclusively via an online store. Worldwide tours by Erasure and Depeche Mode have been recorded, as well as documenting significant live events by Blur, Status Quo and Orchestral Manoeuvres in the Dark. Revolutionary in its field, although run independently of Mute, it continues to be involved with Mute recording artists and has recently released live recordings by New Order.

Mute Irregulars (2007–2009) Set up for Mute by Barry 7 of Add N To (X) and involved closely with the influential 'underage' music scene established by his teenage son Sam Kilcoyne, later part of Mute group S.C.U.M. Released music by prodigiously young artists, including New York band Tiny Masters Of Today – with siblings Ivan (thirteen) and Ada (eleven) joined by Blues Explosion drummer Russell Simins – and Alice Costello's first band Pull In Emergency, all aged between thirteen and fifteen.

Liberation Technologies (2012→) An electronic label set up by Patrick O'Neill to release one-off recordings in the form of limited-edition 12-inch singles and high-definition downloads. Releases include Powell, Laurel Halo, British Murder Boys and Mark Fell.

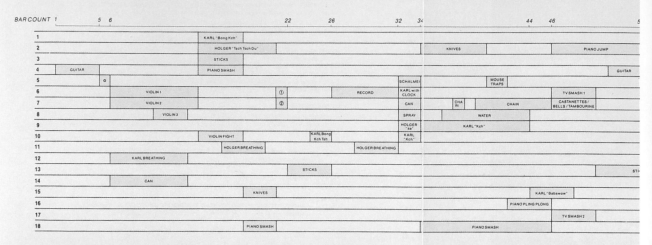

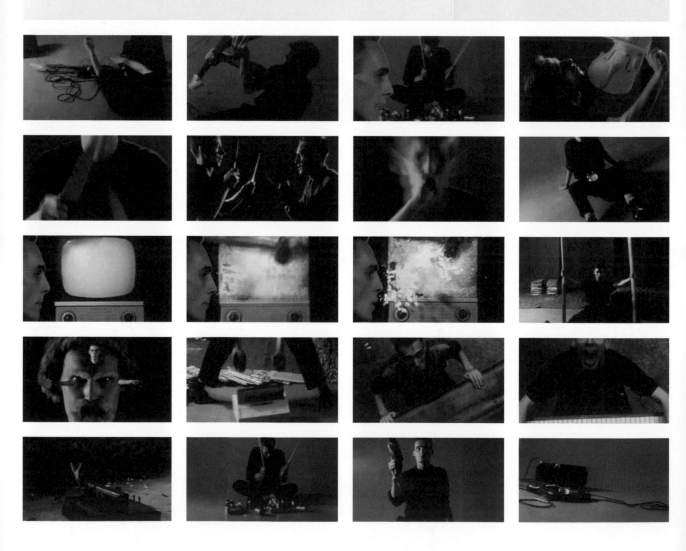

1983 – 1989   OHI HO BANG BANG

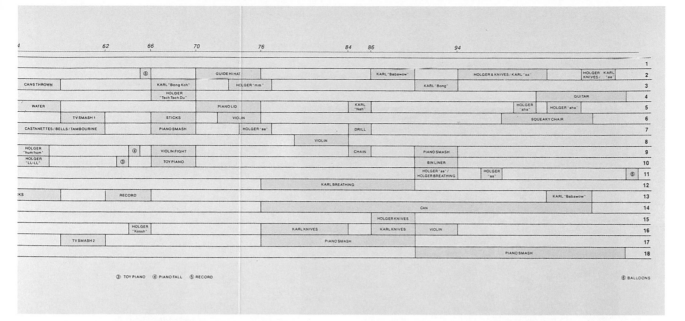

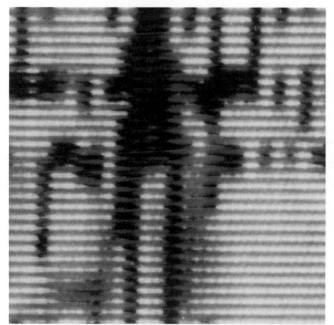

MUTE072

MUTE072 / 'The Three' / Video Stills / Cover / Sequence / 1988 /
Former vocalist with Palais Schaumburg, Holger Hiller had already released his Mute solo debut, *Oben Im Eck*, in 1986. Ohi Ho Bang Bang was a one-off collaboration with Renegade Soundwave's Karl Bonnie and Japanese video artist Akiko Hada. They were filmed making noises with the human voice and items or instruments that were readily available; clips were then edited to produce the final audio-visual piece. While the simultaneous rhythmic sampling of audio and video would later become commonplace with developments in digital technology, Ohi Ho Bang Bang is all the more impressive given that Hada used analogue video-editing equipment and cutting techniques. The cover seen here is that of Mute's CD Video release; the format was a short-lived precursor to the DVD that brought together the technologies of the compact disc and LaserDisc and was obsolete by the early 1990s.

12MUTE138

STUMM63

STUMM85

STUMM100

STUMM90

CDSTUMM152

STUMM85

MUTE138 / 'Cocaine Sex' / Front / 1992 / STUMM63 → STUMM152 / Albums Discography / 1989–96 / *Soundclash* (1989); *In Dub* (1990); *Howyoudoin?* (1994); *The Next Chapter of Dub* (1995); *RSW 1987–1995* (1996).

STUMM85 / *In Dub* / Artwork Board / 1990 / Formed in London in 1986, Renegade Soundwave were noted for their early use of digital sampling and skilled fusion of hip hop, dub and industrial genres. *In Dub* (1990), with its artwork by Slim Smith, was a huge influence on the British dance scene.

STUMM67

STUMM214

STUMM381

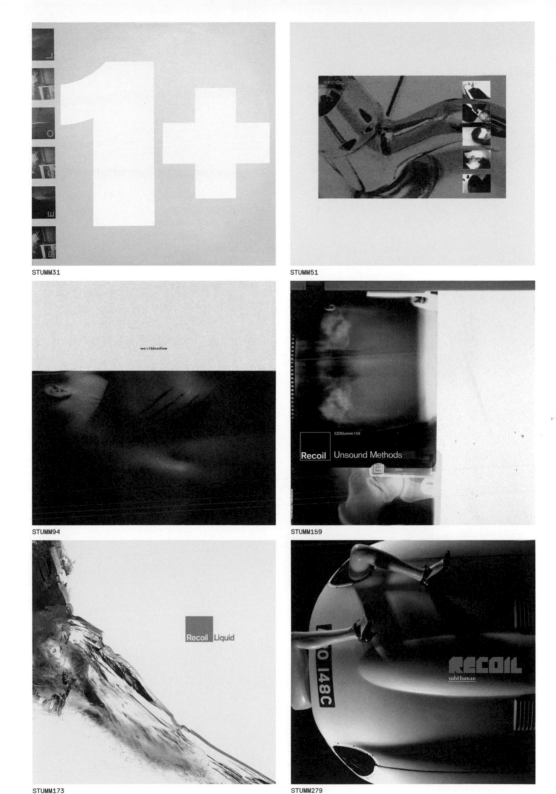

STUMM31

STUMM51

STUMM94

STUMM159

STUMM173

STUMM279

STUMM67 → STUMM381 / EP + Albums Discography / 1989–2015 /
Martin Gore's solo debut, *Counterfeit²*, was another collection of cover
versions. The album's artwork featured photography by Anton Corbijn
accompanied by simple graphics from Shaughn McGrath of Four5one.
The packaging and graphical design for Gore's 2015 *MG* took its
inspiration from the Joy Division compilation album *Still*.

STUMM31 → STUMM279 / Albums Discography / 1986–2007 / For his solo
project, Alan Wilder sought a distinctive design style intended to establish
his albums as more than just a Depeche Mode side project. 'The design styles
reflect Alan's perfectionist nature as he oversaw all elements of the artwork
including the ground-breaking interactive enhanced CD element on "Liquid".'
Paul A. Taylor, art director, Mute.

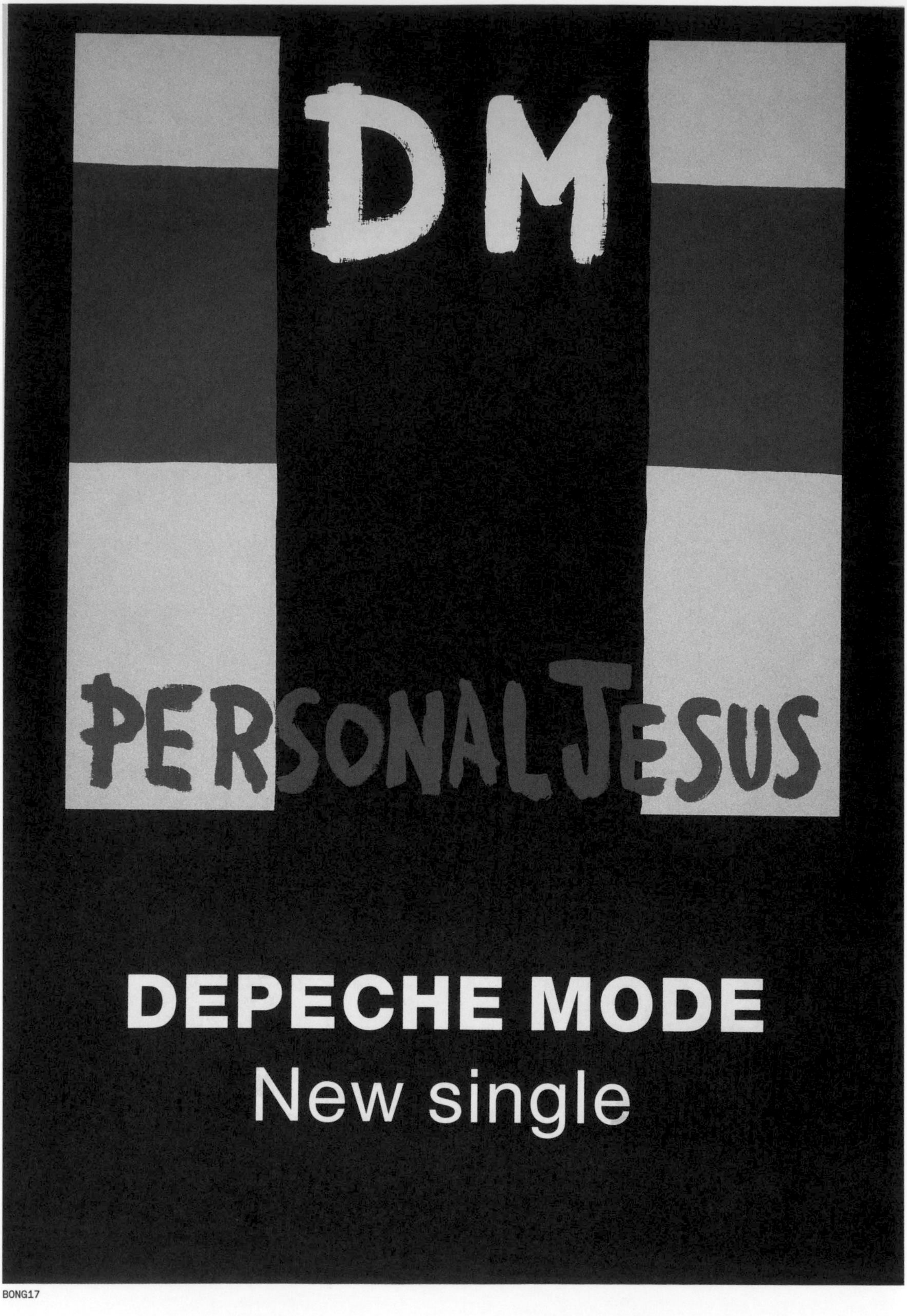

BONG17

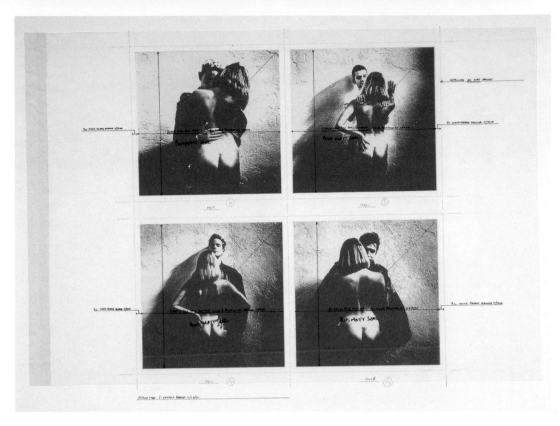

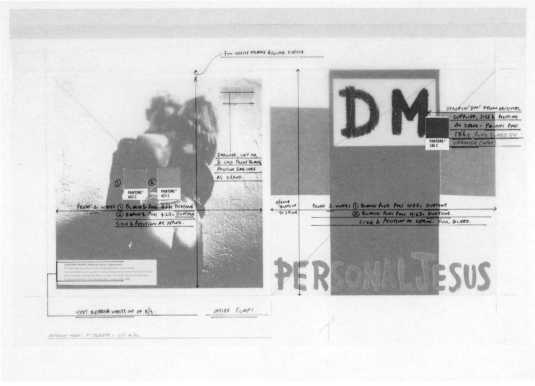

BONG17 / 'Personal Jesus' / Poster / Artwork Boards / 1989 / 'The poster for "Personal Jesus" (left) followed the teaser street campaign we did featuring simple stickers and large street posters in Helvetica Bold font, white out of black, with "Your own personal Jesus" and a phone number. If you phoned the number you got to hear an exclusive excerpt of the song. Genius pre-internet marketing in action! The flat board artwork layouts (above) with the hand-written instructions for the reprographic company were done by Richard Smith at Area, Anton Corbijn's design collaborator at that time.' Paul A. Taylor, art director, Mute.

1990

1999

01

02

'SPREADING THE NEWS AROUND THE WORLD'

The 1980s had ended on a positive note for the Mute label, as Depeche Mode's global appeal broadened with each new release. The single 'Personal Jesus' charted across the world, spending an impressive 23 weeks in Germany's Top 40. Inspired, according to composer Martin Gore, by Priscilla Presley's autobiography *Elvis And Me*, 'Personal Jesus' is one of the band's most lauded songs, and was later famously covered by both Johnny Cash – stripped back to a bare acoustic guitar – and Marilyn Manson.

January 1990 saw the release of the band's most successful single. With a smart Anton Corbijn video built around the children's book *The Little Prince*, 'Enjoy The Silence' was a Top 10 single in every major record-buying market – except Japan, which remained singularly resistant to the Depeche Mode sound. Unsurprisingly, it won a BRIT award for the Best Single.

Violator, the album containing these two important hit singles, shattered Mute's previous sales records, selling over a million copies in the USA for the first time. As an indicator of the band's growing popularity, an album signing event at a Los Angeles music store had to be abandoned for security reasons when more than twenty thousand fans turned up. When the band left early, a riot ensued.

The album heralded a new phase for Depeche Mode. Miller recalls: 'The recordings were produced by long-time Mute collaborator Flood [Mark Ellis], and mixed by François Kevorkian, which turned out to be a brilliant combination – François had mixed Kraftwerk's *Electric Café*.'

Yet Depeche Mode's new success wasn't all plain sailing. 'When you've gone from starting your career to selling 10 million records in a short period of time,' Miller remarks, 'whether you like it or not, the pressure starts to build and your time isn't your own any more. A lot of things changed after the *Violator* tour.'

From 1992 to early 1993, Depeche Mode recorded arguably their most enduring album, *Songs Of Faith And Devotion*. They rented a large house in Madrid, and had a studio constructed inside. The early results, however, were not promising. 'When I turned up after a couple of weeks, the vibe was different,' Miller recalled. 'They were really not working together as a band.' The sessions were abandoned and later resumed in Hamburg.

In spite of the difficulty in recording the album, *Songs Of Faith And Devotion* was a global phenomenon, both critically and commercially. It entered the charts at No.1 on both sides of the Atlantic, and was one of the biggest-selling releases of the year.

The *Devotional* Tour that followed was similarly successful. Anton Corbijn created a lavish stage set and the band, who already had a reputation for being one of the great live acts, took it to another level. The tour still ranks as one of the greatest live shows ever staged; it lasted eighteen months, and took its toll on the group. By the end, exhaustion had overpowered them. Alan Wilder made the decision to leave the band and concentrate on his Recoil project, whilst Dave, Martin and Fletch decided they needed a lengthy time out from the band.

With few signs of activity during the ensuing four years, the press speculated that Depeche Mode had simply stopped. As a tentative step, Miller suggested that they reconvene to record an EP. 'Everybody was feeling fragile and nervous,' he recalled. And yet, 'Somehow it became an album.' It was, he admits, 'a transitional record, both in their personal lives and in the structure of the band – with Alan's departure it was the first time they'd worked together as a three-piece since Vince had left.' 1997's *Ultra* charted almost as strongly as its predecessor. It was no great surprise, however, when they decided against touring the album, playing only a pair of short promotional sets in London and Los Angeles.

03

04

Nevertheless, the decade drew to a close on a high note for Depeche Mode. With no new material from the band, and seemingly no great desire to enter the studio, Mute maintained public interest with the release of a second compilation. Selling over 2 million copies worldwide, *The Singles 86–98* was supported by a four-month world tour that gave Depeche Mode a new impetus to move forward into the 21st century. The artwork for the campaign was put together by Anna Bergfors at The Intro Partnership, and was shot on location during a road trip from San Francisco to Las Vegas with photographer Rick Guest. It went on to win numerous design awards.

At a very different position on the pop music spectrum, at the beginning of 1990 Mute teamed up with the Inspiral Carpets, a popular unsigned band on the 'Madchester' indie-dance scene, whose self-pressed single 'Move' had only just missed out on the Top 40. The Inspirals had an appealing, gently psychedelic sound based around a vintage Farfisa organ – not to mention a neat line in T-shirts, most famously a cartoon cow smoking a cigarette accompanied by the caption 'Cool As Fuck'. Although the band were originally only active until around 1995, during that time they scored eleven Top 40 hit singles, and three Top 10 albums.

As the decade progressed, another of the established Mute families, Nick Cave And The Bad Seeds, acquired more mainstream success as Cave began to find a wider audience. With his 1988 Southern Gothic-style debut novel *And the Ass Saw the Angel*, Cave had already achieved a degree of literary respectability. The 1992 release of the compelling *Henry's Dream*, recorded in California with Neil Young's producer David Briggs and featuring artwork and photography by Anton Corbijn, not only appeared on many end-of-year lists, but also took Cave into the UK Top 30 album chart for the first time. 'It was clear to us even in

the eighties that Nick's music had the potential to reach a very wide audience, and that just happened over a long period of time. Among other things, he wrote the film script for *The Proposition*, which was well received and which made people outside his core audience take him more seriously – now he's in *The Guardian*.'

Cave's career continued to grow throughout the decade, 1994's *Let Love In* closing in on the Top 10. Two years later Cave enjoyed his biggest success to date when *Murder Ballads*, an album that mixed new and traditional songs, reached the Top 3 in the UK and charted throughout most of Europe. It also brought about a rather unlikely Top 20 single – with an even more unlikely partner – when he duetted with Australian pop star Kylie Minogue on the song 'Where The Wild Roses Grow'.

The decade also saw two of Cave's Bad Seeds producing notable solo works for Mute. Former bass player Barry Adamson had already gained attention with his own takes on the concept of a soundtrack-to-a-movie-that-never-existed. His third solo album, *Soul Murder*, was nominated for the 1992 Mercury Prize. He followed this with *Oedipus Schmoedipus* (1996), a stylish album featuring collaborations with Pulp's Jarvis Cocker, Billy MacKenzie from The Associates and Nick Cave, which really highlighted his versatility as a songwriter and musician. Adamson would also contribute soundtrack material to high-profile movies by David Lynch and Oliver Stone.

Meanwhile, Cave's long-term right-hand man, multi-instrumentalist Mick Harvey, stepped out to produce a pair of cover albums of Serge Gainsbourg songs – *Intoxicated Man* (1995) and *Pink Elephants* (1997). Both were rightly admired cult hits. Indeed, Harvey has arguably done more than any other musician to bring Gainsbourg's work to English-speaking audiences. (Both albums featured another Bad Seeds collaborator, Anita Lane, who recorded her first solo album for the label in 1993.) Harvey would continue

01 Depeche Mode (David Gahan) / 'Personal Jesus' / Video Still / 1989
02 Depeche Mode (David Gahan) / 'Enjoy The Silence' / Video Still / 1990
03 Inspiral Carpets / *Cool As Milk* Promotional Bottles / Lancashire Dairies / 1990
04 Nick Cave And The Bad Seeds (Nick Cave) / 'Where The Wild Roses Grow' /
     On-Set Photograph / 1995

05

06

to revisit the great Frenchman with *Delirium Tremens* in 2016 and *Intoxicated Women* a year later.

Another band to find a home on Mute, West Berlin's Einstürzende Neubauten, made an impact in the early 1980s with a sound that combined piledrivers, drills and custom-built apparatus made from scrap with more conventional instruments. By the mid-1980s, founder Blixa Bargeld had also become a full-time member of The Bad Seeds – and former Bad Seed Anita Lane would later sing with Neubauten. Mute had already released a compilation of the band's early recordings in the 1980s, but in 1993 they made their studio debut for the label with *Tabula Rasa*, their sixth album. It represented a slight shift in how they used the sound and noises they created with their unorthodox approach. The overall effect may have seemed more conventional, but in fact it was pushing the boundaries further still. It penetrated the mainstream, particularly in Germany, and its influence can be felt in the music of many artists – particularly, and surprisingly, U2.

Mute remains arguably the most significant label to have taken an active and committed interest in the experimental music scenes, not only with Einstürzende Neubauten, but through their long-term relationship with Boyd Rice / NON and in releases by Diamanda Galás, Laibach, Irmin Schmidt, Simon Fisher Turner, Swans, Nitzer Ebb and Blast First's Pan Sonic and Suicide. Mute's Grey Area would also reissue the influential Can, Cabaret Voltaire, Virgin Prunes, Swell Maps and Throbbing Gristle back catalogues.

One of the more unexpected releases of this period, *The Sporting Life* saw avant-garde vocalist Diamanda Galás paired with a bona fide rock star in the shape of Led Zeppelin's John Paul Jones. In another rare example of a record label giving sustained backing to even the most uncompromising of musicians, Galás has recorded many albums for Mute over a twenty-eight-year period. Her voice is, quite possibly, the most unique you will ever hear, and she

uses it in thought-provoking and challenging ways. Having also performed vocals for fellow Mute artists Erasure and Recoil, she is hard to pigeonhole and is clearly viewed as an important figure by her label. Miller makes the point: 'We don't see a Mute artist in terms of one song or album, but want to support them as they evolve over a long period.' He continues, 'Mute simply reflects my own tastes, and those of the people who work here.'

While Depeche Mode were now one of the most commercially successful bands of the decade, Mute Records found itself with another less likely global superstar on its hands. In 1993, the label signed New York electronic dance music producer Richard Melville Hall, better known (having tried out a variety of other pseudonyms) as Moby.

Miller saw him as a perfect fit for Mute: 'Moby was looking for a label. He made very musical dance music, his live performances were spectacular, and when I listened to the music he was working on at the time it was really varied. It was clear that he was a very versatile musician. He was an ideal Mute artist, someone who was self-contained and adventurous.'

Moby's 1995 label debut *Everything is Wrong* was a modest success, generating three singles that hovered around the lower reaches of the UK Top 40 as well as being rated one of the best albums of the year in *Rolling Stone* magazine. But a year later he confounded everyone by following it with an album of guitar punk metal. Changing musical direction from album to album would become a Moby trademark.

'His first album was a great electronic pop record,' Miller notes, 'but then he recorded *Animal Rights*. Nobody really got it as a concept – everyone just went, "Why?" Just as electronic artists like The Prodigy and Fatboy Slim were taking off on a global scale, he decided to make a complete U-turn and came up with a punk rock record.'

07

08

The release was a commercial disaster that came close to ending Moby's career. 'He needed to do it and we supported it. It was a good record and it pissed a lot of people off, but really alienated his audience,' Miller admits.

At this time, Moby apparently contemplated leaving the music business altogether and was even reported to have been contemplating a career in architecture. He nevertheless spent much of the next two years in his home studio. 'He was writing electropop songs that were all OK, but nothing really stood out. And then he came up with one great track that had an entirely sampled vocal. His manager Eric [Härle] and I both encouraged him to take that direction.'

The recordings for the resulting album made extensive use of vocal samples taken from Alan Lomax's field recordings from America's Deep South in the first half of the 20th century. 'Sample clearance for the album came from the same source, which made the clearances easier and benefited everyone involved.'

On its release, *Play* looked set to bomb in much the same way as its predecessor. '*Melody Maker* gave the album a full-page write-up and then awarded it zero out of ten!' Miller recalled. After the release of three singles, Moby was finding airplay difficult to come by, and *Play* was simply not selling. A creative solution came in the form of licensing tracks from the album to appear in television adverts.
'*Play* came out at a time when most artists didn't want their music on ads – now, of course, everybody wants it all the time,' Miller remarks. 'When the offers came in he approved them. We thought it was a good way of getting the music out there, and Moby agreed. When a few music supervisors started using tracks from *Play*, others started to follow. And after that it did finally start to get airplay.'

The ultimate slow burner, on release in May 1999 *Play* sold just 6,000 copies in its first week. It took until April 2000, after a fourth single, 'Why Does My Heart Feel So Bad' had been a hit, for the album to reach No.1 in the UK. It has since sold in the region of 12 million copies worldwide.

In 1996, Moby's lawyer had mentioned to Mute that Jon Spencer was looking for a partner for work outside North America. As The Jon Spencer Blues Explosion, Spencer had released two hugely acclaimed albums with Matador – one of which, *Orange* (1994), featured the remarkable 'Bellbottoms' single – and he wanted stronger support in territories where Matador didn't then have a foothold. It wasn't a long conversation; who wouldn't want to work with 'the greatest rock 'n' roll band on the planet'?

Spencer's vision for imagery and videos was always very clear, exact and singular: nothing less than perfection was acceptable. The artwork for the classic *Now I Got Worry* (1996) consisted of layers of black-on-black subtlety, as well as type treatments that had gone through multiple fax/photocopy processes.

Spencer's next three Mute albums continued to push visual boundaries with limited-edition packaging. *Acme* (1998) was designed by David Warner and packaged in a sweet-packet-style wrapper sourced by Artomatic. Later albums *Plastic Fang* (2002) and *Damage* (2004), both designed by legendary comic-book graphic designer Chip Kidd, respectively mimicked hanging bags for joke shop Dracula teeth and adopted flip-up matchbook-style packaging. Innovative packaging solutions had become key.

05 Anita Lane / *Dirty Pearl* / Outtake / 1993
06 Einstürzende Neubauten (N. U. Unruh / Mark Chung / Alexander Hacke / Blixa Bargeld / F. M. Einheit) / *Tabula Rasa* / Outtake / 1990
07 Diamanda Galás / *Plague Mass* / Promotional Poster / 1991
08 Moby / New York / 1990s

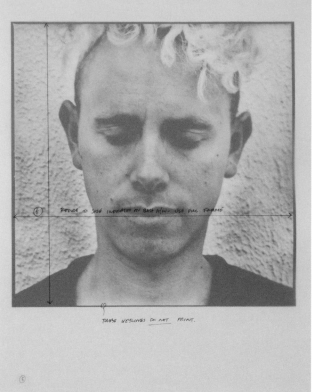

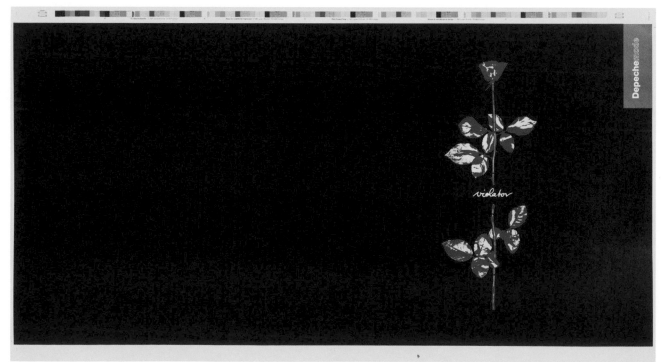

STUMM64

STUMM64 / *Violator* / Artwork Boards / Proofs / 1990 / The release of *Violator* saw Depeche Mode and the Mute label reaching a new level of commercial success. The album became a *Billboard* Top 10 album in the USA. During this period, Anton Corbijn began to take on an all-encompassing, conceptual role in the band's presentation, from photography and album sleeves to video creation and stage design. This fruitful collaboration continues to the present day.

12BONG18

L12BONG18

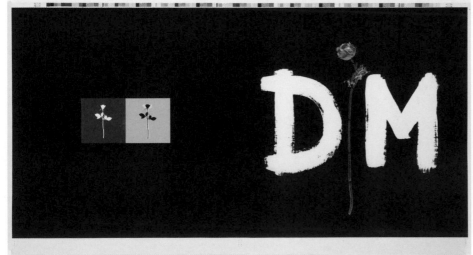

XL12BONG18

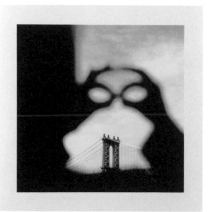

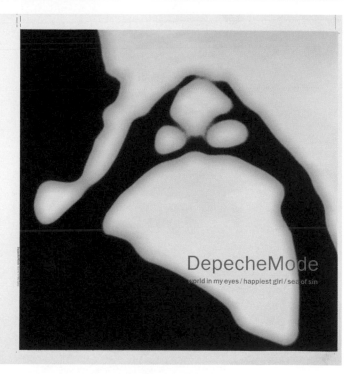

DepecheMode

world in my eyes / happiest girl / sea of sin

BONG18 / 'Enjoy The Silence' / Proofs / 1990 / The second single release from *Violator*. Cementing the album campaign's visual identity, Anton Corbijn re-appropriated his rose motif. Corbijn's video for the single remains one of the most iconic music videos of all time; he later made a pastiche of it with Coldplay for their single 'Viva La Vida'.

BONG20 / 'World In My Eyes'/'Happiest Girl'/'Sea Of Sin' / Test Shots / Proof / 1990 / For the artwork of 'World In My Eyes', the four members of Depeche Mode were photographed using hand shapes to create eyes to see the world through. The six images at the top of the page are test prints of Anton Corbijn's photos from the reprographic stage.

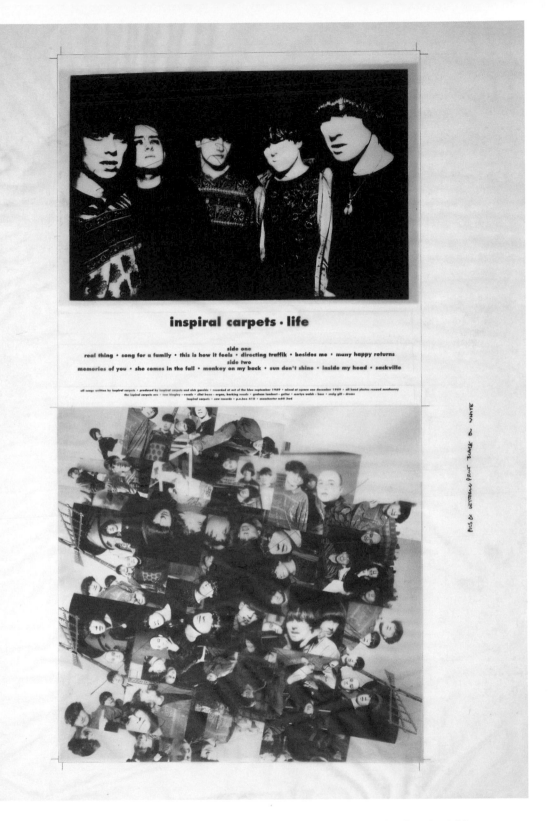

inspiral carpets · life

side one
real thing · song for a family · this is how it feels · directing traffik · besides me · many happy returns
side two
memories of you · she comes in the fall · monkey on my back · sun don't shine · inside my head · sackville

all songs written by inspiral carpets · produced by inspiral carpets and nick garside · recorded at out of the blue september 1989 · mixed at square one december 1989 · all band photos roused meekeney
the inspiral carpets are · tom hingley · vocals · clint boon · organ, backing vocals · graham lambert · guitar · martyn walsh · bass · craig gill · drums
inspiral carpets · cow records · p.o.box 410 · manchester m60 3rd

PICS IN WITERALLY PRINT BLACK ON WHITE

DUNG8 / *Life* / Proof / Artwork Boards / 1990 / 'The *Life* album cover started as a still from our video for the single 'She Comes In The Fall'. The problem was that our original silhouettes from the still didn't actually look clear enough. We were doing moves which were supposed to look as if we were floating in space. Instead, it looked like we were doing the "Dying Fly". We went in search of some better silhouettes and found them in pictures of Spiderman, Al Jolson and Fred Astaire.' Clint Boon, Inspiral Carpets. 'The inner sleeve was taken on our first visit to France to play at a club Haçienda show in late November 1989. We had been supplied with clothes by Joe Bloggs' owner Shami [Ahmed]. He had a catchphrase "If it's good for you, it's good for me." We adopted this through 1990.' Graham Lambert, Inspiral Carpets.

DUNG7

DUNG10

DUNG10R

DUNG11

DUNG13

DUNG15

DUNG16

DUNG17

DUNG18

DUNG20

DUNG22

DUNG23

DUNG24

DUNG26

DUNG31

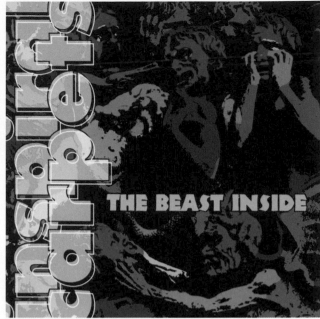

DUNG7 → DUNG31 / Singles Discography / 1990–2003 / 'This Is How It Feels' (1990); 'She Comes In The Fall' (1990); 'Commercial Rain' (1990); 'Island Head EP' (1990); 'Caravan' (1991); 'Please Be Cruel' (1991); 'Dragging Me Down' (1992); 'Two Worlds Collide' (1992); 'Generations' (1992); 'Bitches Brew' (1992); 'How It Should Be' (1993); 'Saturn 5' (1994); 'I Want You' (1994); 'Uniform' (1994); 'Come Back Tomorrow' (2003).

'As with most bands, our sleeves were important. From our first demos to our last album in 2014, we took great pride in our artwork – it was something to behold while the tunes sunk in. We had an aversion to capital letters and I always wanted the type to be bold so it didn't get lost when reproduced. I think this was inspired by New Order. We felt Factory Records always had distinctive art. Mute always let us push through our ideas on the artwork.

Daniel Miller and his core team were always driving our ideas forward, even if now, looking back, some of them were a little crazy.' Graham Lambert, Inspiral Carpets.

DUNG8 → DUNG25 / Albums Discography / 1990–94 / *Life* (1990); *The Beast Inside* (1991); *Revenge Of The Goldfish* (1992); *Devil Hopping* (1994).

'*Revenge Of The Goldfish* got its name and front cover image from an art installation by artist Sandy Skoglund; the design was by Brian Cannon, who later produced the iconic Oasis album sleeves – the band of then Inspirals roadie Noel Gallagher. *Devil Hopping* was named after Belgian producer Pascal Gabriel, who had difficulty pronouncing the word "developing" with his accent.' Paul A. Taylor, art director, Mute.

Diamanda uses her
voice as an instrument
like no other artist can.

Truly remarkable.

STUMM27

STUMM33

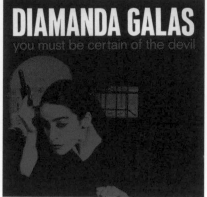

STUMM46

STUMM83

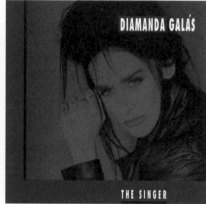

STUMM103

STUMM119

STUMM127

STUMM146

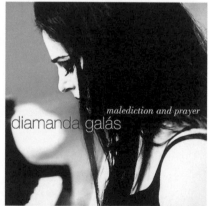

STUMM163

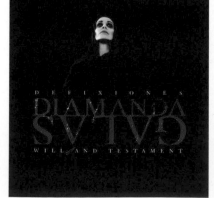

STUMM205

STUUM206

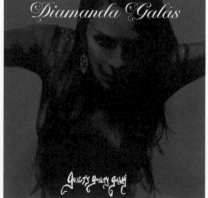

STUMM274

STUMM49

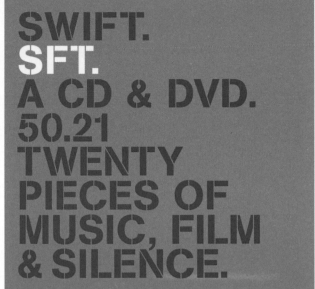

STUMM197

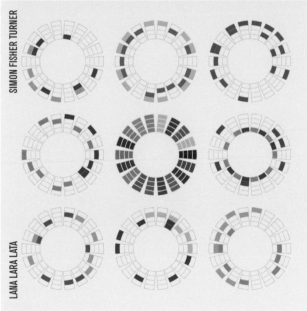

STUMM254

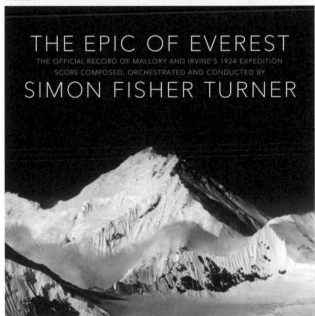

STUMM357

STUMM27 → STUMM274 / Albums Discography / 1986–2008 /
The Divine Punishment (1986); *Saint Of The Pit* (1986); *You Must
Be Certain Of The Devil* (1988); *Plague Mass* (1991); *The Singer*
(1992); *Vena Cava* (1993); *The Sporting Life [With John Paul Jones]*
(1994); *Schrei X* (1996); *Malediction And Prayer* (1998); *Defixiones –
Will And Testament* (2003); *La Serpenta Canta* (2003);
Guilty Guilty Guilty (2008).

Trained as a bel canto opera singer with a three-and-a-half-octave

vocal range, Diamanda Galás has recorded a dozen albums of challenging
avant-garde vocal music for Mute.

STUMM49 / *Blue* / STUMM197 / *Swift* / STUMM254 / *Lana Lara Lata* /
STUMM357 / *The Epic of Everest* / Fronts / 1993–2013 / Variously a child
TV actor and fledgling teenage pop star (as Simon Turner) in the early
1970s and as the King of Luxembourg in the 1980s, Simon Fisher Turner
would later compose and record acclaimed soundtracks for Derek Jarman
and David Lynch.

When I first heard
Barry's ideas for *Moss
Side Story* it was clear
his talents went way
beyond being just
a great bass player.

BARRY ADAMSON
THE NEGRO INSIDE ME
SIX TRACK
LP+CD
NOW AVAILABLE

MUTE RECORDS PRESENT

BARRY ADAMSON's

MOSS SIDE STORY

"IN A BLACK AND WHITE WORLD
MURDER BRINGS A TOUCH OF COLOUR…"

STUMM53

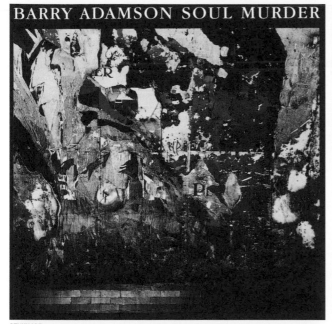

STUMM105

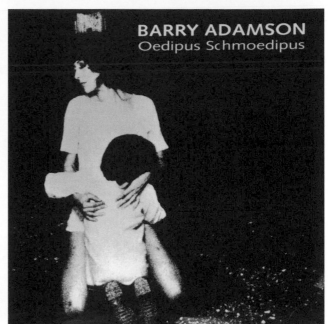

STUMM134

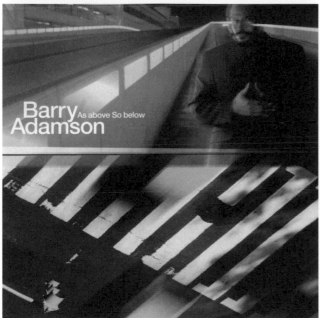

STUMM161

STUMM176

STUMM53 → STUMM176 / Mute Studio Albums Discography / 1989–2002 /
Moss Side Story (1989); *Soul Murder* (1992); *Oedipus Schmoedipus* (1996);
As Above, So Below (1998); *The King Of Nothing Hill* (2002).

'The *Moss Side Story* artwork came about through knowing Malcolm Garrett
at Assorted Images, who was an old friend from Manchester, who had also
done most of the the Magazine record sleeves and others too famous to name.
I knew I was in safe hands. I had a small office/studio at Assorted Images and
had already met the brilliantly scathing art director, Joe Ewart. He had been
working with new photographer – Lawrence Watson – recommended him for
the shoot and a small team was instantly born. We jumped into my seventies
silver Merc and headed north. The weather was perfectly grim as we drove
around under surveillance, stopping off to shoot various Moss Side landmarks.
The Russell Club, The Nile and, of course, Leech's Funeral Services! The image
on the cover was taken and timed in a back alley behind a house I used to live
in. The umbrella seems to suggest that it is not from protection of the usual

incessant rain but from the rubbish that has fallen all around in the background.
There is a nice touch for me in that my shirt cuff and link looks a little like a
silver handcuff as I grip the brolly and my face shows disdain for what I'm tied
to. On returning to London, Joe and I knocked the tag line about and came up
with, "In a black and white world, murder brings a touch of colour". We had it.
Now it was down to Malcolm to give the sleeve itself the kind of Iconic edge
he was used to bringing to the table. He didn't let us down.' Barry Adamson.

'Barry was – and is – one of my heroes. It was the only Mute job I ever
lobbied for. After a meeting with Barry, we started work on the *As Above,
So Below* album. Cover designer Adrian Talbot did the photography. He and
I took Barry on a tour of west London, and shot him in various moody noirish
locations. I remember we drove around in Barry's vintage Jag – a sixties
gangster's car! Very cool! The cover evokes the spirit of Barry's' mildly
paranoiac world view of urban angst and empty rooms. I still play the
record and still enjoy the cover.' Adrian Shaughnessy, founder, Intro.

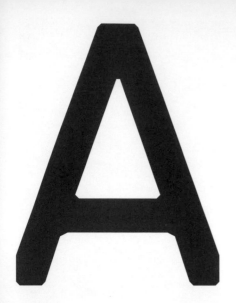

TECHNO MUTE

In the first half of the 1980s, when electronic music began to dominate dance floors, electro and the earliest forms of house evolved using inexpensive (or then unfashionable) analogue synthesisers and drum machines. For a label that had been steeped in electronic music right from the very beginning, and whose founder had himself recorded a seminal electronic single, it might seem strange that the Mute label didn't position itself at the heart of that burgeoning scene.

Miller admits that when fledgling label owners James Horrocks and Martin Heath first played him a selection of house 12-inchers, he wasn't wholly moved. 'I didn't quite get it. It sounded like disco to me, but they had passion, and understood it really well, so we went into partnership and set up Rhythm King.' The label launched in 1986, and within two years had enjoyed a succession of dance-floor hits by British artists such as The Beatmasters, Bomb The Bass, Cookie Crew, S-Express and Betty Boo.

One problematic issue for Miller was that the fast turnaround and fly-by-night fortunes of house and techno artists – almost a defining characteristic of the dance music scene – were at odds with Mute's philosophy of backing artists to develop at their own pace. One of Rhythm King's early signings, Renegade Soundwave, did, in fact, move across to Mute, becoming one of the few dance acts to appear on the label on that time. They were a significant presence on the UK dance music scene – The Chemical Brothers, among many others, citing them as an important influence.

Rhythm King also played a part in the early development of Sheffield's Warp label. Beginning as a shop specialising in techno imports from Detroit and Chicago, as a label Warp found early success with 'bedroom' producers such as LFO and Tricky Disco. When their relationship with Rhythm King stalled, Miller himself advised Warp to develop a catalogue with its own label identity; over the last two decades,

it has become an important purveyor of electronic music, introducing ground-breaking artists such as Aphex Twin and Squarepusher.

After Mute separated from Rhythm King in 1991, Miller launched a dedicated techno subsidiary, once again manned by genre specialists. 'There was a lot of commercial electronic dance music that I didn't like, so we set up Novamute as a purist techno label,' he explains. Initially, Novamute provided UK releases for 12-inch singles licensed from smaller European and American labels, but later began releasing new recordings in its own right. 'We released some legendary records on Novamute, working with relatively unknown producers who became techno superstars, like Speedy J, Richie Hawtin, Luke Slater and Chris Liebing.'

Novamute remained active until 2008, but is still an area of interest for Miller. 'Seth Hodder and Pepe Jansz, who were running it, moved on to other projects and it's been dormant since. But we are relaunching the label.' Meanwhile, some Novamute artists have found a home at Mute proper: under the guise of Plastikman, Richie Hawtin became a key figure in techno as an influential DJ.

Nitzer Ebb was another significant Mute band making electronic dance music. Formed in Essex in 1982, their 1987 debut *That Total Age* was a key influence on early rave and the Electronic Body Music (EBM) genre.

Given the nature of Depeche Mode's sound, it's no great surprise to find that solo releases by members of the band have veered into electronic dance territory. Even before his departure from Depeche Mode in 1995, Alan Wilder had been producing club-oriented music using his long-standing Recoil alias. And since 2011, Vince Clarke and Martin Gore have collaborated for the first time since the early days of Depeche Mode under the name VCMG; their Mute album *Ssss* is a fine example of minimalist techno. Alone, as MG, Martin Gore has also produced some interesting minimalist electronic instrumental releases.

The London duo Fortran 5 were part of the 1990s dance scene. They had originally recorded a pair of electropop albums for Mute in the mid-eighties using the name I Start Counting, but by 1991 had evolved into dance producers. Following their rebrand, they recorded three albums and remixed a diverse array of fellow Mute artists, including Erasure and Laibach. In 1996, the duo made another stylistic shift, this time drifting back toward their early Kraftwerk-influenced roots. This time, they re-christened themselves Komputer.

The sound of everything.

→ EINSTÜRZENDE NEUBAUTEN / 1990s /
(MARK CHUNG / F.M. EINHEIT / N.U. UNRUH /
ALEXANDER HACKE / BLIXA BARGELD)

STUMM14

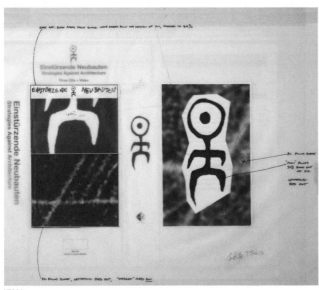

MF001

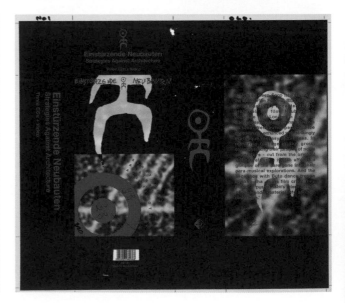

STUMM14 / MF001 / *Strategies Against Architecture* / Posters / Video Artwork Board / Video Proof / 1984–92 / An experimental industrial noise band from Berlin, Germany, although Einstürzende Neubauten did not make their studio debut for Mute until 1992, the label released a compilation of the band's early recordings in 1984. 'I don't want to produce musical notes – there are enough of them already – I want to cause events to happen.' Blixa Bargeld, Einstürzende Neubauten.

Einstürzende Neubauten (Blixa Bargeld / Alexander Hacke) / Copenhagen / 1983 / 'I have seen the death of rock and roll and its name is Einstürzende Neubauten,' hailed British music weekly *Sounds*, after the band's debut performance supporting The Birthday Party at London's Lyceum in March 1983. The on-stage use of angle grinders and piledriver hammers not only provided a literal definition of 'industrial music' but also ensured a spectacular live performance.

EINSTÜRZENDE NEUBAUTEN

TABULA RASA

**The new album available
on Mute compact discs
and digilog cassettes**

BETON106

STUMM14

BETON106

BETON504

BETON602

STUMM182

STUMM201

STUMM221

STUMM137

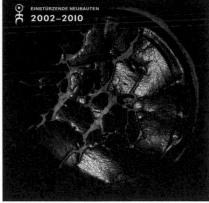

STUMM325

BETON106 / *Tabula Rasa* / Poster / 1992 / The band's Mute studio debut saw a shift in style away from the aggressive industrial sound of their earlier work, one track, 'Wüste', even featuring a string quartet. The cover artwork features a cropped photograph of a still life by Dutch 'Golden Age' painter Ambrosius Boschaert II (1609–45), sometimes referred to as Ambrosius the Younger.

STUMM14 → STUMM325 / Albums Discography/ 1984–2010 / 80–83 Strategien Gegen Architekturen (1984); *Tabula Rasa* (1992);

Ende Neu (1996); *Ende Neu Remixes* (1997); *Silence Is Sexy* (2000); *Strategies Against Architecture III* (2001); *Perpetuum Mobile* (2004); *Kalte Sterne – Early Recordings* (2004); *Strategies Against Architecture IV* (2010).

'Music doesn't have to be entertaining, but between boring and entertaining there is a wide spectrum. The humour in Neubauten is usually completely forgotten. After all, we are Germans – we are not supposed to be funny.' Blixa Bargeld, Einstürzende Neubauten.

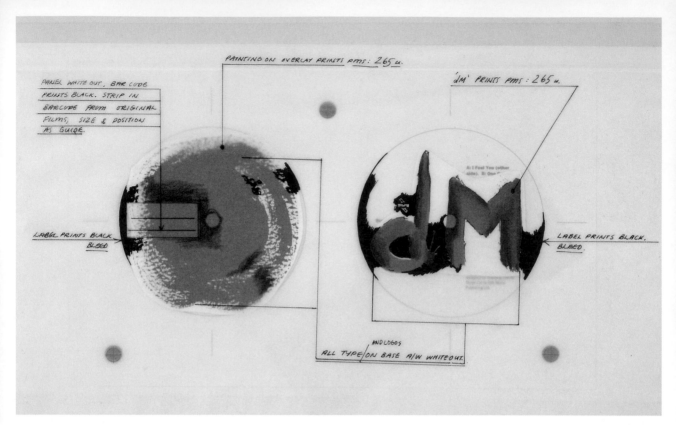

PAINTING ON OVERLAY PRINTS PMS: 265 u.

'dM' PRINTS PMS: 265 u.

PANEL WHITE OUT, BAR CODE
PRINTS BLACK. STRIP IN
BARCODE FROM ORIGINAL
FILMS, SIZE & POSITION
AS GUIDE.

LABEL PRINTS BLACK
BLEED

A: I Feel You (other side). B: One

LABEL PRINTS BLACK,
BLEED.

AND LOGOS
ALL TYPE ON BASE A/W WHITE OUT.

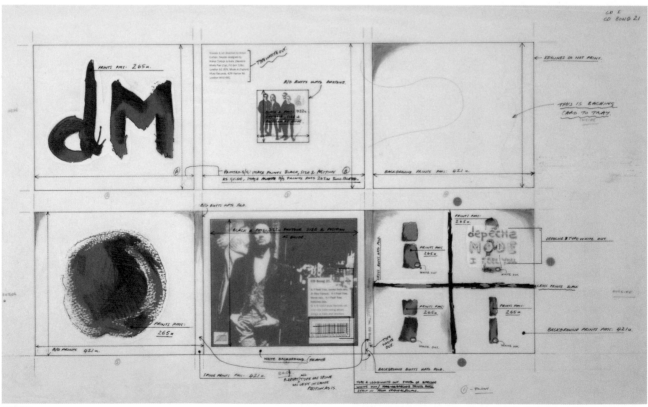

CD I
CD BONG 21

PRINTS PMS: 265 u.

TYPE WHITE OUT.

B/G BUTTS UPTO PHOTONE.

KEYLINES DO NOT PRINT.

THIS IS BACKING
CARD TO TRAY

BACKGROUND PRINTS PMS: 421 u.

PAINTED B/4: IMAGE PRINTS BLACK, SIZE & POSITION
AS GUIDE, IMAGE PHOTO B/G PRINTS PMS 265u THRO BLEED.

B/G BUTTS UPTO FOLD.

BLACK & PHOTO 422 u. PHOTONE SIZE & POSITION
AS GUIDE.

CD Bong 21.

PRINTS PMS:
265 u.

PRINTS PMS:
265 u.

PRINTS PMS:
265 u.

WHITE OUT.

depeche MODE

DEPECHE & TYPE WHITE OUT.

ACROSS PRINTS BLACK

PRINTS PMS:
265 u.

PRINTS PMS:
265 u.

BACKGROUND PRINTS PMS: 421 u.

B/G PRINTS 421 u.

PRINTS PMS:
265 u.

WHITE BACKGROUND FRAMES

WHITE OUT.

BACKGROUND BUTTS UPTO FOLD.

SPINE PRINTS PMS: 421 u.

REPRODUCE ON SPINE
USE IN SAME
POSITION AS IS.

TYPE & LOGO WHITE OUT.

PRINT

12BONG21

L12BONG21

BONG21 / 'I Feel You' / Artwork Boards / Proofs / 1993 / Original board artworks, marked up by Richard Smith at Area with instructions for the reprographic house. Before computer-based graphic design, it could be difficult to see how the artwork would be realised; it was not unusual for there to be two or three changes at proofing stage prior to printing.

'These are the first flat proofs for the "I Feel You" 12-inch singles. Anton and Richard felt that the painted background on the centre spread of L12BONG21 was too distracting, so we changed it to a solid black. There were also housekeeping corrections to the photos and colour work on both.' Paul A. Taylor, art director, Mute.

MUTEL5

BONG29

LMUTEL5

P12MUTEL5

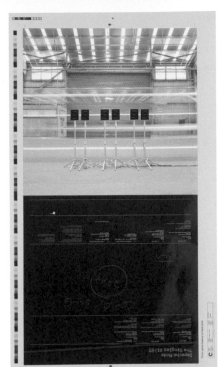

LMUTEL5

P12BONG29

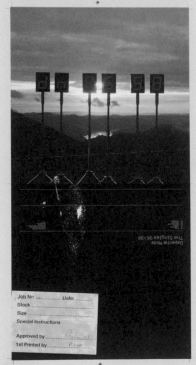

MUTEL5

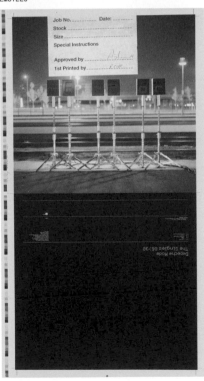

LMUTEL5

MUTEL5 / *The Singles 86 > 98* / BONG29 / 'Only When I Lose Myself' / Campaign / 1998 / 'This was a mega production. The basic idea of LED display units situated in various US locations with Depeche Mode associations came from Intro designer Mat Cook. There was a long, drawn-out process of budgeting and planning. It was an expensive idea to execute. Daniel eventually green-lighted the project, and a small team, led by Mat, was dispatched to the US for a ten-day shoot. The results were wonderful, and I think it was one of the best campaigns we did for Mute. What sticks in my mind is Daniel saying that there would never again be that sort of budget for cover art. That set off a warning signal. We were doing a lot of high-end work at that time for major labels, and this was the first sign that maybe the days of the big album cover budgets – late nineties – were over. It was the early days of Napster, MySpace and illegal downloading. A new attitude was forming in labels. The album cover was less important. Other media channels were taking over. We didn't do many mega-budget projects after that.' Adrian Shaughnessy, founder, Intro.

12BONG26   12"

LCDBONG26   CD

12BONG27   12"

LCDBONG27   CD

12BONG28   12"

CDBONG28   CD

CDBONG29   CD

LCDBONG29   CD

12BONG30   12"

LCDBONG30   CD

CDBONG31   CD

L12BONG31   12"

CDBONG32   CD

DVDBONG32   DVD

CDBONG33   CD

RCDBONG33   CD

CDBONG34   CD

12BONG34   12"

BONG35   7"

12BONG35   12"

CDBONG36   CD   12BONG36   12"

12BONG37   12"   L12BONG37   12"

12BONG38   12"   L12BONG38   12"

CDBONG39   CD   LCDBONG39   CD

BONG40   7"   LCDBONG40   CD

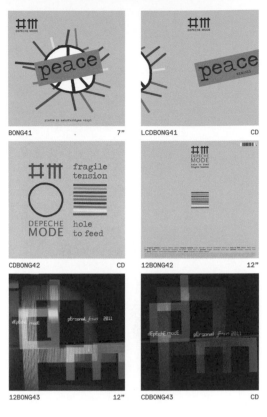

BONG41   7"   LCDBONG41   CD

CDBONG42   CD   12BONG42   12"

12BONG43   12"   CDBONG43   CD

BONG26 → BONG43 / Singles Discography / 1997–2011 / [Page 218, left block] 'It's No Good' (1997); 'Home' (1997); 'Useless' (1997); 'Only When I Lose Myself' (1998); 'Dream On' (2001). [Page 218, right block] 'I Feel Loved' (2001); 'Freelove' (2001); 'Goodnight Lovers' (2002); 'Enjoy The Silence 04' (2004); 'Precious' (2005). [Page 219, left block] 'A Pain That I'm Used To' (2005); 'Suffer Well' (2006); 'John The Revelator'/'Lillian' (2006); 'Martyr' (2006); 'Wrong' (2009). [Page 219, right block] 'Peace' (2009); 'Fragile Tension'/'Hole To Feed' (2009); 'Personal Jesus 2011' (2011).

STUMM5

STUMM9

STUMM13

STUMM19

1-25346

STUMM26

STUMM47

STUMM101

STUMM64

STUMM106

LSTUMM106

STUMM148

MUTEL5

STUMM190

XLCDMUTEL8

STUMM260

DMLHN31

MUTEL15

STUMM300

DMLHN52

MUTEL18

STUMM5 → MUTEL18 / Albums Discography / 1981–2011 / *Speak & Spell* (1981); *A Broken Frame* (1982); *Construction Time Again* (1983); *Some Great Reward* (1984); *Catching Up With...* (1985); *Black Celebration* (1986); *Music For The Masses* (1987); *101* (1989); *Violator* (1990); *Songs Of Faith And Devotion* (1993); *Songs Of Faith And Devotion (Live)* (1993); *Ultra* (1997); *The Singles 85>98* (1998); *Exciter* (2001); *Remixes 81···04* (2004); *Playing The Angel* (2005); *Touring The Angel* (2006); *The Best Of Depeche Mode Volume 1* (2006); *Sounds Of The Universe* (2009); *Tour Of The Universe* (2010); *Remixes 2: 81–11* (2011).

LIBERTY LBS 83279

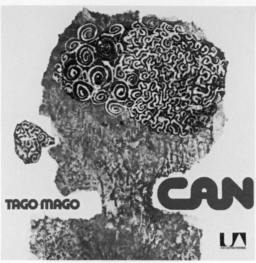

UNITED ARTISTS RECORDS → SPOON6/7

POLYDOR 2310 142

BRAIN 1028

KLING KLANG → STUMM304

KLANGBOX002

KRAUTROCK CONNECTIONS

In the late 1960s, German rock music began to gain a following in the UK. On BBC Radio 1, John Peel introduced British audiences to Faust, Can, Neu!, Amon Düül II and Kraftwerk, while weekly music paper *Melody Maker* began running album and concert reviews. In spite of the diverse sounds produced, these bands were generally filed under the catch-all category of 'krautrock'. ('Kraut' had been a derogatory term used by British soldiers during the two world wars to describe their foe.) As a term, krautrock was never particularly intended to offend, and even though many of the bands themselves disliked the description, it's now been reluctantly accepted as covering German music of a certain time and type.

Many of these bands were an important influence on Daniel Miller and the birth of Mute Records. And it's notable that more than a few of his favourite original recordings have ended up on one of the label's niche imprints, The Grey Area Of Mute Records. 'It's a reissue label of artists we love, who we think are important, and whose work should always be available,' explains Miller. 'And whose work was not originally available on Mute.'

Here, Miller discusses five of his favourite krautrock albums. Although he gives no preferential order, they're listed chronologically.

Amon Düül II *Phallus Dei* (1969)
Growing out of Germany's heavily politicised hippy scene, musicians from the Amon Düül commune split, one faction talking the name Amon Düül II. The title of their debut album *Phallus Dei* means 'God's Penis'. 'This is a bit different from the others as it's the earliest one in the list. It's much more freeform,' Miller declares. 'Probably not the best album in the world, but it made a significant impact on me when I first heard it. And they used all sorts of electric noises and it really appealed to me.'

Can *Tago Mago* (1971)
A benchmark in experimental rock, the third album by Can has been cited as an influence on everyone from Marc Bolan and John Lydon through to Radiohead and The Flaming Lips. 'Can were another huge influence who have recorded so many great albums. It's hard to pick a favourite, but it has to be *Tago Mago*. It just got me addicted – I couldn't stop playing it. I think the relationship we've had with Can, which has [lasted] over twenty-five years now, is a great example of how a band that no longer exists can keep bringing out new material. We've worked really closely with them on the reissues.'

Faust *Faust* (1971)
Originally assembled by producer Uwe Nettelbeck, the idea of Faust was sold to the Polydor label as a German band capable of competing commercially with the likes of the Rolling Stones. The first album that emerged was a commercial disaster but quickly came to be regarded as an avant-rock classic. 'On the very opening of the record, you hear a little bit of "Satisfaction" by the Stones and "All You Need Is

Love" by the Beatles,' recalls Miller. 'And it was all kind of distorted and screwed up. To me, it felt like a relinquishing of the musical past and the birth of something new. When I heard that in 1971 it felt like an amazing statement. It may not have been what they intended, but it was certainly how I interpreted it. It's abstract, melodic, weird, it's got *musique concrète* – it's a really important album.'

Neu! *Neu! 2* (1973)
A pioneering band comprising Michael Rother's proto-ambient guitar and drummer Klaus Dinger's characteristic motorik drum rhythm. Mute tried unsuccessfully to bring the Neu! catalogue to the label: 'We were hoping to sign the Neu! catalogue for years, but could never get Michael and Klaus to talk together,' explains Miller. 'They'd had a falling-out. It was a crazy situation; they both wanted to sign but wouldn't talk to each other. We even had meetings with them in parks in Düsseldorf, but nothing ever came of it.'

Kraftwerk *Radio-Activity [Radio-Aktivität]* (1975)
As the standout pioneers of synthpop, Kraftwerk are the band that perhaps had the most notable impact on the early days of Mute. '*Autobahn* [1974] was an enormous influence on me,' enthuses Miller. 'It combined the experimentation and electronic music I was enjoying at that time plus the pop I'd grown up with as a kid...that was my year zero. My favourite Kraftwerk album would have to be *Radio-Activity*. All of their albums are conceptual, but that one's perhaps the most realized. But really, all of their albums are great.'

In 2009, appropriately enough, Mute Records, took over the reissue of the newly remastered Kraftwerk catalogue. 'They know what a huge fan I am...and they thought being on Mute was a good idea, which was incredibly flattering.'

Krautrock Albums / LIBERTY LBS 83279 / *Phallus Dei*, Amon Düül II (1969); UNITED ARTISTS RECORDS → SPOON 6/7 / *Tago Mago*, Can (1971); POLYDOR 2310 142 / *Faust*, Faust (1971); BRAIN 1028 / *Neu! 2*, Neu! (1973); KLING KLANG → STUMM304 / *Radio-Activity [Rado-Aktivität]*, Kraftwerk (1975); KLANGBOX002 / *Kraftwerk: The Catalogue*, Kraftwerk (2009).

An ideal Mute artist:
a self-contained,
adventurous and
innovative musician
who cannot be
categorised.

He's a law unto himself.

STUMM130

XLSTUMM130

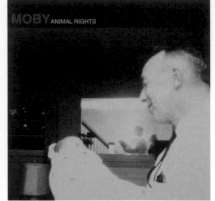

STUMM150

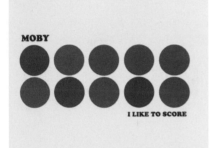

STUMM168

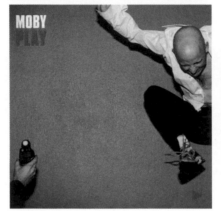

STUMM172

LSTUMM172

STUMM202

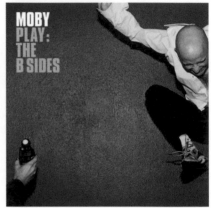

STUMM240

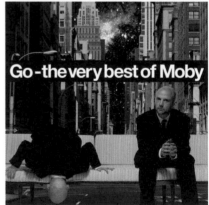

MUTEL14

MUTEL14

STUMM275

LCDSTUMM275

STUMM130 → LCDSTUMM275 / Albums Discography / 1995–2008 /
Everything Is Wrong (1995); *Everything Is Wrong (DJ Mix Album)* (1995);
Animal Rights (1996); *I Like To Score* (1997); *Play* (1999); *Play: The B Sides*
(2000); *18* (2002); *Hotel* (2005); *Go–The Very Best Of Moby* (2007); *Go –
The Very Best Of Moby (Remixed)* (2007); *Last Night* (2008); *Last Night:
Remixed* (2008).

'I love the artifice and glam quality of Helmut Newton's work, which seemed
to fit the concept of the *Last Night* album, as it's about a long, strange
night out in New York.' Moby.

STUMM130 / *Everything Is Wrong* / Album Photography / 1995 /
The photographs for Moby's Mute debut were taken by Jill Greenberg.

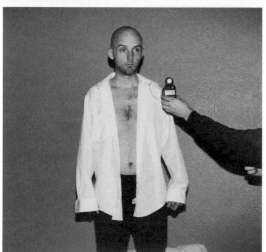

STUMM172

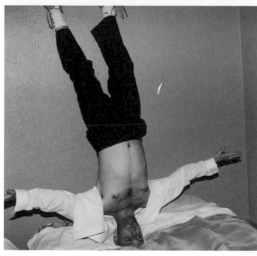

STUMM172 / *Play* / Album Photography / 1998 / 'Working with Corinne [Day, photographer] was great. We spent the day wandering around New York and rented a room at the Chelsea Hotel, where we jumped on the bed and shot the cover image. For the design I just borrowed the triangle image from the universal "play" icon. I named the album after a mural at a playground on Mulberry Street [New York], but later realised that it's a rare album title in that it describes what people did with the record.' Moby.

MUTE218

L12MUTE218

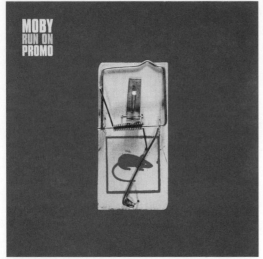

P12MUTE221

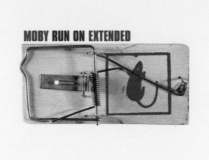

LCDMUTE221

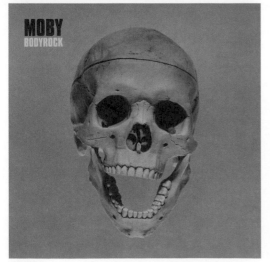

12MUTE225

LCDMUTE225

STUMM202

MUTE218 / 'Honey' / MUTE221 / 'Run On' / MUTE225 / 'Bodyrock' /
Fronts / Limited Editions / 1998–99 / Moby's *Play* album yielded an
extraordinary nine hit singles, among them the three shown here.
The covers of 'Run On' and 'Body Rock' both featured the work
of Swedish still-life photographer Henrik Bonnevier.

STUMM202 / *18* / Counterstand Proof / 2002 / Moby's sixth studio album,
18, debuted at No.1 in the UK and peaked at No.4 in the US *Billboard* chart.
The artwork was photographed by Danny Clinch. 'We just rented an RV
and drove out to the desert with a bunch of odd clothes and cameras.
It was actually quite spontaneous.' Moby.

musik - the new album by plastikman
available on novamute compact discs and cassettes

NovaMute

NOMU22

NOMU30

NOMU37

NOMU61

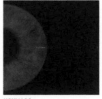

NOMU65

NOMU100

STUMM370

NOMU37 / *Musik* / Poster / 1994 / 'Daniel [Miller], Mick Paterson, Pepe Jansz and I set up Novamute in 1991 from the ashes of Rhythm King, Mute's earlier pop/dance label. We wanted it to be quite a different creature, concentrating its A&R policy on more experimental electronic music and techno. An alliance with legendary Berlin Club Tresor, releasing its compilations, cemented our global reputation.' Seth Hodder, ex-Novamute.

NOMU22 → STUMM370 / Albums Discography / 1993–2014 / Plastikman is the alter ego of producer Richie Hawtin. The Plastikman logo, designed in 1991 by Californian artist Ron Cameron, has an unusual background story. 'I did this for my own skateboard company [Strike].... Someone re-scanned it and sold it to Richie Hawtin in 1992 and claimed ownership. Richie found me around 1997, and everything was settled all cool-like.' Ron Cameron, designer.

Pan sonic

vakio

BFFP118

BFFP132

BFFP149

BFFP166

BFFP180BX

BFFP118 → BFFP180 / Albums Discography / 1995–2004 /
Vakio (1995); *Kulma* (1997); *A* (1999); *Aaltopiiri* (2001); *Kesto (234.48:4)* (2004).

Recording for Mute's Blast First subsidiary label, Pan Sonic formed (originally under the name Panasonic) in 1993, in the Finnish city of Turku, and split up in 2009. Blast First Petite released their last album, *Gravitoni*, in 2010. The group's co-founder Mika Vainio died in 2017.

Pan Sonic (Mika Vainio / Ilpo Väisänen) / Unedited Promo Photo / 1995 /
At the time the hugely influential *Vakio* was recorded, Mika Vainio and Lipo Väisänen were still calling themselves Panasonic. 'We were weeks away from release when we got the news that Panasonic would not allow them to use the name and would sue us if we released their music under that moniker…. We moved forward with the name Pan Sonic, but continued to use the same font as the electronic giant. Retouching tools were used to amend artwork and press photos and off we went.' Paul A. Taylor, art director, Mute.

My name is Holger Hiller.

I have called this CD "Little Present".

It consists of a story and 13 music tracks made from audio recordings of Tokyo. I think the charm of the man-made sounds and images of Tokyo lies in the way these man made objects "talk to you" in a quick and changing succession, interpreting and replacing the "natural" environment.

At the time my son  was living in Tokyo and this is the story of one of my various trips visiting him.

CDSTUMM108

Here is the track listing.
Story and atmospheres are indicated by black numbers,
music tracks by red numbers.

1-2 children's songs...
3-4 ...and favourite videos

5-6 train stations
and their melodies

7-8 happy to go shopping

9-10 CNN

11-12 fresh young girls in commercials

13-14 busy loudspeakers
in Shinjuku

15-16 everybody having a
good time

17-18 drive to Yokohama

19-20 dozing
off in front of
the TV

21-22 toy telephone

23-24 ride through the suburbs

25-26 while leaving

STUMM108 / *Little Present* / Cover / 1995 / The background story to Holger Hiller's touching 1995 *hörspiel*, *Little Present*, is told on the sleeve of the CD. Visiting his four-year-old son – Kentaro – in Tokyo, Hiller made a field recording of his trip, which includes audio clips of ambient street sounds, TV commercials, train stations and his son singing. The artwork was created by Hiller together with Paul A. Taylor, and using photographs of Tokyo taken mainly by Daniel Miller. Hiller would gradually edge away from the music business, and later worked as an English teacher in Berlin.

'Holger came into the Mute office at 429 Harrow Road with this fabulous album he'd made on a trip to Japan; it was unlike anything else he'd done. Created in conjunction with the broadcaster Bayerischer Rundfunk, we had the licence to manufacture and sell a maximum of 500 copies – any more would have breached his agreement. We used Daniel Miller's photos of Tokyo and created a naive design to convey the innocence and spontaneity of the content. Everyone should take time to listen to this wonderful piece of art Holger created.' Paul A. Taylor, art director, Mute.

STUMM132

STUMM154

STUMM184

STUMM236

THE JON SPENCER BLUES EXPLOSION SWEET N SOUR

MUTE271

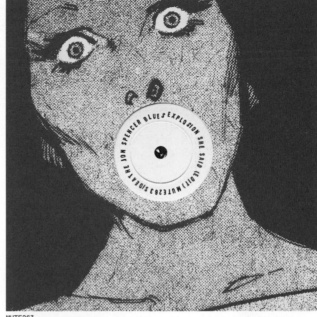

MUTE263

MUTE288

STUMM199

STUMM132→STUMM236 / Albums Discography / 1996–2004 / *Now I Got Worry* (1996); *Acme* (1998); *Acme-Plus* (1999); *Plastic Fang* (2002); *Damage* (2004).

'Jon always wants to push the boundaries of what you can achieve with design and packaging. Everything he wanted to do with the design and in the printing process for *Now I Got Worry* flew in the face of convention. The printer even said it wouldn't work and we had to sign a waiver of responsibility for them. It did of course work and looks amazing. I learn something new from all our artists and from the fabulous creatives we get to work with on our releases. Jon never fails to blow my mind.' Paul A. Taylor, Art Director, Mute.

MUTE271 / 'Sweet N Sour' / MUTE263 / 'She Said' / MUTE288 / 'Shakin' Rock 'N' Roll Tonight' / STUMM199 / *Plastic Fang* / *Plastic Fang* Campaign / 2002 / Award-winning New York graphic designer Chip Kidd produced the cover for *Plastic Fang* and its associated singles. 'It was a dream-come-true for me to have Chip Kidd design Plastic Fang. I had just read the *Jack Cole and Plastic Man* book that he had designed, loved it, and basically cold-called Chip (we had never met) to ask if he'd like to do my band's new record … Chip's final design so perfectly captured what I had in mind, what I was wished to articulate, and the album's themes. Plus it was cool and clever as fuck.' Jon Spencer.

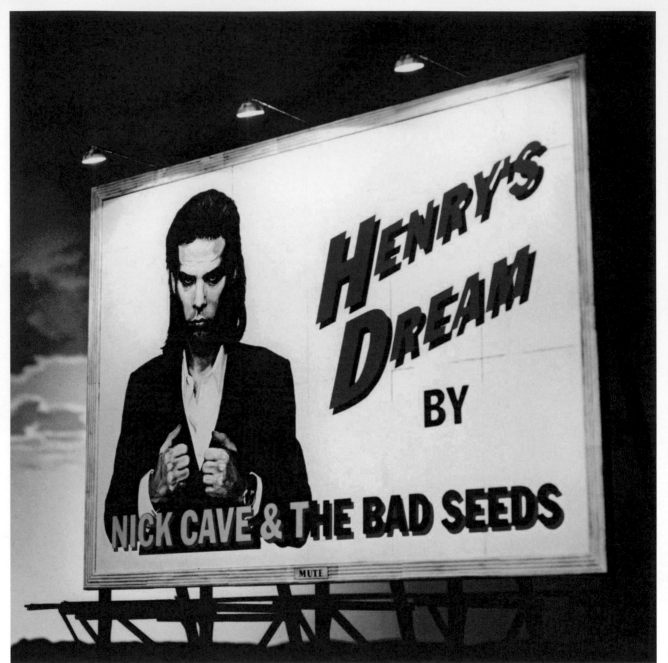

STUMM92

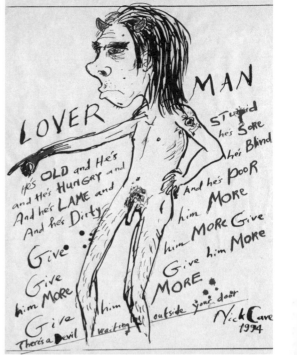

STUMM123

STUMM92 / *Henry's Dream* / Front / 1992 / Art directed by Anton Corbijn and also featuring his photography, *Henry's Dream* was designed by Richard Smith at Area and ironically enough, the first Bad Seeds album not to feature a photograph of Nick on the cover. The front cover billboard was painted and initial pressings of the vinyl came with an art print of the image.

STUMM123 / *Let Love In* / Poster / Loverman Promotional Postcard / CD Inner Artwork / 1994 / *Let Love In* was photographed by collaborator, Polly Borland. Initial pressings of the album came with a set of postcards, including one showing Nick's hand drawn Loverman. The vinyl inner sleeve and CD tray feature the above photograph of Nick's working environment for the album.

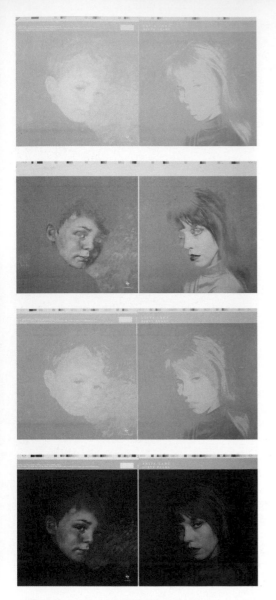

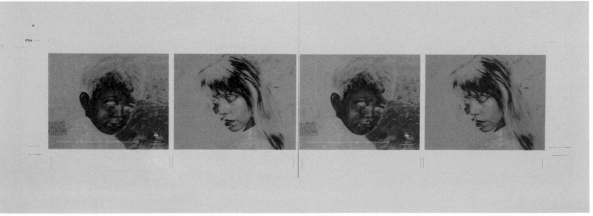

STUMM81

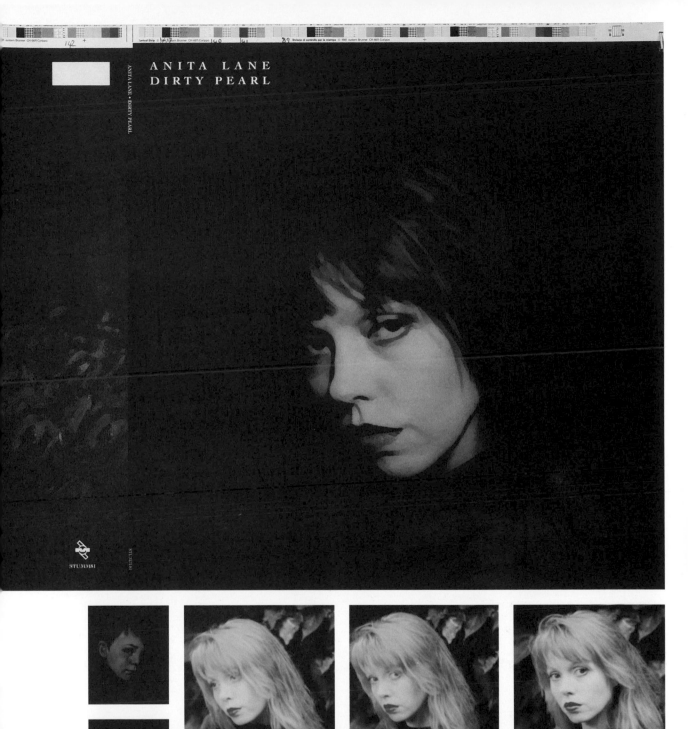

ANITA LANE
DIRTY PEARL

ANITA LANE · DIRTY PEARL

STUMM81

STUMM81 / *Dirty Pearl* / Colour Separation / Printing Plates / Proof / Manipulated Photography / 1993 / Australian singer-songwriter Anita Lane's album of her collected work features one of Giovanni Bragolin's famous 'Crying Boys' paintings on the back cover, the front cover image is a photo-manipulated image of Anita by designer Slim Smith, created to echo the back cover painting. A brief member of Nick Cave's Bad Seeds, Anita has collaborated with various members of The Bad Seeds throughout her musical career.

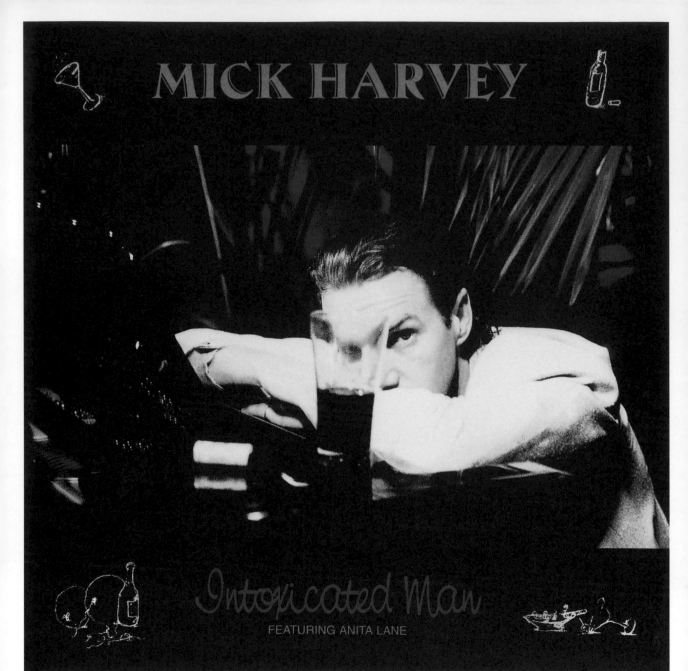

STUMM144

MICK HARVEY

Intoxicated Women

STUMM396

STUMM144 / *Intoxicated Man* / Front / 1995 / STUMM396 / *Intoxicated Women* / Front / 2017 / Bad Seed Mick Harvey released the first of his four albums of Serge Gainsbourg covers in 1995. 'The original photo for *Intoxicated Man* was taken by Mick's partner, the painter Katy Beale. It seemed to evoke the mood of Serge Gainsbourg perfectly – at a piano

with a drink to hand – whilst retaining an identity of its own. Mick very much wanted to echo the mood of that photo for the *Intoxicated Women* artwork 22 years later, working with film-maker and photographer Lyndelle-Jayne Spruyt, again at the piano, drink close by, deep thoughts closing in.' Paul A. Taylor, art director, Mute.

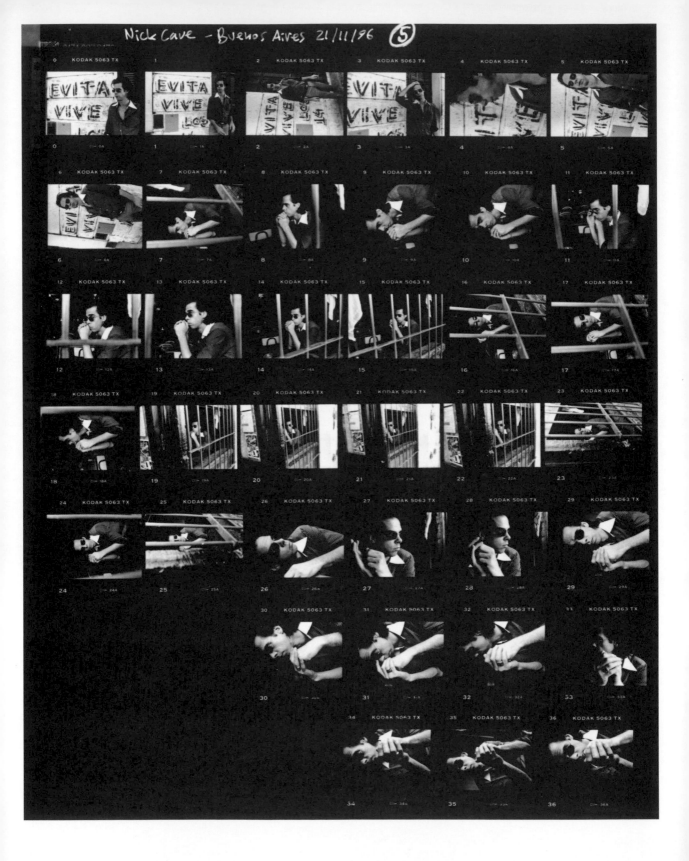

1990 – 1999   NICK CAVE + THE BAD SEEDS

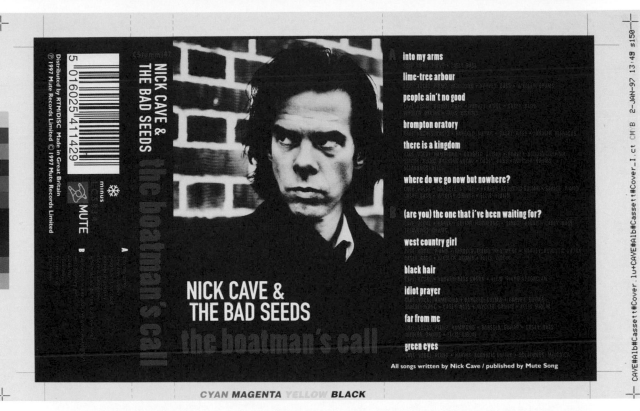

CSTUMM142

Nick Cave / Contact Sheet / Buenos Aires / 1996 / Nick Cave And The Bad Seeds embarked on a brief, four-date South American tour In November 1996. The selection of photographs shown here was taken earlier in the day on 21 November, before the band's performance at the Teatro Opera in Buenos Aires, Argentina.

STUMM142 / *The Boatman's Call* / Proofs / 1997 / 'Nick had a clear idea of what he wanted to do: "A photoshoot with Anton [Corbijn] – just me and him." Anton had one hour available. I told Daniel I was worried that it was not long enough. Daniel said, "It's Nick, he knows what he's doing, and when have you ever seen a bad photo from Anton?"' Paul A. Taylor, art director, Mute.

1990 — 1999 NICK CAVE + THE BAD SEEDS

STUMM277

STUMM277 / *Dig, Lazarus, Dig!!!* / Artwork Drawing / Installation / Photography / Poster / 2008 / The influence of side-project Grinderman can be heard in the raw, live sound of Nick Cave And The Bad Seeds' fourteenth studio album, *Dig, Lazarus, Dig!!!*, which was completed from scratch in five days. The artwork created and photographed for the cover was produced by contemporary British artists Tim Noble and Sue Webster. It was around 8 ft square and incorporated 775 light bulbs. The photographs are from a special-edition mini book and 3" CD that charts the title song's progress from Cave's initial scribblings through the construction and erection of the huge installation.

MUTE032

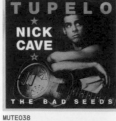

MUTE038

MUTE047

MUTE052

MUTE086

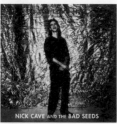

MUTE108

MUTE118

MUTE140

MUTE148

MUTE151

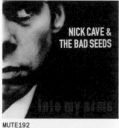

MUTE160

MUTE169

MUTE172

MUTE185

MUTE189

MUTE192

MUTE206

MUTE249

MUTE262

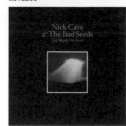

MUTE265

MUTE290

MUTE318

MUTE324

MUTE329

MUTE339

MUTE377

MUTE390

MUTE403

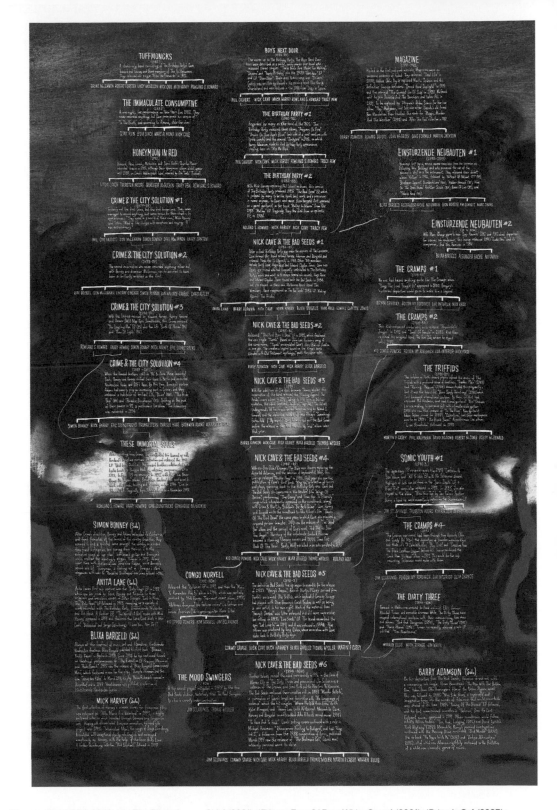

MUTE032 → MUTE403 / Singles Discography / 1984–2008 / 'In The Ghetto' (1984); 'Tupelo' (1985); 'The Singer' (1986); 'The Mercy Seat' (1988); 'Deanna' (1988); 'The Ship Song' (1990); 'The Weeping Song' (1990); 'Straight To You'/ 'Jack The Ripper' (1992); 'I Had A Dream, Joe' (1992); 'What A Wonderful World' (1992); 'Do You Love Me?' (1994); 'Loverman' (1994); 'Red Right Hand' (1994); 'Where The Wild Roses Grow' (1995); 'Henry Lee' (1996); 'Into My Arms' (1997); '(Are You) The One That I've Been Waiting For?' (1996); 'As I Sat Sadly By Her Side' (2001); 'Fifteen Feet Of Pure White Snow' (2001); 'Bring It On' (2003); 'He Wants You'/'Babe, I'm On Fire' (2003); 'Rock Of Gibraltar' (2003); 'Nature Boy' (2004); 'Breathless'/'There She Goes, My Beautiful World' (2004); 'Get Ready For Love' (2005); 'Dig, Lazarus, Dig!!!' (2008); 'More News From Nowhere' (2008); 'Midnight Man' (2008).

Family Tree / 1998 / Created for a promotional box set for *The Best Of* album.

Nick Cave
& The Bad Seeds
The Lyre of Orpheus

Nick Cave
& The Bad Seeds
Abattoir Blues

STUMM233

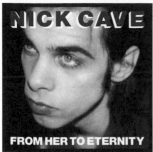

STUMM17

STUMM21

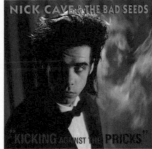

STUMM28

STUMM34

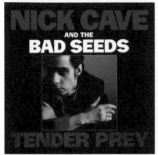

STUMM52

STUMM76

STUMM92

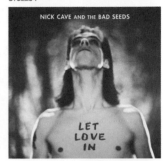

STUMM123

STUMM138

STUMM142

STUMM164

STUMM207

STUMM233

STUMM277

STUMM233 / *The Lyre Of Orpheus/Abbatoir Blues* / Clothbound Special Editon / 2004 / 'Lyre of Orpheus was the first sleeve that Nick and I worked on together. We spoke a lot about exploring this idea of a package that felt very beautiful and delicate on the exterior – hence the imagery of blossoms, the linen wrap and serif typography – almost like an anthology of poetry. But then the music inside was incredibly dark and unsettling. The whole package was about unexpected juxtapositions. I remember Warren (Ellis) describing the two parts of the album to me when we met at the studio, in his words – "The first record's really very beautiful you know, very different for a Bad Seeds album, and the second one – well – it's an absolute fucking ball breaker." It was also a time when physical CD sales were in decline (downloads were on the rise) and so Nick and I wanted to create something that felt really special – like a precious artefact somehow. We wanted to give fans a reason to go into stores and buy a physical copy of the album.' Tom Hingston, designer.

STUMM17 → STUMM277 / Studio Albums Discography / 1984–2008 / *From Her To Eternity* (1984); *The Firstborn Is Dead* (1985); *Kicking Against The Pricks* (1986); *Your Funeral...My Trial* (1986); *Tender Prey* (1988); *The Good Son* (1990); *Henry's Dream* (1992); *Let Love In* (1994); *Murder Ballads* (1996); *The Boatman's Call* (1997); *No More Shall We Part* (2001); *Nocturama* (2003); *The Lyre Of Orpheus/Abbattoir Blues* (2004); *Dig, Lazarus, Dig!!!* (2008).

2000

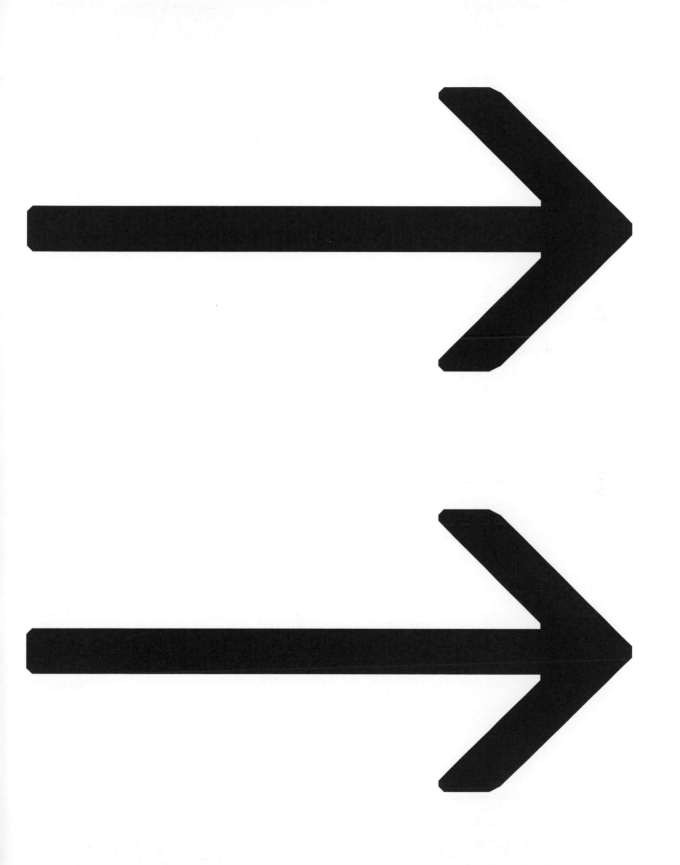

01

02

INTO TOMORROW

The 1990s had ended with Mute's commitment to musical experimentation as fervent as ever. Add N To (X), a three-piece freeform electronics project from Camberwell, had joined the label in 1997 and seemed to be precisely the kind of band guaranteed to capture Daniel Miller's imagination. 'I was very excited when I first saw them because they were bucking the fading Britpop trend of the time,' he reveals, 'I thought they should be on Mute and that we, as a label, could do more for them than anybody else.' Mixing vintage analogue synthesisers – at that time still relatively unfashionable – with frenetic live drumming, their performances were both anarchic and exhilarating. They released three albums on Mute before disbanding in 2003.

Steven Claydon from Add N To (X) also played a key role in the discovery of one of the most significant Mute bands of the new millennium. 'Steve's girlfriend was a singer who'd worked on some of their recordings, explains Daniel Miller. 'Now, one of the worst moments you can have if you run a record label is when one of your artists asks, "Will you listen to my girlfriend/boyfriend's demo?" You have to go, "Yeah, of course" and smile, even though it might be terrible and you wonder how you're going to deal with it. (In fact I had a bad falling-out with one artist over that very thing.) So I put on the CD, and after about forty-five seconds I said to Steve, "I need to sign this!"' The song was 'Lovely Head'; the artist, Goldfrapp.

Alison Goldfrapp's ethereal vocals had already graced recordings by Goldie and Orbital, and in 1999 Goldfrapp had been introduced to multi-instrumentalist and composer Will Gregory. A former session musician, Gregory had played with Tears for Fears in the 1980s. The duo began writing together, Goldfrapp's abstract lyrics paired with Gregory's soundscapes.

Adopting her surname for their band, the duo spent six months locked away in rural Wiltshire. There, they recorded their debut, *Felt Mountain* (2000), which mixed sumptuous instrumentation with diverse influences such as 1960s French pop and the soundtracks of Ennio Morricone. The word 'cinematic' was widely invoked in reviews and interviews. '*Felt Mountain* was very atmospheric, and incredibly beautiful,' Miller acknowledges, 'and by its nature not a very rhythmic record; I think Alison got a bit bored playing it live after a while.'

A key moment came while touring the album, when the duo began ending their shows with an electronic dance version of Olivia Newton-John's 1980s hit 'Physical'. 'It went down an absolute storm,' Miller recalled. 'I loved their arrangement; she told me they wanted more of a party vibe when they played.'

For their follow-up, the band settled at a home studio in Bath, working in relative isolation. Unlike some other Mute artists ('Moby would send us absolutely everything he was doing – every last loop!' Miller remembers), work in progress was never auditioned. 'We didn't hear from them for months and then the first track arrived one day in the post. That was "Train" from the *Black Cherry* album – it was so completely different from everything they'd done before. But that change in direction all came from them.' Both the album and lead single entered the UK charts.

By the time of Goldfrapp's 2005 album *Supernature*, their sound had made a wholesale shift into electropop territory. Glancing back at 1970s glam, the single 'Ooh La La' – featuring a simple riff and heavy, electronic shuffle beat – reached No.4 in the UK charts. *Supernature* produced three further Top 40 hits and narrowly missed the top spot in the album charts.

Subsequent albums have seen Goldfrapp take similar shifts in direction and dynamic, temporarily moving away from electronic dance music with *Seventh Tree* (2008), taking on a starker sound with *Tales of Us* (2013) and returning once

03

04

again to synthpop with *Silver Eye* (2017). 'They've taken some very interesting twists and turns,' notes Miller.

Most of the label's long-established names continued to thrive into the 21st century. Depeche Mode once again became active, and remain one of the most commercially successful bands in world. Although the last two albums were released by Sony, Miller maintains a close working relationship with them, and Mute's logo continues to appear on the back of their releases. During the 2000s, a variety of solo projects also emerged on Mute from within the band. Singer Dave Gahan released his debut album, the single 'Dirty Sticky Floors' reaching the UK Top 20. Martin Gore teamed up with Vince Clarke, his Depeche Mode colleague from thirty-two years earlier, to produce minimalist techno as VCMG and also released albums of his own; Andrew Fletcher set up a Mute subsidiary label called Toast Hawaii.

Nick Cave And The Bad Seeds, meanwhile, went from strength to strength in the new millennium, in 2004 releasing a universally acclaimed double album, *Abattoir Blues / The Lyre Of Orpheus*, which would find a place on many album-of-the-decade listings. At this time, Cave also engaged in the side project Grinderman with other members of The Bad Seeds. Initially formed to experiment with new material, the band eventually began performing live, generating a dynamic, aggressive sound that recalled Cave's days with The Birthday Party.

Among Mute's most interesting 21st-century signings were a unique New York-based noise-rock band called Liars, who were discovered by Mute subsidiary Blast First – a label that had been founded in 1985 to release Sonic Youth albums in the UK. Liars' full debut for Mute was 2004's *They Were Wrong, So We Drowned*, a fascinating concept album based around witchcraft practised in Germany on Walpurgisnacht. A stark contrast to their debut album, which captured the zeitgeist of 2001, *They Were Wrong, So We Drowned* polarised critics – but it is still regarded

as one of their strongest albums to date. Moving to Berlin, two years later Liars released *Drum's Not Dead*, an album filled with heavy drum, distorted drone guitars and Beach-Boys-style harmonies. They continued to wrong-foot audiences and in 2012, with Daniel Miller's guidance, their sound made a sudden shift toward electronic sound on the album *WIXIW*. Liars' unpredictability appeals hugely to Miller, who declares that, 'It only sounds like a Liars album if it doesn't sound like the last one!'

Another signing to fit in with the label ethos was Beth Jeans Houghton. Unusually, perhaps, for Mute, influences of West Coast 1960s psychedelic folk rock could be traced in her 2012 debut, *Yours Truly, Cellophane Nose*, recorded with her band The Hooves Of Destiny. The singer abandoned recordings for a follow-up, however, reinventing herself instead as Du Blonde. In common with others on the Mute roster, Houghton is also a talented illustrative artist, photographer and video-maker – as her visual presentation makes abundantly clear.

Over the years, Mute Records has also earned a reputation for promoting singular artists who might have struggled to find a natural environment elsewhere. Mute provided a fertile environment for the uneasy listening industrial dub of Mark Stewart – once of late-1970s teenage agitprop band The Pop Group – for many years.

At the other end of the spectrum, singer-songwriter Richard Hawley would seem to have been something of an anachronism for a label that also promoted the experimental sound of NON and avant-garde approach of Laibach. Yet it was a relationship that made sense for the artist, Hawley revealing that Miller was 'the only person from the record industry that I've invited within a mile of my house...he just gave me free reign to do what I wanted....He's the only record company guy I trust.'

One of Mute's more recent misfits has been Josh T. Pearson. A Texas-born songwriter with a Southern

05

06

Pentecostal upbringing, in 2001 his band Lift To Experience made one extraordinary album (*The Texas-Jerusalem Crossroads*) before dramatically imploding. Ten years later, he appeared on Mute with the gut-wrenchingly personal neo-folk of *Last Of The Country Gentlemen*, which was heavily lauded by critics. It was not until 2017 that Pearson began working on a follow-up.

Another of Mute's notable 21st-century signings is New York band Yeasayer. With an ever-evolving sound that encompasses psychedelia and a multiplicity of other contemporary pop styles, Yeasayer sport a relatively unorthodox group lineup, with principle songwriters Chris Keating and Anan Wilder also sharing lead vocals. In particular, the band's album sleeves have also garnered praise, having commissioned works from noted artists such as David Altmejd. As Keating remarked, "I think album artwork is increasingly ignored because everyone's listening on their phones, but to me it's still a really important art form. I like picturing what it's going to look like on an LP, especially on a gatefold."

In 2014, Mute signed Factory Records veterans New Order. Formed in Manchester, evolving from Joy Division in 1980, three years later they would transform into a hugely influential electronic act with the release of their 12-inch single 'Blue Monday'. In due course, they found what might have seemed a natural home as part of the Mute family, and the album *Music Complete* (2015) – a decade after their previous release – was their most overtly electronic collection to date, as well as their first without founding member Peter Hook. The album's artwork was also notable; a stark montage of black lines with block colouring, it was designed by long-time collaborator Peter Saville. Supported by a world tour, the album charted on both sides of the Atlantic.

As far as the business was concerned, the most dramatic events in the Mute story took place in 2002. Having owned the independent label for 24 years, Miller took the difficult decision to part with Mute, selling it in its entirety to one of the world's most famous record companies, EMI. As part of the deal, Miller would remain in charge of the label.

Describing the background to the sale, Miller is blunt: 'We were in financial difficulties.' The second half of the nineties had been troublesome for Mute. Britpop had seen a plethora of retro guitar bands overrunning Britain's music business. 'Britpop represented a lot of things I disliked. I found it non-progressive and all-pervasive.'

The label's fortunes had been relieved when Moby's *Play* album finally broke in 2000 ('like the cavalry coming over the hill,' Miller admits), but the experience had been sobering. His decision was the result of a long-standing relationship with former head of Virgin Records France, Emmanuel de Buretel. 'He was a good friend and he understood Mute,' Miller explains. 'He'd actually been trying to buy Mute for years, so when I was ready to take that leap he was the person I went to.'

By this time, de Buretel was running EMI Continental Europe, and was able to guarantee Miller creative control for the existing roster of Mute artists.

'It was a productive relationship until Emmanuel parted company with EMI. But we still operated as an autonomous label within the EMI group.'

Struggling to deal with the uncertain realities of the 21st-century music business, the mighty EMI had fallen into rapid decline, and in August 2007 the group was sold to a private equity company, Terra Firma, for £2.4 billion. EMI underwent a swift and dramatic restructuring programme that saw across-the-board cost-cutting and job losses.

'We came under the cosh a few times when EMI was sold,' Miller reveals. 'There was a signing freeze – no EMI labels were allowed to take on anyone new for three months. And after that it just got messy. It was not a good place to be, for the label or our artists. So in 2010, we made an agreement to separate.'

07

08

Miller set up the new Mute with a licence to the name and logo. Mute Artists was born. 'We left with most of our staff, and moved to Hammersmith. All the artists who were not under contract with EMI came with us – Goldfrapp, Erasure, Liars – and we started signing new artists.' Sadly, this meant that label stalwarts such as Depeche Mode and Nick Cave would no longer be a part of Mute.

With Mute's renewed independence came the desire and the freedom to collaborate with a new breed of groundbreaking electronic artist. When the opportunity arose to work with Sascha Ring on his Apparat project, Mute didn't think twice. *The Devil's Walk*, released in September 2011, was a beautiful piece of work; it enabled Apparat to move into film, television and composition for the theatre (*Krieg und Frieden*, 2013). Ring's other project, Moderat (released by Mute America), continue to tour extensively and, in 2009, topped Resident Advisor's poll for best live act.

Ben Frost, an artist long admired by the label, had been involved with Miller's publishing company, Mute Song, for some time. When Mute heard extracts from *A U R O R A* (2014), they immediately wanted greater involvement.. Uncompromising, inventive and prolific, Frost continues to push boundaries with each soundtrack, theatre score and album he records. 2017's *The Centre Cannot Hold* (recorded with Steve Albini in Chicago), is a piece of work that firmly establishes Frost as a master of his craft.

For several months Mute courted Alejandro Ghersi for his Arca project. The two resulting Mute albums, *Xen* (2014) and *Mutant* (2015), were amongst the most intricate and mesmerising electronic albums to emerge in a long time. He was later hired to produce the music of Kanye West and Björk.

Spending time with Daniel Miller, you quickly gain a sense of a man with his sight placed firmly on the future. Simone Grant, who designed the artwork for the first Mute releases, has known Miller since they were teenagers:

'Daniel has always hated nostalgia. He was only really interested in what was happening next.' Even now, at an age when many would have begun settling into retirement, his fascination for electronic music and technology is undiminished. He continues to work in the studio and as a techno DJ. And above all, he is still seeking out new and interesting music for the label he has now operated for almost forty years.

Age and experience have given Miller some perspective. 'I was a classic case of a person who starts his own company but then finds it difficult to relinquish any kind of control,' he admits. 'But over the years I've come to accept delegating because I gradually realised there were many things I'm no good at – finance, legal, and some practicalities – so I built a team around me who *could* do those things. And who I trusted.'

So how much of the control freak is there left in him? 'Less than there used to be,' he replies, with a laugh.

Miller is quick to acknowledge the importance of those who work as part of the Mute team. Yet at the same time, it's rare for a record label of such note to have been so uniquely entwined with the creative vision of one individual – especially over such a long period. So where does this leave Mute Records in the future? 'That's a good question,' he acknowledges. 'I have no plans at all to retire. Someone might have plans for me, of course!'

05 Liars (Aaron Hemphill / Julian Gross / Angus Andrew) / Promo Photo / 2012
06 Beth Jeans Houghton / London / 2012
07 Josh T. Pearson / Promo Photo / 2010
08 New Order (Tom Chapman / Gillian Gilbert / Bernard Sumner / Stephen Morris /
      Phil Cunningham) / Promo Photo / 2015

They were the antithesis of Britpop, which was going through its final death throes by the late 1990s.

We were made for each other.

→ ADD N TO (X) / 2002
(STEVE CLAYDON / BARRY SEVEN / ANN SHENTON)

a new heart to
ANALOGUE

STUMM170

STUMM170 / *Avant Hard* / Front / Campaign Art / 1999 / Joe Dilworth has worked extensively for Mute since the late 1990s, combining a career as a professional photographer and drummer. 'I was a fan of Add N To (X) before I worked with them, I did a number of shoots in my studio in Camden Road. I would direct the shoots, but they always had a lot of props and ideas. There was a life-size robot in my garden for years after, left over from one of their shoots.' Joe Dilworth, photographer.

MUTE254

MUTE217

MUTE224

MUTE231

MUTE258

MUTE278

STUMM187

STUMM204

STUMM204

MUTE217 → MUTE278 / Singles Discography / 1998–2002 / 'Plug Me In' (2000); 'Little Black Rocks In The Sun' (1998); 'Metal Fingers In My Body' (1999); 'Revenge Of The Black Regent' (1999); 'The Poker Roll' (2001); 'Take Me To Your Leader' (2002).

STUMM187 / *Add Insult To Injury* / Front / 2000 / STUMM204 / *Loud Like Nature* / Front / Gatefold / 2002 / 'I think we always considered the artwork and the videos to be an extension or prosthetic of the band's activities sonically. There was a very strong sense of the synesthetic where sound translated visually and the palpable physical nature of audio catalysed a lot of vivid imagery. There were extended periods of combined input, conceptually, spontaneously and narratively, and that fertile collaboration brewed some curious concoctions. Collage – or more accurately, collision – played an important role. There were always a lot of visual stimuli to hand either in the analogue equipment that had a very particular brutalist aesthetic or the thousands of records and miscellaneous bric-à-brac that we accumulated while touring. There was always a pool of talented people to hand that enabled some of the ideas. The eclectic way we approached the cover design always reflected the way the band operated, so whether the artwork was drawn from found imagery, staged photographs, collage or elaborately designed packaging that was sometimes scented, there was a strong sense of purpose and dynamism. Sometimes the design was aided by practical and perfunctory coincidence. For instance, we had a rubber stamp made in New York which came with a standard generic sans serif type face, that became part of the band's design identity for a couple of years. A stray flash-photograph to find Ann's visor in the undergrowth after a gruelling drinking session while recording in the South of France became the album cover on one occasion. There was always a good dose of serendipity, pragmatism and humour to the design process that we were able to take full advantage of. We had all gone to art school, a fact we played down at the time. This gave a sort of insight into the transmutation of musical experience into visual intent.' Steven Claydon, Add N To (X).

5 016025 911882 >

ck COVER

Goldfrapp

FELT MOUNTAIN SPECIAL EDITION

Lcdstumm188

LOVELY HEAD
PAPER BAG
HUMAN
PILOTS
DEER STOP
FELT MOUNTAIN
OOMPA RADAR
UTOPIA
HORSE TEARS

BONUS DISC
PILOTS (ON A STAR)
U.K. GIRLS (PHYSICAL)
LOVELY HEAD MISS WORLD MIX
UTOPIA NEW EARS MIX
HUMAN CALEXICO VOCAL
HUMAN MASSEYS CRO-MAGNON MIX
UTOPIA TOM MIDDLETONS
          COSMOS VOCAL MIX
VISUAL CONTENT
A TRIP TO FELT MOUNTAIN
PC & MAC COMPATIBLE

Ⓟ 2001 Mute Records Limited © 2001 Mute Records Limited lcdstumm188 Distributed by Vital Made in Great Britain lc5834 www.mute.com
www.feltmountain.com

C	Cro.no	21352	format	special digi
	Title	Goldfrapp - Felt Mountain	version	1
	Customer	Mute Records	date	14.08.01
	Cat No.	LCDSTUMM188	colours	4
		CYAN MAGENTA YELLOW BLACK		

STUMM188 / *Felt Mountain* / Proof / 2000 / Goldfrapp were signed by Mute in 2000 after Daniel Miller was played a demo of the track 'Lovely Head'. The debut release, *Felt Mountain*, was also made available as an 'enhanced' CD, with a seven-minute video, *A Trip To Felt Mountain*, included. 'Alison has a very definite aesthetic that I tried to respond to, and we talked a lot about pictures before we did anything. I made the split-tone print for the cover of *Felt Mountain*, but it was Alison's idea to mirror-image it during the design process at the Mute office in Harrow Road. My sister found the picture of the Alps on the back from a friend who worked in an old picture library.' Joe Dilworth, photographer.

STUMM250

                        GOLDFRAPP

CDMUTE342 — CD	L12MUTE342 — 12"	LCDMUTE342 — CD	DVDMUTE342 — DVD
CDMUTE351 — CD	12MUTE351 — 12"	PCDMUTE351 — CD	DVDMUTE351 — DVD
CDMUTE356 — CD	12MUTE356 — 12"	L12MUTE356 — 12"	DVDMUTE356 — DVD
CDMUTE361 — CD	12MUTE361 — 12"	LCDMUTE361 — CD	XXLIMUTE361 — DIGITAL

STUMM250 / MUTE342 / MUTE351 / MUTE356 / MUTE361 /
Supernature Campaign / 2005–06 / 'Alison is very visually minded.
Our relationship has mutated, depending on the album. *Supernature*
required a very different visual landscape, as Alison was keen on the cover
being darker and more mysterious. An early inspiration was 1970s fashion
photographer Guy Bourdin. I seem to remember we had the phrase

"Electric Garden" quite early on as a way of contextualising the concept.
We commissioned set designer Rachel Thomas to make a series of pieces,
ranging from a glittery apple to a large-scale plug and collection of fantasy
instruments. Alison devised the idea of the peacock for the cover and
worked closely with the late Cathy Edwards to bring the costume to life.'
Mat Maitland, art direction and design, Big Active.

Goldfrapp

Seventh Tree Singles

MUTE389

MUTE392

MUTE401

SATIN BOYS, FLAMING CHIC

Goldfrapp

Goldfrapp
NUMBERED
LIMITED EDITION
PICTURE DISC

0013

MUTE368

MUTE389 / MUTE392 / MUTE401 / *Seventh Tree* Singles / Front / Picture Discs / 2008 / '*Seventh Tree* was sonically a very different record, more psychedelic and pastoral. This lead us to the work of Serge Leblon, a fashion photographer shooting on film in a style that fitted very well with the music. Alison often says it's her favourite shoot. It really was a magical few days and everything seemed to work; there were so many amazing images. This was also partly because Serge shot everything on film, so there were no digital tests or screens to look at while shooting,

which can sometimes become a hindrance.' Mat Maitland, art direction and design, Big Active.

MUTE368 / 'Satin Boys' / 'Flaming Chic' / Limited-Edition Picture Disc / 2006 / A 7", double-A-sided picture disc limited to 5,000 copies featuring a remix by The Flaming Lips of 'Satin Chic' from Goldfrapp's third album, *Supernature*. On the flip-side was an acoustic cover of The Ordinary Boys' 2005 hit 'Boys Will Be Boys'. Designed and art directed by Alison Goldfrapp.

STUMM188

STUMM196

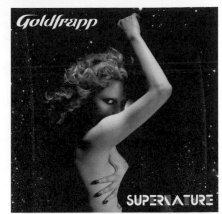

STUMM250

STUMM280

STUMM320

STUMM356

STUMM399

Alison Goldfrapp / Collage / 2017 / For the 2017 album *Silver Eye*, Alison Goldfrapp elected to take full control of the art direction herself, a decision that reflected the importance of photography in her creative life. The shoot took place on Fuerteventura, one of the Canary Islands, where the local black volcanic rock provided a dramatic backdrop. This collage was created by Alison herself, using one of the photographs she took for the campaign. Alison also directed the video for 'Systemagic', the second single from *Silver Eye*.

STUMM188 → STUMM399 / Albums Discography / 2000–17 / 'The *Head First* album was again an exhilarating change of direction for the band. The work of Japanese airbrush artist Harumi Yamaguchi was quite a key reference and a Jacksons album cover from 1984 also gave us the idea of a road disappearing into the sky, as seen on the single cover for "Rocket". The album cover image came out of the post-production process. Alison and I have often worked this way, using the shoot as raw material to create something unexpected.' Mat Maitland, art direction and design, Big Active.

STUMM251

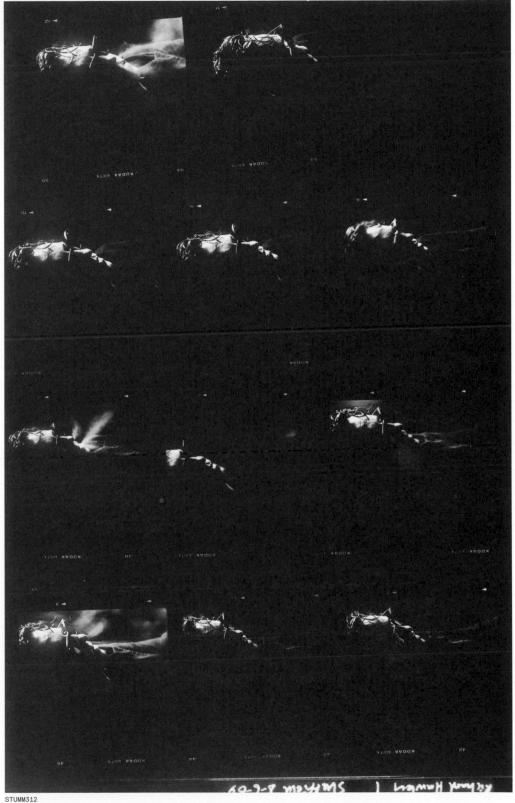

STUMM312

STUMM251 / *Coles Corner* / Front / Outtake / 2005 / For his breakthrough album, Richard Hawley and photographer Gareth James recreated the long demolished Coles Corner, a famed Sheffield romantic meeting place, at the Stephen Joseph Theatre, Scarborough.

STUMM312 / *Truelove's Gutter* / Cover Photography Contact Sheet / 2009 / 'Richard texted me a reference for the cover and we both knew that Steve Gullick was the man to capture such a photo. The album was named after another landmark from his beloved Sheffield.' Paul A. Taylor, Art Director, Mute.

GRINDERMAN
GET IT ON

PANTONE 504 C

17:27:18

06-12-06

101051_Grinderman_7Single

101051_Grinderman_7Single

Written by Grinderman
Produced by Grinderman and Nick Launay
℗2007 Mute Records Limited
©2007 Mute Records Limited
LC05684 SDBM laser. Printed in the EU
MUTE370. 5099468590721
www.grinderman.com

Limited edition

MUTE370

STUMM272

MUTE373

MUTE370 / 'Get It On' / Proof / STUMM272 / *Grinderman* / Front / MUTE373 / 'No Pussy Blues' / Front / 2007 / A Bad Seeds side project initially known as Mini Seeds, the band's name was inspired by Memphis Slim's 'Grinder Man Blues' (1940), which Nick Cave purportedly began to sing during the course of an early band rehearsal. 'Grinderman had a much more raw, impulsive feel to it – both musically and visually. I think that's why everything consequently felt more humorous and lighter somehow, because it wasn't carrying the full weight of The Bad Seeds on its shoulders. It definitely didn't take itself too seriously.... It was all about mixing metaphors; synthetic and primal, sinister and pantomime...' Tom Hingston, designer.

Grinderman

STUMM299

12MUTE441

12MUTE447

12MUTE449

12MUTE452

MUTE441

STUMM299 / MUTE441 / MUTE447 / MUTE449 / MUTE 452 / *Grinderman 2* Campaign / 2010–11 / Grinderman's second album yeilded four singles: 'Heathen Child', 'Worm Tamer', 'Palaces Of Montezuma' and 'Mickey Mouse And The Goodbye Man', with the last two covers illustrated by Ilinca Höpfner.

MUTE441 / 'Heathen Child' / Video Stills / Grinderman's 'Heathen Child' video was directed by Cave's long-time collaborator John Hillcoat. 'The video follows the fortunes of a worryingly young white girl as she sits in a bath, confronted by the panoply of fiends that occupy her subconscious.' Nick Cave.

STUMM321

STUMM346

LSTUMM346

STUMM387

2000 →→   YEASAYER

STUMM321 → STUMM387 / Albums Discography / 2010–16 / *Odd Blood* (2010); *Fragrant World* (2012); *Good Evening Washington D.C.* (2013); *Amen & Goodbye* (2016).

Yeasayer's breakthrough album *Odd Blood* was designed by virtual sculpturist Benjamin Phelan and set the tone for the successful campaign that was to follow its release.

Silly Me / Preparatory Drawings / Storyboard / Video Stills / Stop Motion Models / 2016 / The prequel to the *I Am Chemistry* video, *Silly Me* is almost entirely made of 3D models created by New Media Ltd, which were scanned, animated with motion capture and thrust into a world of singing and dancing forest animals, giants, and partying constellations. 'We use a pretty unique approach; nearly everything in every frame is handmade and hand-painted. We then 3D scan all of it, bringing it into the computer so it's entirely recreated digitally. We record motion-capture of performers and apply the data to the characters for the animation. The lighting is all done in the computer. So while the final product is ostensibly CGI, pretty much everything you're seeing is a digital record of something we directed or fabricated in real-life. Best of all worlds.' Mike Anderson, director.

STUMM364

STUMM389

STUMM364 / *To Be Kind* / Cover Package / 2014 / Swans was formed in 1982 by Michael Gira, and most of their albums are released on his own Young God label. Swans worked with Mute when they released *Children Of God* on subsidiary label Product Inc in 1987. *To Be Kind* was the first album to be released in their latest collaboration with Mute. The artwork featured artist Bob Biggs' portraits of babies, which Michael had first seen many years before. 'I look at Bob's baby images as something like the Mona Lisa – utterly inscrutable, but aching to reach up to the surface. Or like one of Jasper Johns' flag paintings – I just can't figure them out, but they keep calling me back.' Michael Gira, Swans.

STUMM389 / *The Glowing Man* / Cover Package / 2016 / Michael Gira designed the cover for Swans' fourteenth studio album himself: 'I'd thought about using different characters from different languages on each panel, like a Chinese character on the front, say, a Japanese character on the back...but once I'd gathered them I thought it looked really new agey and I was appalled!...So I drew some kind of elliptical characters myself.... We use raw cardboard to print on – that's a sort of theme we've been doing with Swans music...and I want to carry on that theme.' Michael Gira, Swans.

THE MUTE SYNTH

Right from the beginning, music tech has featured at the heart of many of the Mute label's most memorable releases. And in conversation, it's abundantly clear that Daniel Miller has endless enthusiasm not only for the classic vintage 1970s and 1980s analogue synthesisers and drum machines that were used on his own recordings, and those he produced by the likes of Depeche Mode, but also for 21st-century software and Eurorack modular systems. So it's no great surprise to find that the Mute name has been applied to a line of quirky, experimental synthesisers – indeed, perhaps it's more surprising that it took until 2011 for it to happen.

'Electronic music is a big part of our history,' Miller affirms, 'and we thought it would be fun and appropriate to have a Mute synth.'

The man who made this happen was John Richards, a musician and academic whose own Dirty Electronics had already produced an array of experimental circuits used for improvised electronic noise performances. 'After completing my PhD, I became involved with what I guess you might call the "new wave of DIY electronic music", which I think was a little bit of a reaction against the digital way of doing stuff. I designed some interesting etched circuit boards that were quite minimal, and were usually quite focused on visual appearance. I gradually began doing more and more DIY workshop events, and then in 2011, when Daniel was planning his Mute Short Circuit festival at the Roundhouse, we discussed doing something just for that event.'

For Miller, the idea of a visually powerful electronic noise-making device was irresistible. 'We wanted to make something that was fun and not too expensive. And that anyone could play around with and make some sounds. John Richards came in, and we put him together with Adrian Shaughnessy to do the visual design part of it.'

'Mute synths was a strange experience for me,' Shaughnessy recalls. 'I'm not really a product designer and due to technical and budgetary restraints there was limited possibility for radical modelling. So my function was mainly graphic...and to make the objects as interesting as possible. Working with John was rewarding. He is acutely aware of the need for good visual and ergonomic design. I tried to include the printed circuitry (normally hidden in electronic products) into the design.

'I took in some prototypes,' Richards continues, 'and between us we gradually refined it. But I thought – I *knew*, actually – that people would want one of these beyond the Short Circuit festival. They're desirable objects; they feel like they're valuable in some way!'

The synth was a simple battery-operated handheld device that used the conductivity of the operator's skin to make connections between the copper rails on the circuit board, and so create and alter sounds. Visually, the outline of the circuit board, and the copper conductors on the PCB, were cleverly designed to mimic the Mute 'walking man' logo.

'It was very primitive in some ways,' admits Richards, 'and some people complained that you couldn't play it properly! It was quite indeterminate and unorthodox, but it was actually a lovely thing to use.'

Always intended as a limited edition, the Mute Synth was presented as a PCB with components for self-assembly at Richards' workshops, or was sold fully constructed by Mute. Around a thousand circuit boards were produced.

A second collaboration took place between Mute and Dirty Electronics two years later. 'We had fun with the first one,' recalls Miller. 'With the Mute Synth II, we decided to make something a little more sophisticated.'

'For me, that was a good opportunity to try to put across a different way of engaging and making music with these sorts of objects,' Richards recalls, 'but it took quite a long time to be realised. I'd meet Daniel and Paul A. Taylor at Mute, I would bring a prototype along with me, and we'd have it out on the table, and then Adrian would come along and we'd discuss shapes and designs and artworks. There were a lot of meetings!'

The second Mute synth was more obviously 'usable' than the first, with the inclusion of a patchbay and a number of tangible rotary controls. 'I wanted to create a synth that was generative in nature,' Richards explains, 'that starkly challenged the relationship between man/woman and machine, and also retained the indeterminate noise characteristics of previous designs.'

A cult, collectable object that nonetheless sold for considerably less than £100, the three limited-edition runs sold out almost immediately.

This is an area that clearly interests Miller, who continues to keep an eye on interesting new people and developments in this area, with more conventionally playable modules a possibility for the future. 'I'd really love to do more of these projects,' he concludes.

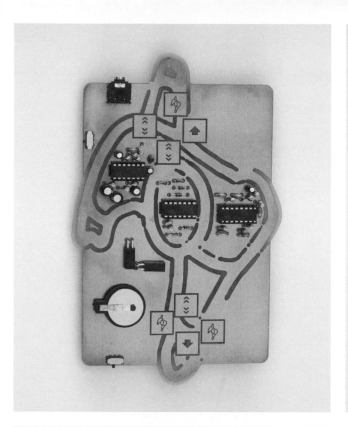

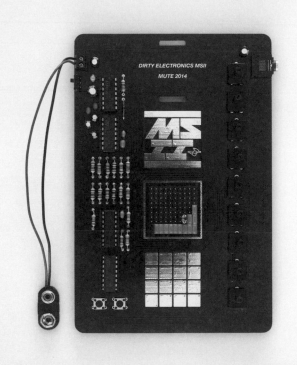

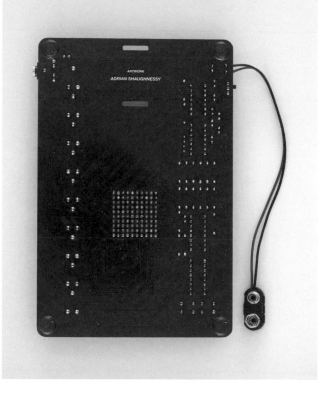

Dirty Electronics / Mute Synths / 2011–14 / The original Mute Synth (top) was produced for the 2011 Short Circuit festival; the more sophisticated Mute Synth II (bottom) appeared three years later.

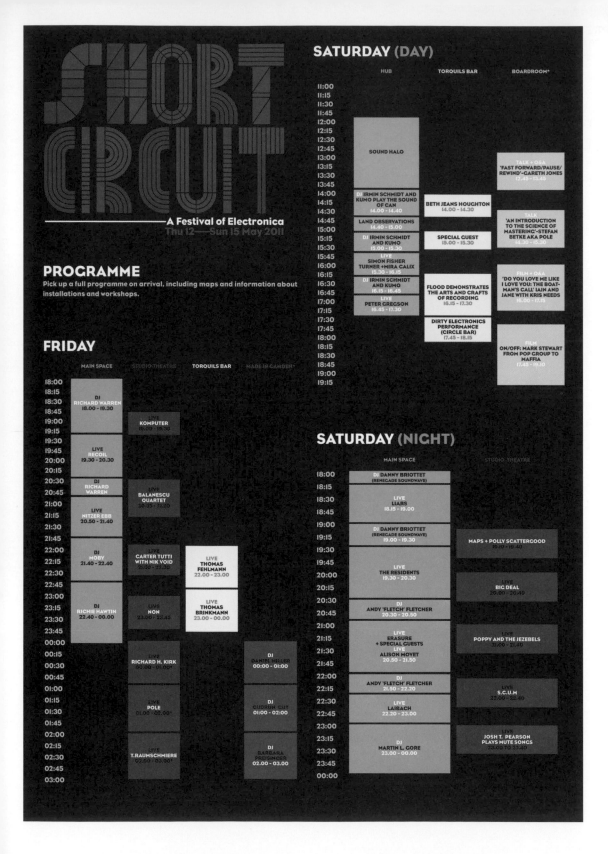

SHORT CIRCUIT

A Festival of Electronica
Thu 12 — Sun 15 May 2011

PROGRAMME

Pick up a full programme on arrival, including maps and information about installations and workshops.

SATURDAY (DAY)

	HUB	TORQUILS BAR	BOARDROOM*
11:00			
11:15			
11:30			
11:45			
12:00			
12:15			
12:30	SOUND HALO		
12:45			TALK + Q&A
13:00			'FAST FORWARD/PAUSE/
13:15			REWIND'—GARETH JONES
13:30			12.45 – 13.45
13:45			
14:00	DJ IRMIN SCHMIDT AND KUMO PLAY THE SOUND OF CAN 14.00 – 14.40	BETH JEANS HOUGHTON 14.00 – 14.30	
14:15			
14:30			TALK
14:45	LAND OBSERVATIONS 14.40 – 15.00		'AN INTRODUCTION TO THE SCIENCE OF
15:00	DJ IRMIN SCHMIDT AND KUMO 15.00 – 15.30	SPECIAL GUEST 15.00 – 15.30	MASTERING'—STEFAN BETKE AKA POLE 14.30 – 15.30
15:15			
15:30	LIVE SIMON FISHER TURNER +MIRA CALIX 15.30 – 16.15		
15:45			
16:00		FLOOD DEMONSTRATES THE ARTS AND CRAFTS OF RECORDING 16.15 – 17.30	FILM + Q&A 'DO YOU LOVE ME LIKE I LOVE YOU: THE BOATMAN'S CALL' IAIN AND JANE WITH KRIS NEEDS 16.00 – 17.15
16:15	DJ IRMIN SCHMIDT AND KUMO 16.15 – 16.45		
16:30			
16:45	LIVE PETER GREGSON 16.45 – 17.30		
17:00			
17:15			
17:30		DIRTY ELECTRONICS PERFORMANCE (CIRCLE BAR) 17.45 – 18.15	
17:45			FILM ON/OFF: MARK STEWART FROM POP GROUP TO MAFFIA 17.45 – 19.10
18:00			
18:15			
18:30			
18:45			
19:00			
19:15			

FRIDAY

	MAIN SPACE	STUDIO THEATRE	TORQUILS BAR	MADE IN CAMDEN*
18:00	DJ RICHARD WARREN 18.00 – 19.30			
18:15				
18:30		LIVE KOMPUTER 18.30 – 19.30		
18:45				
19:00				
19:15				
19:30	LIVE RECOIL 19.30 – 20.30			
19:45				
20:00				
20:15				
20:30	DJ RICHARD WARREN	LIVE BALANESCU QUARTET 20.35 – 21.20		
20:45				
21:00				
21:15	LIVE NITZER EBB 20.50 – 21.40			
21:30				
21:45				
22:00	DJ MOBY 21.40 – 22.40	LIVE CARTER TUTTI WITH NIK VOID 22.00 – 22.50	LIVE THOMAS FEHLMANN 22.00 – 23.00	
22:15				
22:30				
22:45				
23:00	DJ RICHIE HAWTIN 22.40 – 00.00	LIVE NON 23.00 – 23.45	LIVE THOMAS BRINKMANN 23.00 – 00.00	
23:15				
23:30				
23:45				
00:00				
00:15		LIVE RICHARD H. KIRK 00.00 – 01.00*	DJ DANIEL MILLER 00:00 – 01:00	
00:30				
00:45				
01:00				
01:15		LIVE POLE 01.00 – 02.00*	DJ GUDRUN GUT 01:00 – 02:00	
01:30				
01:45				
02:00				
02:15		LIVE T.RAUMSCHMIERE 02.00 – 03.00*	DJ BARBARA PREISINGER 02.00 – 03.00	
02:30				
02:45				
03:00				

SATURDAY (NIGHT)

	MAIN SPACE	STUDIO THEATRE
18:00	DJ DANNY BRIOTTET (RENEGADE SOUNDWAVE)	
18:15	LIVE LIARS 18.15 – 19.00	
18:30		
18:45		
19:00	DJ DANNY BRIOTTET (RENEGADE SOUNDWAVE) 19.00 – 19.30	
19:15		MAPS + POLLY SCATTERGOOD 19.10 – 19.40
19:30	LIVE THE RESIDENTS 19.30 – 20.30	
19:45		
20:00		LIVE BIG DEAL 20.00 – 20.40
20:15		
20:30	DJ ANDY 'FLETCH' FLETCHER 20.30 – 20.50	
20:45		
21:00	LIVE ERASURE + SPECIAL GUESTS	LIVE POPPY AND THE JEZEBELS 21.00 – 21.40
21:15		
21:30	LIVE ALISON MOYET 20.50 – 21.50	
21:45		
22:00	DJ ANDY 'FLETCH' FLETCHER 21.50 – 22.20	
22:15		LIVE S.C.U.M 22.00 – 22.40
22:30	LIVE LAIBACH 22.20 – 23.00	
22:45		
23:00		LIVE JOSH T. PEARSON PLAYS MUTE SONGS 23.00 – 23.40
23:15	DJ MARTIN L. GORE 23.00 – 00.00	
23:30		
23:45		
00:00		

DISOBEY, IRREGULAR, SHORT CIRCUIT AND THE FESTIVAL OF MUTE

Since the early 1990s, the Mute label has been responsible for organising or curating a broad selection of live events, predominantly in the UK, but also running as far afield as Mexico.

It began with a series of programmes at the Scala cinema in London's King's Cross in 1991. These including showings of little-known or obscure films that related to Mute's Grey Area reissue label, along with art installations in the foyer.

Disobey was a series of Blast First-curated club nights launched in 1995 that took place at assorted London and Manchester venues, including the legendary Haçienda club and The Garage. These featured performances from a diverse group of artists, including Aphex Twin, George Melly, Jimmy Cauty, Keijo Heino and Merzbow – and also included artwork made for the events by the Chapman Brothers.

The year 1998 saw the introduction of Mute's Irregular gigs, staged in small venues around London. 'These were irregular both in time and content – hence the name. We did four or five.' Among those involved were Holger Hiller, Cabaret Voltaire's Richard H. Kirk, Pole, Echoboy and Appliance as well as Suicide's Alan Vega.

Mute's most ambitious festival moment came in 2011 when they were invited to curate the annual Short Circuit Electronic Music Festival in north London's famous Roundhouse. The festival (Short Circuit Presents Mute) took place on 13–14 May and included performances by most of Mute's established names as well as related events such as talks and films.

'It was a lot of work, but it was an incredible experience. There were people there who had travelled from all over the world, and it was at the Roundhouse in Chalk Farm, London, which made it even more special. Pretty much every Mute artist did something; they either performed in their own right or in collaboration or they did DJ sets.'

On the Friday, Alan Wilder's Recoil were followed by Nitzer Ebb, Richard H. Kirk, Chris Carter and Cosey Fanni Tutti (both of Throbbing Gristle) – as Carter Tutti – playing with Factory Floor's Nik Void, Boyd Rice and The Balanescu Quartet playing their baroque string versions of Kraftwerk. Saturday saw performances by Erasure, The Residents, Laibach, Liars and then Alison Moyet teaming up with Vince Clarke for one last time to perform some of Yazoo's hits – and there was also the first and only live appearance by The Assembly when Feargal Sharkey joined Vince to sing their sole release 'Never Never'.

Elsewhere, Can's veteran keyboard player Irmin Schmidt, techno star Richie Hawtin (Plastikman), Depeche Mode's Martin Gore and Daniel Miller himself all performed DJ sets.

'There were talks and we showed films, producers Flood and Gareth Jones talked about their Mute productions; and Anton [Corbijn] presented his visual contributions.' There was even a music technology workshop in which the hand-held Mute Synth was introduced. Attendees had the chance to personally solder the synthesiser together.

'Short Circuit was such a big thing for us,' says Miller. 'And thinking about it now, I can't quite imagine how we got it together. But we did. The artists and the fans were amazing and really embraced the event. It was a very special moment.'

The mood of the event was well captured by *The Quietus* magazine when it remarked: 'There's a sense that the one person most sorely missed from the line-up is the late Frank Tovey [Fad Gadget]. For it was his evolution from tar and feathered electronic art punk to guitar toting folk singer that perhaps best sums up Mute's long journey.'

March 2015 saw the label operating further afield with Daniel Miller curating Festival Mute Mexico. Held in Tlaquepaque, a small, picturesque city 300 miles west of Mexico City, it formed part of a cultural exchange between the two countries. Staged on 21 March, the programme featured live performances by Liars, Ben Frost, Land Observations and non-Mute guests Orchestral Manoeuvres in the Dark (OMD). There were also DJ sets from Vince Clarke, Irmin Schmidt and Apparat. 'Sadly, a last-minute health reason meant that I couldn't play at the event,' Miller recalls, 'but it was a great success and we hope to do something similar again in the future.'

Short Circuit: A Festival Of Electronica / Programme / 2011 / Performance listings for the three-day Short Circuit festival at London's Roundhouse. 'For me it was a really moving experience.'

A truly innovative
electronic music
artist. From the start
we felt compelled to
work with him. I'm
extremely proud of
the two albums he
recorded for us.

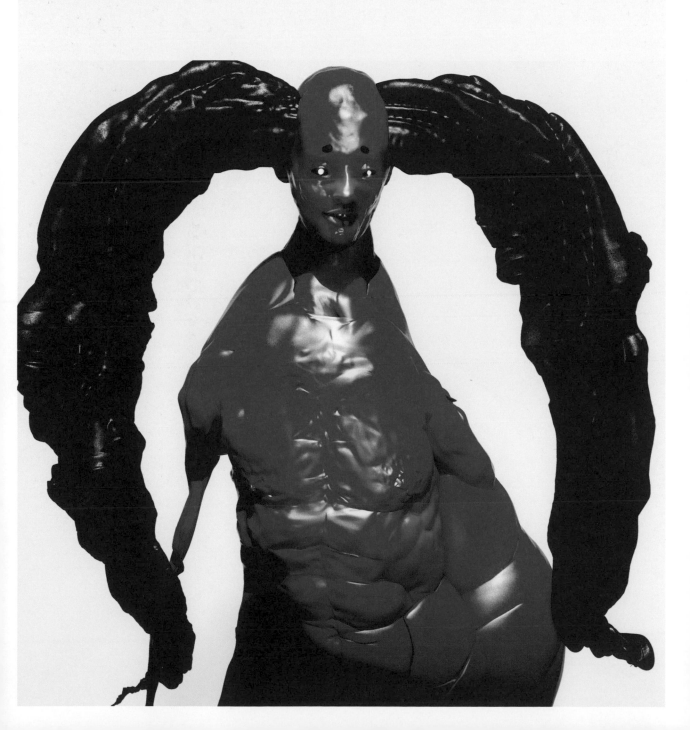

STUMM374

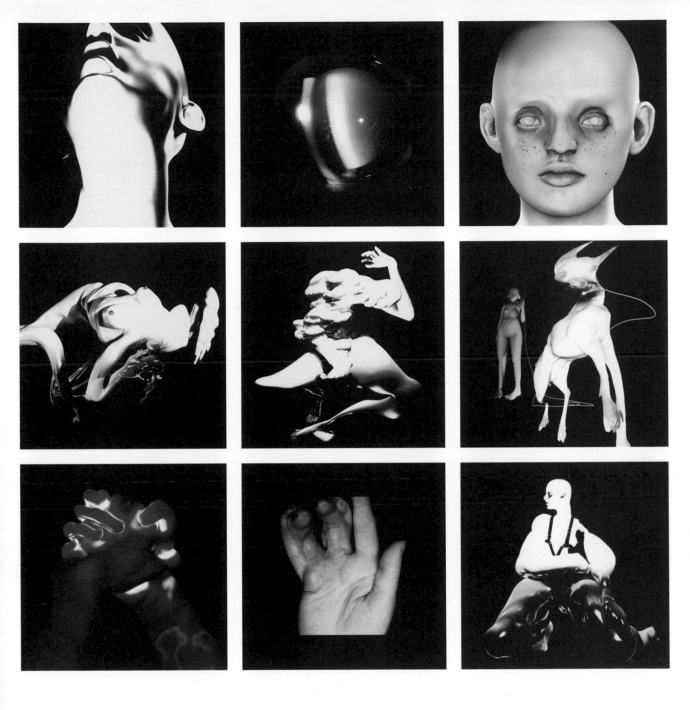

STUMM374 / *Xen* / Front / Artwork / 2014 / Arca is the pseudonym of London-based Venezuelan producer and DJ Alejandro Ghersi, who since 2012 has contributed to releases by the likes of Kanye West, Björk and FKA Twigs. His debut album, *Xen*, was released by Mute in 2014, and features the arresting visuals of Japanese-born/Canadian-raised artist Jesse Kanda. Unusually, Ghersie and Kanda became close friends online as fifteen- and thirteen-year-olds living on different continents, and didn't meet in person for another seven years. They later became housemates in Dalston, east London, collaborating on album and film projects. The title of the album is a reference to Ghersi's 'feminine spirit', portrayed in the album artwork and videos. 'Arca and I have been best friends for over ten years, so we've talked and worked together every day. Our personal work is completely in unison.' Jesse Kanda, artist.

STUMM441

MUTE475

MUTE476

MUTE484

STUMM441 / MUTE475 / MUTE476 / MUTE484 / *Ssss* Campaign / 2011–12
The illustrations for Vince Clarke and Martyn Gore's techno collaboration
were by artist Jan L. Trigg: 'Using up the leftover paint after a session,
I relaxed and let the brushes roll over the paper; gradually these long colourful
slithering snakes appeared. Martyn said they made him think of Matisse.'

STUMM334 / MUTE457 / MUTE460 / MUTE463 / *The Devil's Walk*
Campaign / 2011–12 / Since 2001, Berlin electronic musician Sascha
Ring has operated under the name Apparat. His 2011 album *The Devil's
Walk* and its three associated singles feature illustrations by artist
Hanna Zeckau and were designed by Carsten Aermes.

STUMM326

CDSTUMM398

STUMM326 / *Last Of The Country Gentlemen* / Front / 2011 / A debut regarded by many as one of the key albums of the past decade. '[On the cover] I wanted to be clutching a beautiful girl...just a platonic form of a woman, and me at her mercy – at the mercy of love, basically.' Josh T. Pearson.

STUMM398 / *The Texas-Jerusalem Crossroads* / Digipak / Reissue / 2017 / This double concept album was the only full-length release by Josh T. Pearson's former band Lift To Experience. The design is a homage to the style of Texas-based Pen & Pixel, masters of 'bling-bling' hip-hop cover design.

                                           S.C.U.M

S.C.U.M
AGAIN INTO EYES

MUTE453

STUMM327

S.C.U.M / Promo Photo / MUTE453 / 'Amber Hands' / Artwork / STUMM327 / *Again Into Eyes* / Front / 2011 / S.C.U.M formed in south-east London in 2008, their name a reference to Valerie Solanas' radical feminist *S.C.U.M Manifesto*, written in 1967 – the year before her attempted murder of Andy Warhol. Matthew Stone was responsible for the photography and subsequent collages used on the band's album

Again Into Eyes and single 'Amber Hands' (right). 'I think about the role of the artist in relation to that of the shaman, within a Beuysian tradition. I remember lying in bed when I was a kid playing with balls of invisible energy in my hands and then bouncing them off the walls. What I am doing now feels the same as that, so…I guess it has always been there.' Matthew Stone, photographer.

STUMM337

YANN TIERSEN SKYLINE

MUTE467

YANN TIERSEN MONUMENTS

MUTE468

YANN TIERSEN I'D GONNA LIVE ANYHOW

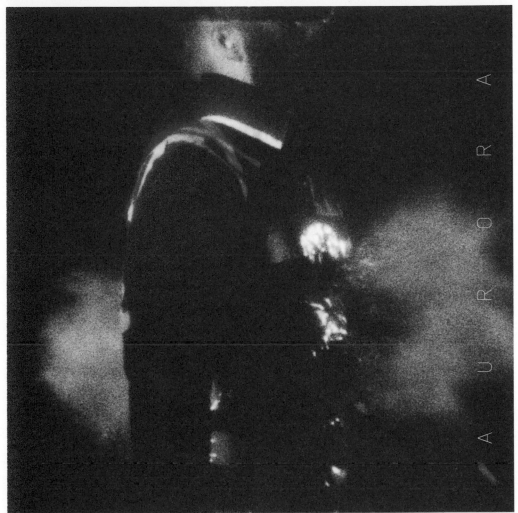

STUMM368

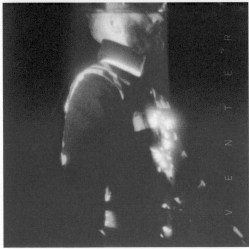

IMUTE514

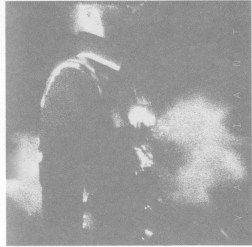

12MUTE525

STUMM337 / MUTE467 / MUTE468 / *Skyline* Campaign / 2011 / Multi-instrumentalist Yann Tiersen worked with a long-term collaborator, the photographer and artist Frank Loriou, on the album campaign for *Skyline*. The simple graphic style – four black bars, always in the same position, superimposed on various images of a skyline also always in the same position – was a simple, effective way to evoke the album's title and meaning.

STUMM368 / MUTE514 / MUTE525 / *A U R O R A* Campaign / 2014 / Ben Frost recorded the powerful *A U R O R A* in 2014. The cover artwork was designed by Rebeca Mendez; the photograph was a collaboration by photographer Richard Mosse and cinematographer Trevor Tweeten. 'Finding Richard Mosse and making that connection had a profound influence on me – seeing possibilities in the kind of hyperrealism of the natural world he found through his art.' Ben Frost.

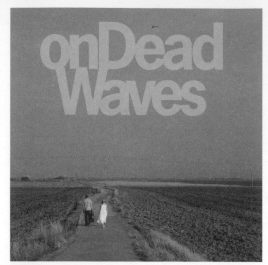

STUMM383

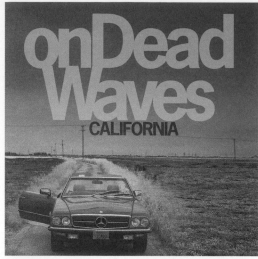

MUTE552

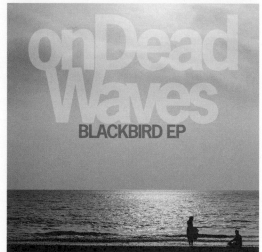

MUTE555

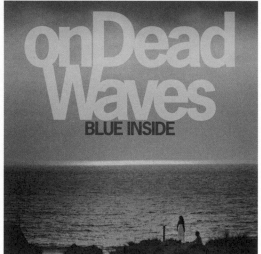

MUTE550

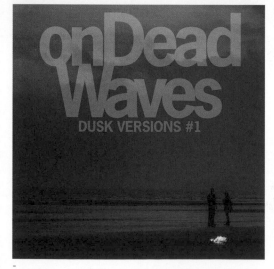

-

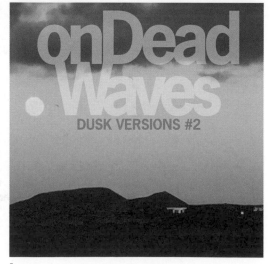

-

LAND OBSERVATIONS

ROMAN ROADS IV–XI

LSTUMM345

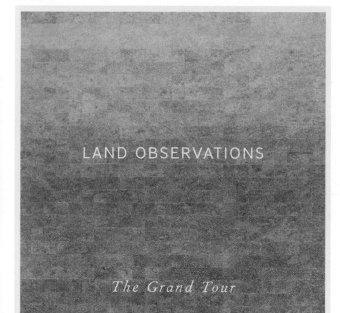

LAND OBSERVATIONS

The Grand Tour

STUMM369

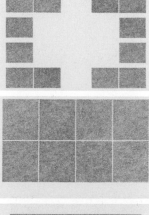

STUMM383 / *On Dead Waves* / MUTE552 / 'California' / MUTE555 / 'Blackbird EP' / MUTE550 / 'Blue Inside' / 'Dusk Versions #1' / 'Dusk Versions #2' / Fronts / 2015–16 / 'The *On Dead Waves* artwork was all about trying to capture a feeling of expansive spaces, with a kind of peaceful emptiness. The sound of the album is quite warm and it was being released in the summer, so we wanted the feel of the images to reflect that. Achieving this in England in January was an interesting task. We worked with a small but amazing team, consisting of the incredible photographer Cat Mook, Mute's art director Paul A. Taylor and Jay Pinxie. We shot the album cover in a road we happened to pass on the way to the beach. The light was hitting the road in a really magical way. It seemed like the perfect image for the album cover.' Polly Scattergood and James Chapman, onDeadWaves.

STUMM345 / *Roman Roads IV–XI* / Front / Artwork / 2012 / STUMM369 / *The Grand Tour* / Front / Artwork / 2014 / Land Observations is a solo project by fine artist James Brooks, who had already recorded four albums for Mute as guitarist and vocalist for the trio Appliance. The releases feature James's original pencil artworks, drawn specifically to accompany the recordings.

Travel recordings: roads, postcards, maps and landscapes	*Drawing as repetition* *Music as repetition*	*Drawing as tone* *Music as tone*
	Drawing as rhythm *Music as rhythm*	*Drawing as movement* *Music as movement*

James Brooks.

STUMM225

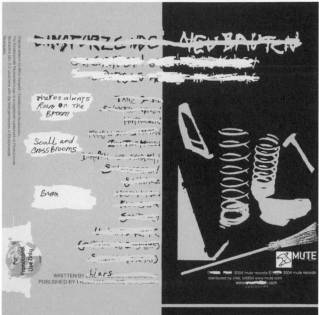

10MUTE317

STUMM225 / *They Were Wrong, So We Drowned* / Front / 2004 /
'During the *Drowned...* and *Drum's Not Dead* era, we worked closely with
Bea Schingelhoff. We'd met at CalArts, where she was doing her Masters
and we were just lowly undergraduates. *Drowned...* was a heavy album
steeped in the folklore of witchery, so we asked Bea to create a tapestry.
It's my favourite album cover of ours.' Angus Andrew, Liars.

MUTE317 / 'There's Always Room On The Broom' / Cover / Record / 2004 /
'Imagine it. You're a young band. You come up with the obnoxious idea of
defacing the logo of one of the most serious industrial art groups in history
– Neubauten. Only one thing stands in your way – you must cold call the
notoriously resolute Blixa Bargeld and ask him point blank over the phone
if he minds. And he doesn't!' Angus Andrew, Liars.

STUMM246

STUMM287

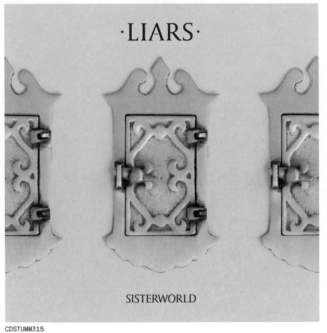

CDSTUMM315

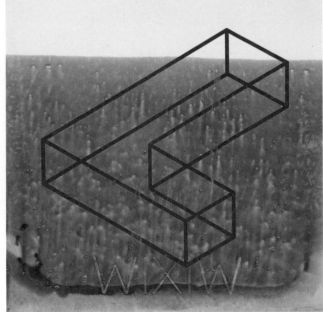

STUMM343

STUMM349

12MUTE517

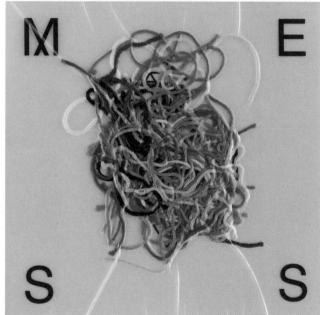

LSTUMM349

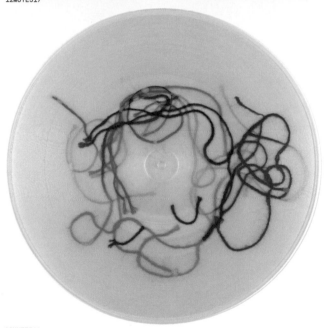

12MUTE511

STUMM246 → STUMM343 / Albums Discography / 2005–14 /
Drum's Not Dead (2006); *Liars* (2007); *Sisterworld* (2010); *WIXIW* (2012).

'Whether by concept or tools, the works are reactions to their forebears,
each album pushing away and against its predecessor. Likewise, the artwork
follows; where once the goal was ornate and personal, next the project calls
for cold and austere.' Angus Andrews, Liars.

STUMM349 / MUTE517 / MUTE511 / *Mess Campaign* / 2014 / 'It's nice to
develop a symbol for an album. Something more than just a logo or a typeface
– something tangible. For *Mess*, we happened upon a ball of multicoloured
string. We unravelled it and saw chaos. Beautiful and positive disorder.
We placed it everywhere, really lived in the stuff, making videos and
costumes until it was no longer just a symbol of *Mess*. It was emblematic.'
Angus Andrews, Liars.

 LIARS

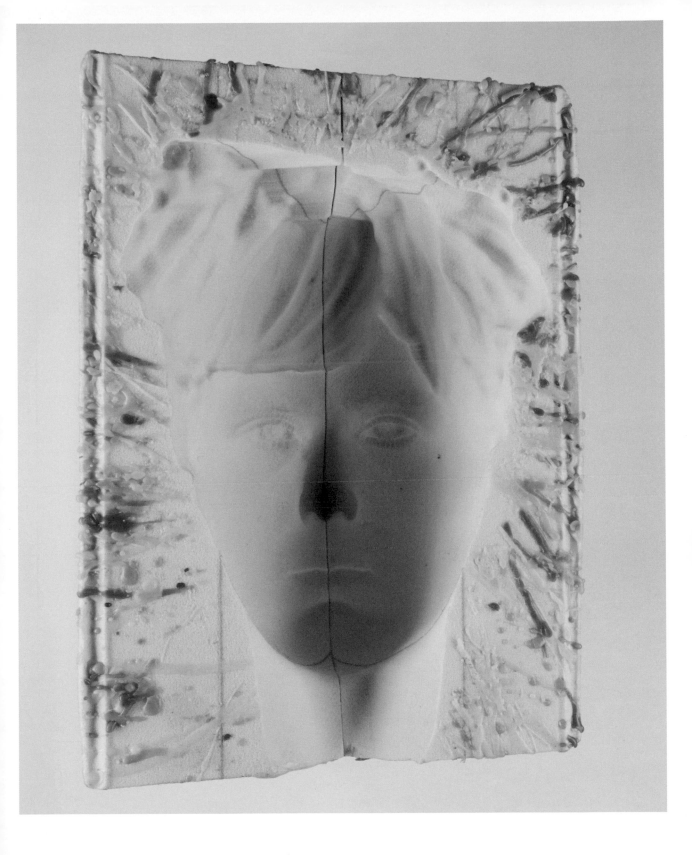

MUTE517 / 'Pro Anti Anti' / Wax Masks / 2014 / Yoonha Park's video for Liars' single 'Pro Anti Anti' demonstrates the process for creating head sculptures for band members Angus Andrew (left) and Aaron Hemphill (right). Brooklyn-based 3D-technology company Direct Dimensions, who had previously produced body scans for Marvel Comics films, provided the technical expertise.

12MUTE541　　　　　　　　　　　　　　12"

CDMUTE541　　　　　　　　　　　　　CD

IMUTE541　　　　　　　　　　　DIGITAL

12MUTE542　　　　　　　　　　　　　　12"

CDMUTE542　　　　　　　　　　　　　CD

IMUTE542　　　　　　　　　　　DIGITAL

12MUTE545　　　　　　　　　　　　　　12"

CDMUTE545　　　　　　　　　　　　　CD

IMUTE545　　　　　　　　　　　DIGITAL

12MUTE553　　　　　　　　　　　　　　12"

CDMUTE553　　　　　　　　　　　　　CD

IMUTE553　　　　　　　　　　　DIGITAL

BXSTUMM390

MUTE541 / MUTE542 / MUTE545 / MUTE553 / STUMM390 /
Music Complete Campaign / 2015–16 / The artwork for New Order's
recording debut for Mute, *Music Complete* – along with its associated
singles – was designed by their long-term collaborator Peter Saville.
The striking design mirrors the stark, characteristic style of his earlier

work with New Order on Tony Wilson's Factory label. Saville's relationship
with the band was not usually a collaborative one: 'More often than not,
New Order would get to see the covers when they were in the stores
– sometimes they liked them and sometimes they didn't,' Saville recalled
in 2013.

STUMM340

2000 →→   CARTER TUTTI VOID / THE CLARKE + WARE EXPERIMENT

CDSTUMM351

STUMM340 / *Transverse* / Front / 2012 / Chris Carter took inspiration from Bridget Riley's 1960s op art when designing the hypnotic packaging for the *Transverse* album, which was a collaboration between him, his partner Cosey Fanni Tutti and Factory Floor's Nik Void.

STUMM351 / *House Of Illustrious* / Box-Set Packaging / 2012 / In the words of Martyn Ware, the brief for this ambitious Clarke And Ware Experiment ten-CD package was to create 'a single desirable object'. It was the work of renowned graphic designer Malcolm Garrett and Artomatic's Tim Milne.

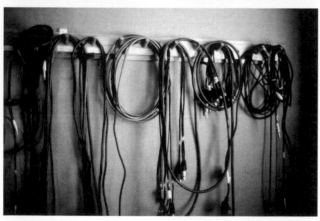

Mute HQ / 429 Harrow Road / London / 1986–2007 / Photographs of the original Mute Records offices and studio, which were located at 429 Harrow Road in north-west London, between 1986 and 2007. All the photography is by Daniel Miller.

Mute Records Demolition Party / 2007 / In April 2007, Mute bade farewell to their headquarters at 429 Harrow Road with live music, DJs...and a pneumatic drill. Each guest leaving the party was handed a small plastic bag containing an authenticated piece of building debris.

Mute059 'Stranger Than Love', Mark Stewart (1987)
Mute060 'Geburt Einer Nation', Laibach (1987)
Mute061 'Victim Of Love', Erasure (1987)
Mute062 'Life Is Life', Laibach (1987)
Mute063 'Marry Me (Lie! Lie!)', These Immortal Souls (1987)
Mute064 'Join In The Chant', Nitzer Ebb (1987)
Mute065 'Dirty Sings', Anita Lane (1988)
Mute066 'The Circus', Erasure (1987)
Mute067 'Kidney Bingos', Wire (1988)
Mute068 'Immobilise', Mkultra (1987)
Mute069 'Lose Him', I Start Counting (1988)
Mute070 'Time Was', A. C. Marias (1988)
Mute071 'Control I'm Here', Nitzer Ebb (1988)
Mute072 'The Three', Ohi Ho Bang Bang (1989)
Mute073 'Could You?', He Said (1988)
Mute074 'Ship Of Fools', Erasure (1988)
Mute075 'Double-Barrel Prayer', Diamanda Galás (1988)
Mute076 'On Every Train', Crime And The City Solution (1988)
Mute077 'The Man With The Golden Arm', Barry Adamson (1988)
Mute078 'Hearts & Minds', Nitzer Ebb (1989)
Mute079 'Bridge Street Shuffle', Frank Tovey (1988)
Mute080 'Sympathy For The Devil', Laibach (1988)
Mute081 'Ra! Ra! Rawhide', I Start Counting (1988)
Mute082 'Biting My Nails', Renegade Soundwave (1988)
Mute083 'Chains Of Love', Erasure (1988)
Mute084 'Silk Skin Paws', Wire (1988)
Mute085 'A Little Respect', Erasure (1988)
Mute086 'Deanna', Nick Cave And The Bad Seeds (1988)
Mute087 'Eardrum Buzz', Wire (1989)
Mute088 'The Phantom', Renegade Soundwave (1988)
Mute089 'Drama!', Erasure (1989)
Mute090 'King Of California', These Immortal Souls (1992)
Mute091 'Across The Universe', Laibach (1988)
Mute092 'Hysteria', Mark Stewart (1990)
Mute093 'Crackers International EP', Erasure (1988)
Mute094 'The Shadow Of No Man', Crime And The City Solution (1989)
Mute095 'Million Headed Monster', I Start Counting (1989)
Mute096 'Shame', Nitzer Ebb (1989)
Mute097 'The Taming Of The Shrewd', Barry Adamson (1989)
Mute098 'In Vivo', Wire (1989)
Mute099 'You Surround Me', Erasure (1989)
Mute100 'Sam Hall', Frank Tovey (1989)
Mute101 'Machineries Of Joy', Die Krupps (1989)
Mute102 'Probably A Robbery', Renegade Soundwave (1990)
Mute103 'Los Niños Del Parque', Liaisons Dangereuses (1990)
Mute104 'Space Gladiator'/'Phantom', Renegade Soundwave (1989)
Mute105 'One Of Our Girls (Has Gone Missing)', A. C. Marias (1990)
Mute106 'Lightning Man', Nitzer Ebb (1990)
Mute107 'So & Slow It Grows', Wir (1991)
Mute108 'The Ship Song', Nick Cave And The Bad Seeds (1990)
Mute109 'Blue Savannah', Erasure (1990)
Mute110 'Faith Healer', Recoil (1992)
Mute111 'Star', Erasure (1990)
Mute112 'Biting My Nails', Renegade Soundwave (1990)
Mute113 'Crazy Earth', Fortran 5 (1990)
Mute114 'I Have The Gun', Crime And The City Solution (1990)
Mute115 'Fun To Be Had'/'Getting Closer', Nitzer Ebb (1990)
Mute116 'Wirtschaft Ist Tot', Laibach (1992)
Mute117 'Final Countdown', Laibach (1994)
Mute118 'The Weeping Song', Nick Cave And The Bad Seeds (1990)
Mute119 'These Boots Were Made For Walking', Barry Adamson And Anita Lane (1991)
Mute120 'Love Baby', Fortran 5 (1990)
Mute121 'The Liberty Tree', Frank Tovey (1991)
Mute122 'As Is EP', Nitzer Ebb (1991)
Mute123 'Gush Forth My Tears', Miranda Sex Garden (1991)
Mute124 'Thunder II', Renegade Soundwave (1990)
Mute125 'Chorus', Erasure (1991)
Mute126 'Groove', Fortran 5 (1991)
Mute127 'The Dolphins & The Sharks', Crime And The City Solution (1991)
Mute128 'Honky's Ladder EP', The Afghan Whigs (1996)
Mute129 'Heart On The Line', Fortran 5 (1991)
Mute130 'Dream Kitchen', Mark Stewart (1996)
Mute131 'Love To Hate You', Erasure (1991)
Mute132 'Ab Ovo', Bruce Gilbert (1996)
Mute133 'I Give To You', Nitzer Ebb (1991)
Mute134 'Am I Right?', Erasure (1991)
Mute135 'Godhead', Nitzer Ebb (1991)
Mute136 'Look To The Future', Fortran 5 (1992)
Mute137 'Kray Twins', Renegade Soundwave (1992)
Mute138 'Cocaine Sex', Renegade Soundwave (1992)
Mute139 'Play', Miranda Sex Garden (1993)
Mute140 'Straight To You'/'Jack The Ripper', Nick Cave And The Bad Seeds (1992)
Mute141 'There Can Only Be One', Simon Bonney (1992)
Mute142 'Breath Of Life', Erasure (1992)
Mute143 'Time To Dream', Fortran 5 (1993)
Mute144 'Abba-esque EP', Erasure (1992)
Mute145 'Ascend', Nitzer Ebb (1992)
Mute146 'Renegade Soundwave', Renegade Soundwave (1994)
Mute147 'Women Respond To Bass', Renegade Soundwave (1992)
Mute148 'I Had A Dream, Joe', Nick Cave And The Bad Seeds (1992)
Mute149 'Cinema Is King', Barry Adamson (1992)
Mute150 'Who Needs Love Like That (Hamburg Mix)', Erasure (1992)
Mute151 'What A Wonderful World', Nick Cave And The Bad Seeds with Shane MacGowan (1992)
Mute152 'Always', Erasure (1994)
Mute153 'Run To The Sun', Erasure (1994)
Mute154 'Sunshine', Miranda Sex Garden (1993)
Mute155 'Kick It', Nitzer Ebb (1995)
Mute156 'Push For The Love Of Life', Parallax (1993)
Mute157 'Persian Blues', Fortran 5 (1993)
Mute158 'Move', Moby (1993)
Mute159 'Bullet Proof Zero', Parallax (1993)
Mute160 'Do You Love Me?', Nick Cave And The Bad Seeds (1994)
Mute161 'Hymn', Moby (1994)
Mute162 'Big Red Balloon', Spell (1993)
Mute163 'Peepshow', Miranda Sex Garden (1994)
Mute164 'I Thought', Nitzer Ebb (1995)
Mute165 'Brixton', Renegade Soundwave (1995)
Mute166 'I Love Saturday', Erasure (1994)
Mute167 'Don't Walk Away From Love', Simon Bonney (1996)
Mute168 'Dun' Like A Kipper', Hoodwink (1997)
Mute169 'Loverman', Nick Cave And The Bad Seeds (1994)
Mute170 'In The Army Now'/'War', Laibach (1995)
Mute171 'Do You Take This Man?', Diamanda Galás with John Paul Jones (1994)
Mute172 'Red Right Hand', Nick Cave And The Bad Seeds (1994)
Mute173 'Feeling So Real', Moby (1995)
Mute174 'Stay With Me', Erasure (1995)
Mute175 'Komputer EP', Komputer (1996)
Mute176 'Everytime You Touch Me', Moby (1995)
Mute177 'The World's A Girl', Anita Lane (1995)
Mute178 'Fingers & Thumbs (Cold Summer's Day)', Erasure (1995)
Mute179 'Into The Blue', Moby (1995)
Mute180 'Rock Me Gently', Erasure (1996)
Mute181 'Go Further', Armed Response (1995)
Mute182 'Positive ID', Renegade Soundwave (1996)
Mute183 'Movieology', Barry Adamson (1995)
Mute184 'That's When I Reach For My Revolver', Moby (1996)
Mute185 'Where The Wild Roses Grow', Nick Cave And The Bad Seeds + Kylie Minogue (1995)
Mute186 'The Big Bamboozle EP', Barry Adamson (1995)
Mute187 'Initials B.B.', Mick Harvey (1995)
Mute188 'Can't Get Loose', Barry Adamson (1998)
Mute189 'Henry Lee', Nick Cave with P. J. Harvey (1996)
Mute190 'In My Arms', Erasure (1997)
Mute191 'Trip From The Hip', Hoodwink (1997)
Mute192 'Into My Arms', Nick Cave And The Bad Seeds (1997)
Mute193 'Mouthful Of Pennies', Toenut (1996)
Mute194 'Harley Davidson', Mick Harvey (1996)
Mute195 'Don't Say Your Love Is Killing Me', Erasure (1997)
Mute196 'Adamantine', Thirty Ought Six (1996)
Mute197 'God Is God', Laibach (1996)
Mute198 'On My Own', Peach (1996)
Mute199 'Going To Town', The Afghan Whigs (1996)
Mute200 'Come On Baby', Moby (1996)
Mute201 'From This Moment On', Peach (1996)
Mute202 '2 Kindsa Love', The Jon Spencer Blues Explosion (1996)
Mute203 'Looking Down On London', Komputer (1996)
Mute204 'Wail', The Jon Spencer Blues Explosion (1997)
Mute205 'Made In Vain', Peach (1997)
Mute206 '(Are You) The One That I've Been Waiting For?', Nick Cave And The Bad Seeds (1997)
Mute207 'Test Anxiety', Toenut (1997)
Mute208 'Rain', Erasure (1997),
Mute209 'Drifting', Recoil (1997)
Mute210 'James Bond Theme (Moby's Re-version)', Moby (1997)
Mute211 'More Millionaires', Hoodwink (1998)
Mute212 'Valentina', Komputer (1998)
Mute213 'Consumed – The Remix Wars', Mark Stewart (1998)
Mute214 'Stalker'/'Missing Piece', Recoil (1998)
Mute215 'On My Own', Peach (1998)
Mute216 'Sorrow Town', Peach (1998)
Mute217 'Little Black Rocks In The Sun', Add N To (X) (1997)
Mute218 'Honey', Moby (1998)
Mute219 'What It Means', Barry Adamson (1998)
Mute220 'Terminus', Komputer (1998)
Mute221 'Run On', Moby (1999)
Mute222 'Magical Colours', The Jon Spencer Blues Explosion (1998)
Mute223 'Black Amour', Barry Adamson (2002)
Mute224 'Metal Fingers In My Body', Add N To (X) (1999)
Mute225 'Bodyrock', Moby (1999)
Mute226 'Talk About The Blues', The Jon Spencer Blues Explosion (1999)
Mute227 'Food Music', Appliance (1999)
Mute228 'Chirpy', Komputer (2008)
Mute229 'Pacifica', Appliance (1999)
Mute230 'Why Does My Heart Feel So Bad?', Moby (1999)
Mute231 'Revenge Of The Black Regent', Add N To (X) (1999)
Mute232 'Strange Hours', Recoil (2000)
Mute233 'Jezebel', Recoil (2000)
Mute234 'Agharta – The City Of Shamballa', Afrika Bambaataa And Westbam (1999)
Mute235 'Hilary, Last Of The Pool Sharks', Slick Sixty (1999)
Mute236 'Beatbox Rocker', Westbam (1999)
Mute237 'Frances Says The Knife Is Alive', Echoboy (1999)
Mute238 'Eyes Open', SFT (1999)
Mute239 'Heavy', The Jon Spencer Blues Explosion (1999)
Mute240 'Total Eclipse Of The Sun', Einstürzende Neubauten (1999)
Mute241 'Tanz Mit Laibach', Laibach (2003)
Mute242 'Constantinople', Echoboy (2000)
Mute243 'D4', Appliance (2000)
Mute244 'Freedom', Erasure (2000)
Mute245 'A Gentle Cycle Revolution', Appliance (2001)
Mute246 'Kit And Holly', Echoboy (2000)
Mute247 'Lovely Head', Goldfrapp (2000)
Mute248 'Moon & The Sky', Erasure (2001)
Mute249 'As I Sat Sadly By Her Side', Nick Cave And The Bad Seeds (2001)
Mute250 'Solitude', NON (2000)
Mute251 'Natural Blues', Moby (2000)
Mute252 'Porcelain', Moby (2000)
Mute253 'Utopia', Goldfrapp (2000)
Mute254 'Plug Me In', Add N To (X) (2000)
Mute255 'Why Does My Heart Feel So Bad?/Honey feat. Kelis', Moby (2000)
Mute256 'Telstar Recovery', Echoboy (2000)
Mute257 'Turning On', Echoboy (2001)
Mute258 'The Poker Roll', Add N To (X) (2001)
Mute259 'Human', Goldfrapp (2001)
Mute260 'The Next Man That I See', Anita Lane (2001)
Mute261 'Nothing At All', Luke Slater (2002)
Mute262 'Fifteen Feet Of Pure White Snow', Nick Cave And The Bad Seeds (2001)
Mute263 'She Said', The Jon Spencer Blues Explosion (2002)
Mute264 'Utopia (Genetically Enriched)', Goldfrapp (2001)
Mute265 'Bring It On', Nick Cave And The Bad Seeds (2003)
Mute266 'Land, Sea And Air', Appliance (2001)
Mute267 'Pilots (On A Star)', Goldfrapp (2001)
Mute268 'We Are All Made Of Stars', Moby (2002)
Mute269 'Fireside Favourite'/'Collapsing New People', Fad Gadget (2001)
Mute270 'Extreme Ways', Moby (2002)
Mute271 'Sweet N Sour', The Jon Spencer Blues Explosion (2002)
Mute272 'Stars And Heroes', Luke Slater (2002)
Mute273 'The Snare', Looper (2002)
Mute274 'She's A Knife', Looper (2002)
Mute275 'Solsbury Hill', Erasure (2003)
Mute276 'In This World', Moby (2002)
Mute277 'Automatic Eyes', Echoboy (2003)
Mute278 'Take Me To Your Leader', Add N To (X) (2002)
Mute279 '45/45', Pole (2003)
Mute280 'Sunday (The Day Before My Birthday)', Moby (2003)
Mute281 'The Nasty Show', Pink Grease (2003)
Mute282 'Rough Trade Shops Electronic 01', Various (2004)
Mute283 'Whispering Streets', Barry Adamson (2002)
Mute284 'Love Letter', Nick Cave And The Bad Seeds (2002)
Mute285 'Do That Thing', Anita Lane (2002)
Mute286 'Go Native', Appliance (2003)
Mute287 'I Can Complete You', Luke Slater (2002)
Mute288 'Shakin' Rock 'n' Roll Tonight', The Jon Spencer Blues Explosion (2002)
Mute289 'Rough Trade Shops Rock And Roll', Various (2002)
Mute290 'He Wants You'/'Babe, I'm On Fire', Nick Cave And The Bad Seeds (2003)
Mute291 'Train', Goldfrapp (2003)
Mute292 'Make Me Smile (Come Up And See Me)', Erasure (2003)
Mute293 'Lately Lonely', Echoboy (2003)
Mute294 'Dirty Sticky Floors', Dave Gahan (2003)
Mute295 'Strict Machine', Goldfrapp (2003)
Mute296 'Stardust', Martin L. Gore (2003)
Mute297 'Mountaineers', Mountaineers (2003)
Mute298 'Rough Trade Shops Post Punk 01', Various (2003)
Mute299 '90/90', Pole (2003)
Mute300 'Ripen', Mountaineers (2003)
Mute301 'I Need You', Dave Gahan (2003)
Mute302 'Jam For The Ladies', Moby vs Princess Superstar (2003)
Mute303 'Everyday It's 1989'/'The Stars', Moby (2007)
Mute304 'Fever', Pink Grease (2004)
Mute305 'Shake The Dope Out', The Warlocks (2003)
Mute306 'Jam For The Ladies promo', Moby vs Princess Superstar (2003)
Mute307 'Light Is In Your Eyes', Voodoo Child (2003)
Mute308 'Baby Blue', The Warlocks (2003)
Mute309 'Take It Home', Voodoo Child (2003)
Mute310 'Bottle Living', Dave Gahan (2003)
Mute311 'Twist', Goldfrapp (2004)
Mute312 'Oh L'Amour', Erasure (2003)
Mute313 'Good On TV', Echoboy (2003)
Mute314 'Come Save Us', The Warlocks (2005)
Mute315 'I Gotta Sing', Mountaineers (2003)
Mute316 'The Pink G.R.Ease', Pink Grease (2004)
Mute317 'There's Always Room On The Broom', Liars (2004)
Mute318 'Rock Of Gibraltar', Nick Cave And The Bad Seeds (2003)
Mute319 'Das Spiel Ist Aus', Laibach (2004)
Mute320 'Black Cherry', Goldfrapp (2004)
Mute321 'We Fenced Other Gardens With The Bones Of Our Own', Liars (2004)
Mute322 'Loverman EP', Martin L. Gore (2003)
Mute323 'Predator EP', Modey Lemon (2004)
Mute324 'Nature Boy', Nick Cave And The Bad Seeds (2004)
Mute325 'Strip', Pink Grease (2005)
Mute326 '3 Mount View', Mountaineers (2004)
Mute327 'Burn It Off', Blues Explosion (2004)
Mute328 'Crows', Modey Lemon (2004)
Mute329 'Breathless'/'There She Goes, My Beautiful World', Nick Cave And The Bad Seeds (2004)
Mute330 'Breathe', Erasure (2005)
Mute331 'Sleepwalkers', Modey Lemon (2004)
Mute332 'Hot Gossip', Blues Explosion (2004)
Mute333 'Make Love Fuck War', Moby And Public Enemy (2004)
Mute334 'It's Just Like Surgery', The Warlocks (2005)
Mute335 'Strict Machine 04', Goldfrapp (2004)
Mute336 'Crunchy', Blues Explosion (2005)
Mute337 'Don't Say You Love Me', Erasure (2005)
Mute338 'Rough Trade Shops Indiepop 1', Various (2004)
Mute339 'Get Ready For Love', Nick Cave And The Bad Seeds (2005)
Mute340 'Lift Me Up', Moby (2005)
Mute341 'Bucket Of Butterflies', Modey Lemon (2005)
Mute342 'Ooh La La', Goldfrapp (2005)
Mute343 'Peaches', Pink Grease (2005)
Mute344 'Here I Go Impossible Again'/'All This Time Still Falling Out Of Love', Erasure (2005)
Mute345 'Raining Again', Moby (2005)
Mute346 'Out Of Time Man', Mick Harvey (2007)
Mute347 'The Ocean', Richard Hawley (2005)
Mute348 'Trans Slovenia Express Vol.2: The Club Mixes', Various (2005)
Mute349 'It Fit When I Was A Kid', Liars (2005)
Mute350 'Spiders', Moby (2005)
Mute351 'Number 1', Goldfrapp, (2006)
Mute352 'Coles Corner', Richard Hawley (2005)
Mute353 'Down In The Past', Mando Diao (2005)
Mute354 'The Other Side Of Mt Heart Attack', Liars (2006)
Mute355 'Dream About Me', Moby (2005)
Mute356 'Ride A White Horse', Goldfrapp (2006)
Mute357 'Just Like The Rain', Richard Hawley (2006)
Mute358 'Ordinary Girl', Pink Grease (2006)
Mute359 'Boy', Erasure (2006)
Mute360 'Beautiful', Moby (2005)
Mute361 'Fly Me Away', Goldfrapp (2006)
Mute362 'Born Under A Bad Sign', Richard Hawley (2006)
Mute363 'Alien', Pink Grease (2006)
Mute364 'Anglia', Laibach (2006)
Mute365 'Slipping Away', Moby (2006)
Mute366 'I Could Fall In Love With You', Erasure (2007)
Mute367 'Coles Corner', Richard Hawley (2006)
Mute368 'Satin Boys, Flaming Chic', Goldfrapp (2006)
Mute369 'Carlights', Pink Grease (2007)
Mute370 'Get It On', Grinderman (2007)
Mute371 'New York, New York', Moby (2006)
Mute372 'Prey', Recoil (2007)
Mute373 'No Pussy Blues', Grinderman (2007)
Mute374 'Headphones And Ringtones', Komputer (2007)
Mute375 'It Will Find You', Maps (2007)
Mute376 'Sunday Girl', Erasure (2007)
Mute377 'Dig, Lazarus, Dig!!!', Nick Cave And The Bad Seeds (2008)
Mute378 'You Don't Know Her Name', Maps (2007)
Mute379 'Hotel Room', Richard Hawley (2007)
Mute380 'Alice', Moby (2008)
Mute381 '(I Don't Need You To) Set Me Free', Grinderman (2007)
Mute382 'Tonight The Streets Are Ours', Richard Hawley (2007)
Mute383 'Plaster Casts Of Everything', Liars (2007)
Mute384 'Storm Chaser', Erasure (2007)
Mute385 'Serious', Richard Hawley (2007)
Mute386 'House Clouds', Liars (2007)
Mute387 'Disco Lies', Moby (2008)
Mute388 'Valentine', Richard Hawley (2008)
Mute389 'A&E', Goldfrapp (2008)
Mute390 'More News From Nowhere', Nick Cave And The Bad Seeds (2008)
Mute391 'I Love To Move In Here', Moby (2008)
Mute392 'Happiness', Goldfrapp (2008)
Mute393 'Kingdom', Dave Gahan (2007)
Mute394 'Like A Bird', Komputer (2007)
Mute395 'Hey Mr DJ', Tiny Masters Of Today (2007)
Mute396 'To The Sky', Maps (2007)
Mute397 'Hologram World', Tiny Masters Of Today (2008)
Mute398 'Saw Something'/'Deeper And Deeper', Dave Gahan (2008)
Mute399 'Nitrogen Pink', Polly Scattergood (2007)
Mute400 'I Hate The Way', Polly Scattergood (2008)
Mute401 'Caravan Girl', Goldfrapp (2008)
Mute402 'Rockabilly Radio (From The Film 'Flick')', Richard Hawley And The Feral Cats (2008)
Mute403 'Midnight Man', Nick Cave And The Bad Seeds (2008)
Mute404 'How To Reduce The Chances Of Being A Terror Victim', XX Teens (2008)
Mute405 'Pop! Remixed', Erasure (2009)
Mute406 The Way We Were', XX Teens (2008)
Mute407 'Disco Lies', Moby (2008) UK release
Mute408 'Only You', XX Teens (2008)
Mute409 'Ooh Yeah', Moby (2008)
Mute411 'Skeletons', Tiny Masters Of Today (2009)
Mute412 'Other Too Endless', Polly Scattergood (2009)
Mute413 'Please Don't Touch', Polly Scattergood (2009)
Mute414 'Pop Chart', Tiny Masters Of Today (2009)
Mute415 'I Dream Of Crystal', Maps (2009)
Mute416 'In Your Heart', A Place To Bury Strangers (2009)
Mute417 'For Your Lover Give Some Time', Richard Hawley (2009)
Mute418 'Real Good', Tiny Masters Of Today (2009)
Mute419 'Bunny Club EP', Polly Scattergood (2009)
Mute420 'Phantom Bride EP', Erasure (2009)
Mute421 'Die Happy, Die Smiling', Maps (2010)
Mute422 'Keep Slipping Away', A Place To Bury Strangers (2009)
Mute423 'Open Up Your Door', Richard Hawley (2009)
Mute425 'Percussion Gun', White Rabbits (2010)
Mute426 'Will You Be There?', MiMó / Andy Bell (2010)
Mute427 'Ambling Alp', Yeasayer (2009)
Mute428 'Scissor', Liars (2010)
Mute429 'They Done Wrong'/'We Done Wrong', White Rabbits (2010)
Mute430 'Rocket', Goldfrapp (2010)
Mute431 'Call On Me', Andy Bell (2010)
Mute432 'Alive', Goldfrapp (2010)
Mute433 'Ego Death EP', A Place To Bury Strangers (2010)
Mute434 'The Overachievers', Liars (2010)
Mute435 'O.N.E.', Yeasayer (2010)
Mute436 'Believer', Goldfrapp (2010)
Mute437 'False Lights From The Land EP', Richard Hawley (2010)
Mute438 'I Lived My Life To Stand In The Shadow Of Your Heart EP', A Place To Bury Strangers (2010)
Mute439 'Madder Red', Yeasayer (2010)
Mute440 'Endblood', Yeasayer (2011)
Mute441 'Heathen Child', Grinderman (2010)
Mute442 '15 Years', Pull In Emergency (2010)
Mute443 'The Salesman (Tramp Life)', White Rabbits (2010)
Mute444 'Proud Evolution', Liars (2012)
Mute445 'Non-Stop', Andy Bell (2010)
Mute446 'The Problem', Pull In Emergency (2011)
Mute447 'Worm Tamer', Grinderman (2010)
Mute448 'End Blood', Yeasayer (2011)
Mute449 'Palaces Of Montezuma', Grinderman (2011)
Mute450 'Sweetheart I Ain't Your Christ'/'Country Dumb', Josh T. Pearson (2011)
Mute451 'A Little Respect (HMI Redux)', Erasure (2010)
Mute452 'Mickey Mouse And The Goodbye Man', Grinderman (2011)
Mute453 'Amber Hands', S.C.U.M (2011)
Mute454 'Whitechapel', S.C.U.M (2011)
Mute455 'Woman When I've Raised Hell', Josh T. Pearson (2011)
Mute456 'Famous Last Words', Mick Harvey (2011)
Mute457 'Ash'/'Black Veil', Apparat (2011)
Mute458 'Liliputt', Beth Jeans Houghton And The Hooves Of Destiny (2011)
Mute459 'Chair', Big Deal (2011)
Mute460 'Song Of Los', Apparat (2011)
Mute461 'Faith Unfolds', S.C.U.M (2012)
Mute462 'Distant Neighborhood', Big Deal (2011)
Mute463 'Candil De La Calle', Apparat (2012)
Mute464 'When I Start To (Break It All Down)', Erasure (2011)
Mute465 'Sorry With A Song', Josh T. Pearson (2011)
Mute466 'Black Water' Apparat (2011)
Mute467 'Monuments', Yann Tiersen (2011)
Mute468 'I'm Gonna Live Anyhow', Yann Tiersen (2011)
Mute469 'Sweet Tooth Bird', Beth Jeans Houghton And The Hooves Of Destiny (2012)
Mute470 'Be With You', Erasure (2011)
Mute471 'Big Deal EP', Big Deal (2011)
Mute472 'Faith Unfolds', S.C.U.M (2012)
Mute473 'Talk', Big Deal (2012)
Mute474 'Atlas', Beth Jeans Houghton And The Hooves Of Destiny (2012)
Mute475 'EP1/Spock', VCMG (2011)
Mute476 'EP2/Single Blip', VCMG (2012)
Mute477 'Immigrant Song', Karen O. with Trent Reznor And Atticus Ross (2012)
Mute478 'Amber Hands', S.C.U.M (2012)
Mute479 'Fill Us With Fire', Erasure (2012)
Mute481 'Transverse V2/V3 Edits', Carter Tutti Void (2012)
Mute482 'Dancing Coins EP', Cold Specks (2012)
Mute483 'Big Deal Vs S.C.U.M', Big Deal + S.C.U.M (2012)
Mute484 'EP3/Aftermaths', VCMG (2012)
Mute485 'Blank Maps/Winter Solstice', Cold Specks (2012)
Mute486 'No.1 Against The Rush', Liars (2012)
Mute487 'Temporary', White Rabbits (2012)
Mute488 'Henrietta', Yeasayer (2012)
Mute490 'Longevity', Yeasayer (2012)
Mute491 'Dodecahedron', Beth Jeans Houghton And The Hooves Of Destiny (2012)
Mute492 'Hector', Cold Specks (2012)
Mute493 'It's Not Me', White Rabbits (2012)
Mute494 'Reagan's Skeleton', Yeasayer (2012)
Mute495 'Brats', Liars (2012)
Mute496 'Goddess', Crime And The City Solution (2013)
Mute497 'When The City Lights Dim', Cold Specks (2012)
Mute498 'Wanderlust', Polly Scattergood (2013)
Mute499 'I Heard Them Say', Maps (2013)
Mute500 'In Your Car', Big Deal (2013)
Mute501 'Cocoon', Polly Scattergood (2013)
Mute502 'Subsequently Lost', Polly Scattergood (2014)
Mute503 'A.M.A.', Maps (2013)
Mute504 'Dream Machines', Big Deal (2013)
Mute505 'A.M.A.', Maps (2013)
Mute506 'You Will Find A Way', Maps (2013)
Mute507 'Swapping Spit', Big Deal (2013)
Mute508 'S', Laibach (2013)
Mute509 'Gaudete', Erasure (2013)
Mute510 'Make It Wonderful', Erasure (2014)
Mute511 'Mess On A Mission', Liars (2014)
Mute512 'Thea', Goldfrapp (2014)
Mute513 'In Your Car'/'Catch Up', Big Deal (2014)
Mute514 'Venter', Ben Frost (2014)
Mute515 'A Midsummer Evening', Yann Tiersen (2014)
Mute517 'Pro Anti Anti', Liars (2014)
Mute518 'Were You There? Feat. Neil Tennant', Diamond Version (2014)
Mute519 'Sakura EP', Big Deal (2014)
Mute520 'Abisto', Cold Specks (2014)
Mute521 'Dangerous Days', Zola Jesus (2014)
Mute522 'Elevation', Erasure (2014)
Mute523 'Bodies At Bay', Cold Specks (2014)
Mute524 'Thievery', Arca (2014)
Mute525 'V A R I A N T', Ben Frost (2014)
Mute526 'I'm No Gold', Liars (2014)
Mute527 'Go (Blank Sea)', Zola Jesus (2014)
Mute528 'Reason', Erasure (2014)
Mute529 'Oxygen', Swans (2014)
Mute530 'EX Club Mixes', Plastikman (2015)
Mute531 'Swans', Swans (2015)
Mute532 'Sacred', Erasure (2015)
Mute533 'Hunger', Zola Jesus (2015)
Mute534 'Black Flag', Du Blonde (2015)
Mute535 'Europa Hymn', MG (2015)
Mute536 'Living Signs', Cold Specks (2015)
Mute538 'MG EP', MG (2015)
Mute539 'Europa Hymn (Andy Stott Remix)'/'Pinking (Christoffer Berg Remix)', MG (2015)
Mute540 'Blackbird', onDeadWaves (2015)
Mute541 'Restless', New Order (2015)
Mute542 'Tutti Frutti', New Order (2015)
Mute543 'Sometimes 2015', Erasure (2015)
Mute544 'Nail', Zola Jesus (2015)
Mute545 'Singularity', New Order (2016)
Mute546 'I Am Chemistry', Yeasayer (2016)
Mute547 'I&I', LUH (2016)
Mute548 'Porz Goret', Yann Tiersen (2015)
Mute550 'Blue Inside', onDeadWaves (2016)
Mute552 'California', onDeadWaves (2016)
Mute553 'People On The High Line', New Order (2016)
Mute554 'Beneath The Concrete', LUH (2016)
Mute555 'Blackbird EP', onDeadWaves (2016)
Mute556 'Cold Night', Yeasayer (2016)
Mute557 'Anymore', Goldfrapp (2017)
Mute558 'Lament', Lost Under Heaven (2016)
Mute559 'Threshold Of Faith', Ben Frost (2017)
Mute560 'They're Just Words', ADULT. (2017)
Mute561 'Farfisa Song', Looper (2017)
Mute562 'Love You To The Sky', Erasure (2017)
Mute563 'Falling From Cloud 9', Lift To Experience (2017)
Mute564 'Systemagic', Goldfrapp (2017)
Mute565 'World Be Gone', Erasure (2017)
Mute566 'Everything Is Never Enough', Goldfrapp (2017)
Mute569 'All That You Love Will Be Eviscerated' Ben Frost (2017)
Mute579 'Ionia', Ben Frost (2017)
Mute666 'Evil', Grinderman (2011)

PICTURE CREDITS

9–10	Courtesy Venusnote Limited, collage by Chris Nash
10–11	Photo by David Tonge/Getty Images
12–13	Courtesy BMG Rights Management (UK) Ltd. Photo by Joe Dilworth, art direction by Alison Goldfrapp
14–15	Installation by David Altmejd, photo by Steven Brahms
18t	Courtesy BMG Rights Management (UK) Ltd.
18b	Courtesy Venusnote Limited
21	© Joe Dilworth
22t	The Electricity Club
22c	© Anton Corbijn
23t	Photo by Dave Penny
23c	© Simon Fowler Photography
23b	Outtake, shoot for *Boyd Rice*, Boyd Rice, original self-released pressing, 1977
24tl	Photo by Phoebe Markham
24tc	© Anton Corbijn
24tr	© Tasso Taraboulsi/Polaris/eyevine
25tl	Photo by Frans Schellekens/Redferns Getty Images
25tc	Courtesy BMG Rights Management (UK) Ltd. Photo by Joe Dilworth
25tr	Photo by snapshot-photography/ullstein bild via Getty Images
30l	© BBC
30r	Photo by Brian Shuel/Redferns
31l	Photo by Hildegard Schmidt
31r	Photo by Fröhling/Kraftwerk/Getty Images
32l	Photo by Antoine Giacomoni
33l	Photo by Max Kisman
33r	© simone grant design
37lt–b	Illustrator Adrian Cartwright: Planet illustration
37tr	Courtesy BMG Rights Management (UK) Ltd.
38t	Courtesy BMG Rights Management (UK) Ltd.
38br	Courtesy BMG Rights Management (UK) Ltd.
39	*The South Bank Show*, ITV, 1979, Video Stills
43	© simone grant design
50tl	© Che Seibert
51tl	Photo by Christopher Cooper
51tr	© Steve Cook
52tl	© BBC
53tr	'Downstairs At Erics', *Electronics & Music Maker*, March 1984
61	Courtesy BMG Rights Management (UK) Ltd.
62tl	Courtesy BMG Rights Management (UK) Ltd.
63	Courtesy BMG Rights Management (UK) Ltd.
69	Photo by Peter Anderson
72–73	Courtesy Venusnote Limited
74–75	Courtesy Venusnote Limited
77	© Brian Griffin
80bl	Courtesy BMG Rights Management (UK) Ltd.
80br	Courtesy BMG Rights Management (UK) Ltd.
81	Courtesy BMG Rights Management (UK) Ltd. Photos by Joe Lyons
82	Courtesy BMG Rights Management (UK) Ltd.
86	© Anton Corbijn
96t	*Everything Counts*, Depeche Mode, dir. Clive Richardson, 1983, video still

96tr	*Who Needs Love Like That?*, Erasure, dir. John Scarlett-Davis, 1985, video still
97tl	Courtesy BMG Rights Management (UK) Ltd.
97tr	akg-images/picture alliance/Jazz Archiv/Karsch
98tl	Courtesy BMG Rights Management (UK) Ltd. Photo by Jutta Henglein
98tr	Courtesy BMG Rights Management (UK) Ltd.
99tr	Photo by Antonio Živoković
102t	Courtesy Venusnote Limited
104	Courtesy Venusnote Limited
105t	Courtesy Venusnote Limited
106tl	Courtesy Venusnote Limited
106cl	Courtesy Venusnote Limited
106bl	Courtesy Venusnote Limited
107	Courtesy Venusnote Limited
111	© Bleddyn Butcher, London 1983
112	© Tasso Taraboulsi/Polaris/eyevine
113	© Tasso Taraboulsi/Polaris/eyevine
116–17	Courtesy BMG Rights Management (UK) Ltd.
118–19	Courtesy BMG Rights Management (UK) Ltd.
120–21	Courtesy BMG Rights Management (UK) Ltd.
126	© Anton Corbijn
127	Courtesy BMG Rights Management (UK) Ltd.
133	Courtesy BMG Rights Management (UK) Ltd.
134–35	Courtesy BMG Rights Management (UK) Ltd.
137	Courtesy BMG Rights Management (UK) Ltd.
138–39	Courtesy BMG Rights Management (UK) Ltd.
140	Courtesy BMG Rights Management (UK) Ltd.
141	Courtesy BMG Rights Management (UK) Ltd. Photo by Peter Ashworth
144–45	Courtesy Venusnote Limited
147	Courtesy Venusnote Limited
148–49	Courtesy Venusnote Limited
150–51	Courtesy Venusnote Limited
157	Photo by Igor Škafar
161	Concept by Morten Traavik, design by Valnoir Mortasonge
162bl–br	Courtesy BMG Rights Management (UK) Ltd.
163bl–br	Courtesy BMG Rights Management (UK) Ltd.
165	Courtesy BMG Rights Management (UK) Ltd.
167	Courtesy BMG Rights Management (UK) Ltd.
168–69	Courtesy BMG Rights Management (UK) Ltd.
170tl	Courtesy BMG Rights Management (UK) Ltd.
170b	Courtesy BMG Rights Management (UK) Ltd.
171	Courtesy BMG Rights Management (UK) Ltd.
176b	*The Three*, Ohi Ho Bang Bang, dir. Akiko Hada, 1989, video stills
178t	Courtesy BMG Rights Management (UK) Ltd.
179	Courtesy BMG Rights Management (UK) Ltd.
182–83	Courtesy Venusnote Limited
186tl	*Personal Jesus*, Depeche Mode, dir. Anton Corbijn, 1989, video still
186tr	*Enjoy The Silence*, Depeche Mode, dir. Anton Corbijn, 1990, video still
187tl	Private Collection

187tr	Photo by Dave Tonge/Getty Images
188tl	Courtesy BMG Rights Management (UK) Ltd.
188tr	Photo by Fritz Brinckmann
189tl	Photo by Tom Caravaglia
189tr	S.I.N./Alamy Stock Photo
190–91	Courtesy Venusnote Limited
192–93	Courtesy Venusnote Limited
194–95	Courtesy BMG Rights Management (UK) Ltd.
199	Photo by Ebet Roberts/Redferns/ Getty Images
210tr	Private Collection
210bl	Courtesy BMG Rights Management (UK) Ltd.
210br	Courtesy BMG Rights Management (UK) Ltd.
211	© Robin Skjoldborg
214–15	Courtesy Venusnote Limited
216–17	Courtesy Venusnote Limited
225	Photo by Catherine McGann/ Getty Images
227	Courtesy BMG Rights Management (UK) Ltd. Photos by Jill Greenberg
228–29	Photos by Corinne Day
231	Courtesy BMG Rights Management (UK) Ltd.
235	Photo by Joe Dilworth
241tr	Courtesy BMG Rights Management (UK) Ltd.
241b	Courtesy BMG Rights Management (UK) Ltd.
242–43	Courtesy BMG Rights Management (UK) Ltd.
244	Courtesy BMG Rights Management (UK) Ltd.
246	Courtesy BMG Rights Management (UK) Ltd. Photo by Steve Gullick
247	Courtesy BMG Rights Management (UK) Ltd.
248	Photos by Tim Noble and Sue Webster
256tl	Courtesy BMG Rights Management (UK) Ltd. Photo by David Titlow
256tr	Photo by Alison Goldfrapp
257tl	Photo by Travis Shinn
258tl	Photo by Zen Sekiszwa
258tr	Photo by Richard Gray
259tl	Photo by Steve Gullick
259tr	Photo by Nick Wilson
261	Photo by Joe Dilworth
263	Courtesy BMG Rights Management (UK) Ltd.
266–67	Courtesy BMG Rights Management (UK) Ltd.
272	Collage by Alison Goldfrapp
274b	Photo by Gareth James
275	Photo by Steve Gullick
276	Courtesy BMG Rights Management (UK) Ltd.
279	*Heathen Child*, Grinderman, dir. John Hillcoat, 2010, video stills
281	*Silly Me*, Yeasayer, Dir. Mike Anderson, 2016, video stills. Models and drawings by Mike Anderson/New Media Ltd.
291	Artwork by Jesse Kanda
296–97	Photos by Matthew Stone
301	Artwork by James Brooks
306–07	Video directed by Yoonha Park, casts by Direct Dimensions
311	© Daniel Miller
320	© Daniel Miller

INDEX

ACKNOWLEDGEMENTS

Terry Burrows would like to thank:
Thames and Hudson – Tristan de Lancey, who conceived and oversaw the project; Jane Laing for her usual editorial and management expertise; Phoebe Lindsley for her tirelessly heroic efforts from beginning to end; and Rob Dimery for his fine edits.

Mute – Daniel Miller for sparing his very limited time to chat about analogue synthesisers and, occasionally, the record label he founded, which has contributed so much to the soundtrack of my life; Paul A. Taylor, for sharing some of his vast expertise accrued through nearly three decades working with Daniel.

All the musicians, photographers and art directors connected with the Mute label who were interviewed or provided commentary used throughout the book.

Daniel Miller would like to thank:
All the artists who have worked with Mute since 1978 and in the future; without their creative vision and inspiration there would not be a visual document of Mute.

All the art directors, photographers, designers and illustrators who have helped Mute and our artists realise such a strong, innovative and varied collection of visuals to accompany the music we release.

For taking time to contribute to the book's content, Monica Axelsson, Nicole Blonder, Bleddyn Butcher, Anton Corbijn, Joe Dilworth, Simon Granger, Simone Grant, Brian Griffin, Anne Haffmans, Tom Hingston, Seth Hodder, Mat Maitland, John Richards, Adrian Shaughnessy, Jan L. Trigg.

Paul A. Taylor (Mute's art director since 1990) for his dedication. Without him, this book would not have been possible.

Tristan de Lancey and all at Thames & Hudson for the passion in wanting to show the world through Mute's eyes – and for being patient while we sent through yet another correction.

Terry Burrows for writing the text after so many interviews, and allowing the Mute voice to be heard.

All of the staff who have ever worked at Mute.

My parents, Hanna and Martin, for giving me the space.

The publisher would like to extend a special thanks to Paul A. Taylor for his enormous and steadfast contribution to the content and accuracy of the book.

First published in the United Kingdom in 2017 by Thames & Hudson Ltd, 181A High Holborn, London WC1V 7QX

Mute: A Visual Document © 2017 Thames & Hudson Ltd, London

Introduction © 2017 Daniel Miller

Designed by Daniel Streat, Visual Fields

British Library Cataloguing-in-Publication Data
A catalogue record for this book is available from the British Library

ISBN 978-0-500-519721

Printed and bound in China by Everbest Printing Co. Ltd.

To find out about all our publications, please visit
www.thamesandhudson.com. There you can subscribe to our e-newsletter, browse or download our current catalogue, and buy any titles that are in print.

Below: Daniel Miller / Photograph / Mute Studio / 429 Harrow Road